# INTO THE HEART
# OF TEACHING

By
**Rosalie J. Johnson**

INTO THE HEART OF TEACHING

Printed in the United States of America

For ordering information contact us at:

Pro-Ed Books
403 Maple Lane
Valatie, NY  12184

ISBN:  0-9625842-0-7

It is with deepest gratitude that I acknowledge three professional educators and dear friends. Their technical advice, creative ideas, genuine interest, and constant encouragement contributed greatly to the successful completion of this book:

Mr. Paul V. Clause

Mrs. Elizabeth Powhida

Mrs. Gail Wheeler

A special note of thanks must be given to the illustrator. Her drawings portray a sensitive, familiar, and even humorous observation with which many of us in the teaching profession can identify.

Mrs. Nancy M. Peterson

All authors know the great value of a thorough proofreader - mine devoted many hours to the task of polishing this book. I am indebted to her.

Mrs. Edna M. Lenehan

# INTRODUCTION

Since you have decided to read my book, let me introduce myself to you. My name is Rosalie Johnson, and I am a teacher! I hold a Bachelor of Arts degree in history from Nyack College and a Master of Arts degree in education from the University at Albany, State University of New York. I taught social studies courses (grades eight, eleven, and twelve) in a public school for ten and a half years and at a private school for one year. I have been a faculty member at The College of Saint Rose for eight years and at the University at Albany for three years serving as a student teacher supervisor. I have also served on two different Boards of Education, for a total of eight years. Additionally, I am a consultant for an educational research and evaluation company. I am happily married and am the mother of three sons.

During my first five years of teaching, I had no children so I often was involved in a variety of activities. My opportunities included being a softball and bowling coach, softball umpire, Senior Class Advisor, member of the teacher-administration liaison committee, a cooperating teacher for a student teacher, and writer of a New York State grant for funding a law education workshop.

As I gained teaching experience, I not only realized the importance of time in the classroom, but I attempted to use time efficiently for the benefit of my students and myself. My goal in teaching became more defined, simply stated, it was to increase my skills and impact as a teacher while limiting the time spent on teaching duties so that I had time for my family. Many of you will come to the same conclusions, and hopefully this book will assist you to reach your goals.

My goal in writing this book is to inform you of some ideas and practices I have used, as well as some methods used by other teachers. In each unit, I have attempted to be both concise and realistic in stating my rationale for methods used and my observations about their success. I hope the ideas presented in this book will help you to perform your teaching duties more professionally and that your teaching career will be somewhat easier and more enjoyable.

**As you read this book, think about and react to the ideas and methods described, then feel free to adopt, adapt, or avoid any of the suggestions presented!**

# TABLE OF CONTENTS

# PART I

# THE MANY FACETS OF TEACHING

**(CHALLENGES AND REWARDS)**

**Chapter 1**

# WELCOME TO THE FACULTY!

As you enter the exciting and challenging vocation of teaching, you will discover a world of demanding expectations combined with exceptional opportunities! Your impact as a teacher will be a direct result of your understanding of the role of a teacher, how you guide individuals, and how you orchestrate opportunities. It is necessary to fully understand and integrate the many aspects of being a teacher.

## How do you define the term "teacher"?

When people begin to define the term, they realize the word "teacher" includes many ideas, practices, and expectations. Listed below are a few words which should be considered when defining what a school teacher is or should be. It is important to review the meaning of each idea as used in this book.

**EDUCATOR**. An educator is "a specialist in the science of education; an authority on educational methods, theories, and problems" (*Webster's New World Dictionary of the American Language*). This means the person has received training in a wide variety of teaching methods, understands different schools of thought pertaining to how people learn, and can apply those different theories in varying situations. This person is also familiar with the many problems and challenges existing in the educational system.

**MASTER**. The master is an expert in a particular field of knowledge or specialized skill and has a great love for that specific area of knowledge. This person also has a wide range of interests and a deep respect for learning.

**PROFESSIONAL**. A professional is a person who has received in-depth training which should allow her/him to do well in a particular type of work. The person is well-prepared, acts responsibly, and is worthy of respect.

So far, we have seen that a teacher is a person who understands educational theory and practice, is an expert in a specialized field of knowledge, and has been trained to share her/his expertise with others in a responsible way. A teacher is (or should be) far more than a "well-trained individual." There is more to being a teacher than what is included

3

in the ideas of educator, master, and professional; there is a personal quality that must be present. Consider the following additional ideas:

**INSTRUCTOR.** The instructor teaches or trains other people by demonstrations, explanations, and discussions. The instructor also provides resources and direction for further study. All instructors' efforts should be aimed at imparting and increasing knowledge, expanding students' understanding, and deepening their insights. This is accomplished through systematic teaching, which is the combining of teaching methods (Educator), knowledge of subject area (Master), and past training of the individual (Professional).

**MENTOR.** The mentor is an instructor who is willing to share knowledge, interests, and experiences, with another person who wants to learn; however, that is not all that is shared by the mentor. The mentor shares a sense of humanity, kindness, sympathy, understanding, and tolerance for differences of opinions or life-styles. The mentor is a person who recognizes difficult situations and shares observations and possible solutions. *Webster's New World Dictionary of the American Language* summarizes the mentor well: "loyal friend and wise advisor."

**FACULTY MEMBER.** The word "faculty" can refer to a number of ideas, but when referring to teachers, the word carries three distinct meanings. They are: 1) "all of the teachers in a school," 2) "all of the members of a learned profession," and 3) "those having authority" (*Webster's New World Dictionary of the American Language*). The word "member" refers to being a part of some "body or group" - not complete when alone. School teachers are members of a group, a team. It is vital for the members of the team to function well together, to recognize the talents of each member and to be responsive to each other's needs.

**TRUSTWORTHY ADULT FRIEND.** As much as possible, we, as teachers, should be friends to our students. The previous statement does not mean that teachers are to socialize with students or to be "best buds" with students; it simply means that we are trustworthy adults who are available to our students in times of personal need as well as for the purpose of increasing their learning. It is in this arena of teaching that our own humanity shows through, our own vulnerabilities appear, and we are recognized as caring individuals. When we appear as "real people" to our students we can help them the most. At times we need only to be friendly to the shy student, to quietly talk with a sad student, or to joke with a cheerful student. At other times we must attentively listen to the hurting student who needs to talk, or discuss options with the student who is searching for answers.

After reading the previous listed descriptions of a teacher, you may decide there is a noticeable overlap of ideas. You may not even agree with all of the ideas presented (that is permissible); however, it is important for you to be informed of the personal qualities and professional practices required of teachers as presented in this book.

To summarize, teachers are a group of well-trained people who share knowledge and experience with their students and with each other. Teachers are caring people who reach out to others and make a difference in their lives. As teachers, we must be knowledgeable in curriculum content and committed to continual personal growth. It is vital for us to commit to the practice of making learning relevant, exciting, and challenging. We must set reasonable standards for our students, create requirements which are challenging yet fair and attainable, encourage and expect our students to do their best then compliment their successes. We must be responsive and available to our students.

We have chosen a worthy vocation in which we can grow as individuals and professionals. We can and should be happy in our teaching experiences. We have the opportunity to touch the lives of many people and we can be even more of a positive influence for them and to their futures than we ever thought possible. Take each opportunity and make the most of it!


**OPPORTUNITIES FOR REFLECTION:**

1. **What elements described in the previous reading are most important to you?**

2. **What other ideas would you include in a definition of "teacher"?**

3. **As you traveled through your formal educational process, you met many teachers and experienced a variety of teacher styles and expertise. What ideas and practices have you highly valued (or will you avoid) as a result of the teachers who have been a part of your life?**

**Chapter 2**

# TEACHER ROLES

Many times it seems to teachers that they must be "all things, to all people, at all times." One soon becomes acutely aware of many different groups represented within a school setting and each group has defined interests and goals. Interacting with the varying groups can at times be fulfilling, exacting, or even difficult. The most recognizable groups are administrators, parents, students, faculty members, staff members, and the teachers' association. Added to the groups are the issues and mandates of state education departments, boards of education, contracts, unions, departments within a school, personal teaching priorities and individual career goals. Teachers deal with many of these groups and issues at some time in their career, but all challenges must be kept in perspective. It is most important for teachers to remember their highest commitment should be to their students and meeting their intellectual and human needs.

In the intellectual realm, we teachers are to instruct our students and inspire intellectual curiosity. We must aid students in developing major concepts and understandings of specific subject areas. We must challenge students to think, rather than to simply repeat learned information or react to situations on an emotional level.

In the human realm, we are to encourage the development of our students' social survival skills: a sense of responsibility and of caring, commitment, kindness, and the ability to learn from each other. We are often called upon to be an adult advisor, confidante, or mediator. In that role, we often help our students find their individual strengths, gain confidence, and reach potentials so they will fully develop as individuals and be able to contribute in a positive manner to our society.

As we attempt to reach the goals of expanding the intellectual abilities of our students and meeting their human needs, we teachers are seen as qualifiers or role models. How we perform, what we do, the style in which we teach, the standards we set, the manner in which we reach out to our students -- all are very important roles and opportunities; however, there are many other expectations for teachers to accomplish. Consider the following collection of ideas:

The teacher is expected to be an effective large-group instructor. This requires a solid foundation of knowledge in a particular subject area, as well as the ability to communicate (explain) the subject content to other people. Teachers must have the ability to control the students in their classroom so that teaching and learning can take place. Teachers should be able to share their knowledge and experience with students in an involving and challenging manner. Teachers must inspire their students to listen, create, reason, and respond. The teaching aspect of our position also includes being a tutor to each student, for we must evaluate each one and whenever possible, design our presentations to meet their individual needs.

The teacher is expected to be a general educator which means the teacher must be able to combine several disciplines and instruct in them. For example, an American History teacher should be able to correct students' grammar, improve their analytical skills, and assist them in mastering both research and presentation skills.

Teachers are recognized and accepted as "role models - an exacting responsibility. We present our own personality, our moral qualities, and our values. Teachers have always been role models: sometimes positive, sometimes negative - but always role models. It is important for us to be positive role models without being hypocritical. Allow your humanity to be seen in your dealings with your students; be fair, be honest, be kind, and be consistent.

Teachers are expected to aid their students in the development of positive, life-long attitudes and skills. Students need to develop personal responsibility, good study/work habits, personal strengths, and a desire to contribute in a positive manner to our society.

The teacher is expected to be a good administrator. This means teachers should have the ability to work well with people, guide programs, and efficiently process the paperwork.

The teacher is expected to be a good evaluator. Teachers are always evaluating students' abilities and their completed assignments, educational programs (including course content, textbooks, requirements), and in-school policies.

The teacher should be congenial. Since teachers are members of the educational team, they must have the ability to get along with other faculty members and successfully work with them. The educational program of a school is strengthened considerably when the teachers are working together as a unit rather than as splintered groups with competing individuals.

The teacher must have the skills of a diplomat, for teachers are constantly involved in matters concerning students, parents, administrators, and colleagues. Whether or not the situations are confidential, all of them need to be handled with finesse.

In addition to the leadership role in the classroom, the teacher is often expected to be a leader in the school community. Teachers are needed to take an active part in the extracurricular life of the school. Teachers support a wide range of programs, clubs, organizations, and sporting activities by advising or coaching, and by attending school functions. Being an advisor to a class, organization or club, or coaching a sports team takes many hours of work, coordinating skills, a willingness to learn, and a desire to help. Why should a teacher become involved with extracurricular activities if they are so time-consuming? Involvement with extracurricular activities provides many opportunities for the teacher to become acquainted with students in a setting other than the classroom. Additionally, one's involvement with extracurricular activities can be fun - an enjoyable diversion from the school routine and demands - and it may provide an excellent opportunity for exercise and stress reduction.

If you decide to advise or coach an activity and later discover that you do not enjoy the activity, complete the assignment to the best of your ability. Then, at the end of the scheduled activity or season, if you still do not like it, inform the administrator in charge that you do not wish to continue that specific assignment in future years. The next school year, choose another activity within your range of interests and ability. It is important to maintain your involvement in the extracurricular activities available within your school as long as possible; it's well worth your time and effort.

Often, a teacher is viewed as a substitute parent by students who are seeking guidance. We have this role because we spend so much time with our students and we are interested in them. Teachers act as a sounding board for their students; someone who will listen and who can be trusted to give thoughtful advice. Sometimes the teacher listens to one student, sometimes to an entire class. We are expected to encourage our students who are troubled by academic problems, counsel them about job or college placement, and sustain them during times of emotional distress. This is one of the aspects of being a teacher that can cause significant teacher stress. Be considerate toward your students, but at the same time be careful not to overextend your ability to deal with the emotional problems of your students.

Once in a while, a teacher may even substitute in work areas normally assigned to the custodial or cafeteria staff. I have cleaned student desk tops to remove valuable information just before giving a major test or simply to remove offensive language. One time, I helped serve hot dogs in the cafeteria to students who were snow-bound in the building. It was fun for one day, but I would not care to do it on a regular basis.

Teachers are expected to be involved in the usual events within the school day. We must always be aware of those situations that threaten the health and safety of students and school personnel. Sometimes teachers must break up a fight between students (my policy was to yell at the combatants while staying one arm's length away), interrupt students who are defacing school property, or report threatening comments or actions to a building administrator. Other duties, all of which I have done, can include extinguishing a fire in a locker, reporting a suspected drug sale, or picking-up a stepped on peanut butter and jelly sandwich (at least that is what I thought it was!).

Are you feeling overwhelmed yet? The first year of teaching can be overwhelming, but remember you have acquired knowledge, learned skills, and there are colleagues who will assist you if you seek their guidance.

In teaching, job variety and challenging situations abound; seldom is there a boring day. Countless occasions exist to influence and improve your students' lives. Be encouraged to take each opportunity that comes your way and always do your best for each student.


**OPPORTUNITIES FOR REFLECTION:**

1. **What do you accept as the most important roles of a teacher?**

2. **What extracurricular activities are of interest to you?**

3. **What do students need from teachers and what are the boundaries to guide teacher responses to student needs?**

**Chapter 3**

# PHILOSOPHY OF EDUCATION: IDEALS, CREATIVITY, EXPERIENCE

Many ideas and theories exist which attempt to explain successful teaching methods and effective student learning outcomes. It is very difficult for new teachers to decide which ideas and theories are most valid and which ones to incorporate in their personal beliefs about the art of teaching. However, new teachers are not alone in recognizing the differences presented by various and changing educational philosophies, veteran teachers also navigate in the revolving educational environment.

The ideas about teaching and learning held by educators develop over a period of time and evolve as a result of experience. Not everyone has the luxury of experience, so before entering the classroom all teachers should develop some basic ideas by which to direct the learning experience to be offered in their classroom. Along with developing a basic understanding of their own role in the classroom, teachers must define curriculum initiatives, student behavior expectations, and classroom management priorities.

Perhaps the following list of ideas will assist you in establishing some of your priorities or expand a number of your presently held ideas.

There are two types of people in a classroom: the teacher and the student. They each have definite, yet interdependent roles for they both teach and learn from each other and they must work together.

It is the teacher's responsibility to facilitate learning and it is the student's responsibility to learn; both responsibilities require skill and effort.

Each student must be viewed by the teacher as an important individual. Some students may be more enjoyable than others, but all are worthy of our attention and our caring. The truly successful teacher has a genuine love for young people combined with a love of learning.

A congenial atmosphere aids learning and provides pleasant learning experiences.

Mutual respect between teacher and students is important <u>and</u> possible.

In teaching, it is more successful to inspire students than to threaten them.

The teacher must be the one who is "in charge of the classroom." This does not mean that the teacher is the only one who participates in classroom activities; it simply means that the responsibility for classroom decorum belongs to the teacher and must be maintained by the teacher.

When students participate in classroom activities they learn more easily.

Practice may increase abilities and sharpen skills but motivation is the true key to learning. Creating the motivational environment is one of the teacher's greatest challenges and privileges.

Students need the guidance and leadership provided by their teachers. Students also need patient understanding from a respectable adult.

Students are influenced by their surroundings; therefore, teachers should use all opportunities possible to encourage the recognition of their goals, such as: a clean, orderly room can indicate focus; a neatly dressed teacher indicates personal recognition of the importance of teaching; and updated, often changed visuals throughout the room attracts student curiosity.

A well-managed classroom atmosphere helps students to keep "on task" with work assignments.

Teachers should tell their students what is required of them and then expect the students to produce accordingly. When a student strays from the stated directions, it is the teacher's responsibility to address the problem promptly and find an effective means to re-direct the student.

Teachers must adequately prepare their students for learning situations. Teach both concepts and skills. New learning and retention of that learning is increased when concepts and skills are taught together and when students are actively involved in the learning environment.

Teachers must accept the idea of accountability whether or not it is part of a written professional standard. We should not be in the teaching profession if we are not willing to do our best to educate our students.

Successful teachers encourage excellence, strive for improvement, and thank students for their efforts.

Combining numerous ideas into a solid understanding of the components of a successful teaching and learning environment can be a stimulating, engaging activity for new teachers. "The ABC's of Successful Teaching" chart shown below and the explanation of it (next page) present three vital components for a successful classroom experience: Academics, Behavior Management, and Classroom Environment. Throughout each classroom experience, these three components must be integrated with each other and fully functioning at the same time. When one of the components is not functioning as it should, a positive learning environment is interrupted, diminished, and may completely disappear.

The ABC's of Successful Teaching
(a maintained balance)

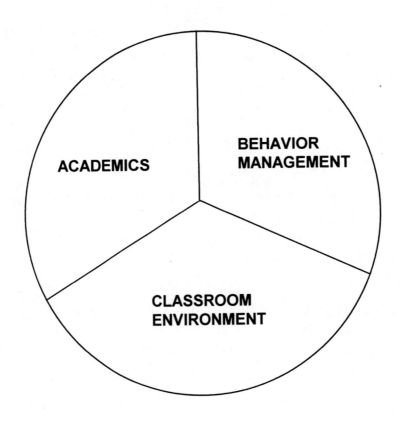

### ACADEMICS:

- Knowledgeable, prepared teacher.
- Defined curriculum content.
- Student centered activities.
- Focused, yet flexible presentation.
- Aligned with curriculum guides and state requirements.
- Varied and engaging teacher presentations.
- Knowledge and skills taught together.

### BEHAVIOR MANAGEMENT:

- Reasonableness - defined expectations.
- Respect to and by all members of the classroom.
- Fairness, consideration, and consistency displayed by teacher during interactions with students.
- Recognized importance of communication between teachers and parents.
- Teacher application of school discipline code.

### CLASSROOM ENVIRONMENT:

- Purposeful - time used efficiently, productively.
- Identified learning expectations.
- Student opinions respected.
- Comfortable, positive atmosphere.
- Organized activities and resources which support academic goals.
- Often changed, thought-provoking visuals posted throughout the classroom.

Now that you have reviewed the chart and component explanations, think about how the loss of one component would negatively impact the learning experience. For example, a teacher has a well developed academic background and has a thoroughly planned lesson with a variety of activities and resources. However, the teacher was highly unorganized and forgot to photocopy several resource sheets for students (and at class time could not even find the masters), thus student enrichment activities are unavailable and the learning opportunity is negatively impacted. Another scenario: the teacher was always well prepared for class presentations, yet is so sarcastic that students detest attending the class and often engage the teacher in verbal warfare, thus interrupting the full delivery of the lesson. One more scenario: the teacher was well prepared for the day's lesson, and began the class presentation even though several students were disruptive. The teacher ignored those students and they become more disruptive. As the teacher continued with class activities other students lost their focus. Finally, in desperation, the teacher stopped the class presentation and stated a homework assignment. The disruptive students remained uncooperative, the lesson presentation was incomplete, and the positive learning opportunity disappeared. Last scenario: the teacher was not well prepared for class, was often late in arriving to class, only reviewed the textbook, and seldom corrected negative student behavior. In this scenario, all components are malfunctioning. If this continues, several events will occur - positive learning will totally disappear, students will quickly adopt this teacher's example and misbehavior will dramatically increase. The final consequence is that the teacher will be replaced.

You can, I am sure, think of additional examples and results. It is easy to understand that when one component is interrupted or removed, the other parts are adversely affected and a positive classroom experience ends. Maintaining a positive balance between academics, behavior management, and classroom environment is, for all teachers, a daily challenge - yet it is possible to achieve this balance. Simply stated, teachers must be well prepared for each day, treat students with respect while guiding them, and determine to consistently enforce academic and behavior standards.

**OPPORTUNITIES FOR REFLECTION:**

1. **What guiding ideals are most prominent in your philosophy of education?**

2. **What are your professional and personal goals as an educator for the school year which you are about to begin? Prepare a short list (2 - 3 items for each category), then post it where you will read it often.**

3. **How will you manage the learning experience offered in your classroom?**

4. **How does the "ABC's of Successful Teaching" chart and explanation assist you as you reflect on the teaching year you are now experiencing or the year ahead? Are there additional ideas which you would add to the descriptions for each category of the Successful Teaching chart?**

# Chapter 4

# TRUE SATISFACTION!

Last night I attended a tenth-year class reunion. I had been the class advisor to these people during their senior year. The evening was very pleasant and enjoyable as we mingled and talked. I renewed friendships with former students and teachers with whom I had worked. I learned of some of the successes and accomplishments these people had enjoyed, and of some of the disappointments they had faced. I felt as though I had taken a giant leap forward in time! They all had changed during the past ten years and now, they were adults. One young man put his arm around me and said, "Mrs. Johnson, it's so good to see you again." I replied, "It's great to see you again too!" "Who are you?" He was one of the students I had been looking for but did not recognize!

Time passed quickly that evening. The dinner was tasty, the speeches were short yet sensitive, the music was loud, and people were happy. The celebration was altogether delightful, but for me, the highlight of the evening came quietly. I was sitting at a table talking with several guests when a former student approached us. He reached out to shake my hand and said, "Hi, do you know who I am?" I said, "Yes," and told him his name. He seemed pleased that I remembered him. Then he asked me this question: "Do you remember the time you asked me to stay after class for a short talk?" I replied, "No, what did we talk about?" He then recounted how he had been planning to quit school and I had evidently learned of his plan. He described how I had taken the time to explain to him that his proposed plan to quit school was a big mistake, and how I urged him to stay in school. He went on to tell me that for the next three weeks I continued talking with him, encouraging him to stay in school and try a little harder. He then thanked me for the guidance I had given to him and explained how happy he was that he had stayed in school, finished his studies, and graduated. He is now married, has children, and very much enjoys his job.

Needless to say, I was elated! I reminded myself teaching does have its rewards, rich rewards, some arriving even ten years later. As I reflected on the pleasure of visiting with my former students I was reminded again of the countless opportunities we teachers have to influence our students' lives in a meaningful way and how very important it is to take each opportunity presented to us.

# PART II

# THE FIRST YEAR
# OF TEACHING

**(A SALUTE TO *THE LITTLE ENGINE THAT COULD*)**

**Chapter 5**

# A ONCE IN A LIFETIME EXPERIENCE

Ask any teacher, "What do you remember about your first year of teaching?" and you will receive a rush of memories. That first year can be described by single words, or by stories; in either case, there are many recollections.

Most teachers would agree that the first year of teaching is exciting in many ways. It is wonderful to secure your first teaching position after years of studying, training, and expense. The future looks full of promise. Thoughts of your adoring students, in a well-organized classroom full of books and teaching resources, fill your mind. Added to those thoughts are the teaching methods you want to try. It is inspiring to think you can influence the lives of your students, and it is wonderful to work with other professionals. Teaching can be a fulfilling career offering daily opportunities or it can be the stepping stone toward an administrative position. Whatever your future is to be in the field of education, remember this: most people going into their first year of teaching have high expectations and a somewhat unrealistic view of what lies ahead.

## So, what should I expect to face in my first year of teaching?

The first year of teaching offers unlimited opportunities for personal growth; it is a year full of change and adjustments. When I was first offered a teaching position, I was assigned five classes of eighth grade American history. It was exactly the teaching position I desired. When I went to the school during the summer to obtain a set of textbooks, I was told my teaching assignment had been changed. I would be teaching two eighth grade classes and three twelfth grade classes. During the fall semester I would have three preparations, and in the spring semester I would pick up a fourth preparation. Not fully understanding all that was involved, and knowing how difficult it was to find a job (in the 1970's there were far more teachers available than needed), I said, "Oh, that's fine with me!"

After accepting this teaching position and, most especially after I was assigned to instruct twelfth grade students, I began to wonder about the academic challenge of dealing with advanced students. After a day or two with my students, I realized that I was very capable of leading the class, and years ahead of my students in the areas of knowledge, experience, and maturity.

Many adjustments must be made once the school year begins. The first week of school is difficult. After meeting many different people, attending numerous meetings, organizing my classes, and making many decisions I began to ask: "Why did I accept this job?" New teacher orientation days were busy and even before meeting my students, I was facing a sudden avalanche of papers and was in the "overload" mode before I knew what happened. Then, the students arrived! That first week of school passed like a blur; somehow all of the new teachers survived it. Each of us quickly realized that the total responsibility for our classes was in our hands; no longer were we supported by a supervising teacher who efficiently guided us through each day. We became full-fledged members of the faculty and were expected to carry our full share of the work load. We soon learned that becoming truly competent teachers was an evolving process. Many of us were struggling, yet we were making progress toward teacher independence and solid expertise.

Further adjustments involve acclimating one's self into "the school routine." The beginning months of my first year of teaching can easily be described: everything I did was somehow related to school. My morning started early, around 5:30 or 6:00 A.M. I studied for a half hour and then got ready to leave for school. The entire day at school was spent on school related activities. I seldom took any time off to relax. At the end of the "official" school day I often attended a required meeting or met with my mentor. Then, I went home and graded papers. I looked forward to the one or two-hour break from school work which cooking supper, cleaning the kitchen, and watching the news on television, involved. Then, it was back to the school work for another couple of hours. The next day was simply a repeat of the same time routine but with different topics. Friday nights I relaxed - at the laundromat! Saturdays, and a good share of Sundays, were given to school work as well; Saturday to catch up, and Sunday to plan ahead. There was always more work to do and I never seemed to be able to get away from the stress that the extra demands created. Teachers are always aware of past assignments which must be graded, current work assignments to complete, and future planning (short and long term) which must be designed. New teachers should be happy if they are not married or even seriously dating, for there is little time for a social life.

The swirl of the beginning school year keeps new teachers very busy, but eventually things begin to settle down. Then, Thanksgiving vacation arrives. Never before had I been so thankful for this holiday! What it really amounted to, was one day off for celebrating and three working days at home. I returned to school with new vigor and a highly developed sense of anticipation related to the Christmas vacation!

The long cold winter common to upstate New York was beginning and this seemed to have a settling effect on students. If you live in a geographical area that receives snow, one day you may wake up to a beautiful white blanket covering the ground. Quickly estimate the depth of the snow covering, then rush to your television to learn if your school has a delayed opening time or is closed for the day. It's so wonderful to see the name of your school district followed by the word "closed!" What is so amazing is that you were not even aware a snowstorm had been forecast. Since your lesson plans are completed, you are tempted to return to bed and sleep for the entire day. Instead you get up, have an enjoyable breakfast, then begin to grade book reports and unit tests. That night, since your lessons are already planned, you have sufficient time to turn on the television and see for the first time one of the new "Fall" shows. Without guilt, you think: "This was a very nice day!"

The next few weeks pass on schedule. Then you hear Christmas carols being sung in the hallways and someone dressed up as Santa Claus interrupts your class as your students are taking a test. Christmas vacation has finally arrived and it is a welcomed time. Although the thought of giving gift certificates to all relatives and purchased cookies to friends had crossed your mind, you have somehow managed to complete your Christmas shopping. You enjoy the holidays for several days and then begin to remember all the school work which must be done. One must get caught up and get a little ahead during this vacation if there is to be any hope of surviving until June. For some reason, after the Christmas vacation the school routine begins to progress more smoothly. Maybe the experience gained in the previous few months is beginning to make a difference as new skills are mastered and experience is increased.

Occasionally as the school year progresses, new teachers may have some doubts which never seem to disappear. Teachers may wonder about the quality of their performance as a teacher and will they be able to maintain the demanding pace of their commitments for the entire year? Will their contract be renewed? Are students increasing their knowledge and being intellectually challenged as a result of the teacher's instructional presentations? Some of the doubts are reduced after a successful classroom observation or two, but somehow, the observations may not be enough. You can generally evaluate your success by noticing trends within your classroom and teacher practice. Are your students asking questions and participating in classroom activities in a constructive manner? Are your students well behaved and your classes well organized? Are your record-keeping practices current and descriptive? Are your scheduling and grading abilities improving? Do you enjoy being in your classes? If you are looking for the same kind of encouragement you received from your supervising teacher during your student teaching days, you will probably be disappointed. Often, general encouragement or compliments are few and far between. If your classes are going well and there are no major problems known to you, then yes, you are doing well in your teaching position.

Another unforgettable memory from the first year of teaching is an incredible tiredness. Your tiredness comes from the many hours of "burning the midnight oil" as well as from the strain of the first year of teaching. Face it, this is a tough year.

Another adjustment to teaching in a public school is related to class size. During my student teaching days, class enrollment was approximately eighteen students. When I started the second semester of full-time teaching, my new (and fourth) preparation was a senior elective course in economics. There were thirty-five students on my class list. Students outnumbered the available desks in the room and for a few days some of the students sat on cabinets in the back of the room. It seemed as though it was going to be impossible to adequately teach that many students. So, I began the course by asking if anyone wanted to drop the course; no one volunteered to do so. As unprofessional as some may judge this to be, I was determined to make the workload so demanding that several students would drop the course. The students received their textbooks and the course work began.

During the first week in this class, I heard "moans and groans" as I piled on the many and varied assignments. The first week ended and no students had dropped the course or indicated they were planning to do so. Most of the students were completing the assignments and showing evidence of learning. I convinced myself that the students needed more time to consider transferring to another course. The second week arrived and the work assignments remained demanding. At the end of the second week, no one had dropped the course. More desks were added to the room and additional textbooks arrived. I began to recognize that classroom management techniques were an important key to successful teaching practice.

As the third week ended and no students had dropped the course, I accepted the fact that my class enrollment for this course was going to remain at thirty-five students. I also realized that my students had ceased complaining about the workload and were responding in a positive manner to the course demands and routine. I concluded the course was moving along nicely. However, there was one noticeable difficulty: I was having a terrible time keeping up with all of the assignments, writing many quizzes, and then grading all of the student papers I received!

We all somehow continued to work at this demanding pace for the entire semester. We studied many topics and had numerous interesting discussions. The textbook was excellent. Best of all were the students, they were lively individuals who participated often and seemed genuinely interested in the course. I believe many of the students benefited from the course and I, too, enjoyed it.

At the end of the semester, I purchased an introduction to economics workbook at a local university and used many questions from it to construct the final exam for this course. It was a tough exam but all of my students passed it. I was extremely proud of my students and truly glad that none of them transferred out of the course.

As a result of this course, I learned many valuable lessons such as: challenge your students to do more than they think they are capable of doing, be well prepared for each class, supplement the textbook with meaningful assignments, combine current events to illustrate course content, be focused and directive, take time to think about your plans and to review your methods. I have always been grateful for the students in that economics class, for the experiences we shared, for the lessons they taught me, and for the positive impact they had on my entire teaching career.

The first year continues to move on, and very slowly, in March. By the time April arrives new teachers feel they have passed from "rookie" to "veteran" and they know whether or not their contract has been renewed. The sense of "straining to survive" has been replaced by an awareness of refined skills. May finally arrives, flowers bloom, yearbooks are seen everywhere, and final exams must be written. Before long, the wonderful month of June appears on our calendars and with it award assemblies, final exams to grade, graduation, and the final day of the school year. As this school year ends, the new teacher becomes a regular faculty member who has gained a year of experience, a sense of confidence, and a feeling of accomplishment. We all know the next school year will offer many of the same challenges, surprises, and opportunities, but it should be somewhat easier.

The first year of teaching has now been completed. Was it a good year? It certainly was a year to remember! Take some time to reflect on the events of the past year. Savor the accomplishments and learn from the mistakes.

There are several ideas teachers should remember from their first year of teaching and practice in succeeding years. Take care of yourself - eat properly, get sufficient sleep, and exercise regularly - those ideas are vital to personal stress management and will reduce the threat of burnout. "Bond" with your colleagues and enjoy your students.

After the school year has ended, teachers face what they think will be several months of "vacation." Actually, they will be involved in a variety of activities (caring for their own children who too quickly become bored without the school routine, taking summer education courses in overcrowded rooms which do not have air-conditioning, or working at some menial, temporary job) none of which actually fall under the category of a "vacation." Then, too, there is the ever-present thought that notes and papers from the past school year should be organized and plans should be developed for the next school year. During this "vacation" you may even have several quick occasions when you begin to look forward to the opening day of the next school year. You will not have long to wait - the opening day of the new school year is never far away!

* Author's note.

*My first year of teaching was demanding, and at times, difficult; still it was a good year. In January of that year I even had enough time to begin dating the man I later married!

# Chapter 6

# ADVICE FOR NEW TEACHERS

Often, new teachers wonder how they can make an easy transition into the teaching profession. They are aware of the many demands which will be placed upon them, yet they do not have the benefit of a wide range of experiences from which to draw practical solutions. Many of my colleagues were asked: "What advice would you give to new teachers which would assist them in their professional practice?" Some of the responding teachers were veterans of many years of teaching service, while others were relatively new to teaching; nevertheless, they all had important ideas to submit for your careful consideration. Those ideas, listed in no particular order, are varied in content, thought-provoking, and practical.

**Work with other teachers**. Being new to the teaching profession as well as a new teacher in a particular school district is a double challenge. You will need to prove yourself; however, you do not need to do this alone. When help is needed, seek the assistance of a friendly teacher or your department chairman. Carry your share of the workload in study halls and other assigned duties; become a member of the faculty "team."

**Learn from other teachers**. Find an excellent teacher who is willing to work with you and then learn all you can from that person. Discuss all aspects of the teaching profession, particularly various classroom management techniques and teaching methods. It can be helpful if this experienced teacher is in the same department as you, but it is not a requirement.

**Seek assistance when needed**. If you are having specific difficulties (controlling your class, planning lessons, grading papers), choose a teacher with whom you feel comfortable and discuss the problem(s). Many skilled teachers are willing to share their experience with new teachers in an effort to help them. After discussing the problems and possible solutions, try some of the solutions and see if they work for you.

**Classroom sharing**. When sharing a classroom with another teacher, be sure to leave the room as soon as possible after your class has ended. Do not linger in the room while the incoming teacher is trying to begin class. Also, the room should be left in good condition: the writing boards

Colleagues are a source of help. Seek their advice.

should be clean, all materials and equipment should be properly stored, and student desks should be neatly arranged.

**Memos, memos, and more memos**! Read, note, and remember important announcements. It is necessary to know when changes are made in the regular school schedule due to activities such as assemblies, field trips, testing, or picture-taking. There may also be changes in the regular schedule of meetings or an unexpected, yet required, meeting may be scheduled. It is the responsibility of all teachers to be aware of those schedule changes and to make appropriate adjustments to their individual plans. Important information should be noted in the plan book or written on a calendar of events.

**Classroom atmosphere**. Aside from lesson content, much of what occurs in the classroom is simply the application of good common sense.

**Short rules**. Be fair, be consistent, be kind.

**Another short rule**. Teacher paperwork must be completed on time, and if it is not done on time, never tell your students!

**Review school policies, discipline codes**. As quickly as possible, become well acquainted with school policies (which apply to your responsibilities), operating procedures related to your school, and the school's student disciplinary code. Knowing the policies and operational procedures will assist you in meeting numerous job requirements and knowing the disciplinary code increases your options for dealing with troublesome students.

**Control your temper**. A school setting is the wrong workplace for a hot-tempered individual who has little self control. Working with students requires patience or, at the very least, a willingness to try to be patient. You will accomplish little if you constantly lose your self-control.

**Talk can be expensive**. Be careful in what you say and how you say it, for often there is an active, well-developed grapevine in a school. When you are told something in confidence, keep it to yourself. Earning the trust of colleagues and students takes time, losing that trust takes only seconds.

**Create positive student behavior expectations**. All teachers want well behaved students, but that does not "just happen." Discuss with your students your expectations and limit the number of rules you make. Do not make rules to cover every possible situation, for you will be so busy enforcing rules you will not have time for instruction. When an individual is behaving poorly tell the student to behave. If you are sufficiently knowledgeable regarding the discipline code, inform the student of the consequences of continued unacceptable behavior. In dealing with disruptive student behavior, the consistency and fairness displayed by the teacher are both extremely important.

**Build a positive relationship with parents.** At the beginning of the school year, try to make a positive contact with the parents of your students. A note, letter, or telephone call to the parents can be very effective in establishing a mutual support base.

**Teacher preparation and life experiences**. Do not fear that your students may know more than you do even though your first teaching position might be in the twelfth grade. Many students are intelligent and academically advanced; however, as a teacher you have accomplished many goals, completed many requirements, and learned a great deal in four or more years of college. In addition to your training and knowledge, you have gained much in personal experience. Be confident in your knowledge, abilities, and leadership.

**True friends?** Avoid deep involvement in small cliques; they stifle opportunities, friendships, and personal development.

**Time to think**. When facing a problem related to academic preparation, presentation skills, classroom management, or student behavior, teachers must take time to think about the difficulty. Define the problem, list its causes, then create workable solutions.

**Teacher hours**. The teachers' contract with a school district usually lists the arrival and departure times for the school day. Teachers are expected to arrive promptly and to stay until the day has officially ended. When the school day is listed as, for example, from 8 A.M. until 3 P.M., one should realize that is somewhat misleading! Plan to spend many, many more hours preparing for class presentations, grading papers, attending meetings, discussing issues or topics with students or other faculty members, and assisting students with extracurricular activities. During your first year of teaching, you will "live" teaching; it will amaze you how much time your teaching duties and responsibilities will consume. It will become less time-consuming as your experience grows, but it always requires more than forty hours per week.

**Learn about your school**. All new teachers in a school need to learn about the life of the school: its strengths and weaknesses, its successes and failures, its policies and practices, and maybe some of its history and future plans. Before suggesting solutions to solve major school problems, learn about previously attempted plans. After being integrated into the faculty, new teachers may voice, with earned respectability, their observations and opinions about school problems and possible solutions.

**Reality check.** Often, first-year teachers are very idealistic, enthusiastic, and confident in their teaching ability and knowledge. However, the first-year teacher often fails to recognize the wide gulf which exists between theory and practice, and between training and experience.

**Never throw anything at students.** It seems incredible that this statement must be made, but some teachers will throw a piece of chalk or an eraser at a bothersome student. It is a mistake - a major mistake! First, it may result in a serious student injury. Second, it sets a poor example of self-control. Third, the wrong student may be hit. Fourth, it may result in disciplinary action taken against the teacher (see next topic). Teachers must employ a safer method for getting a student's attention and changing the undesirable behavior.

**Avoid the use of corporal punishment.** Using any means of physical punishment is totally unacceptable teacher behavior. There may be times when you briefly consider corporal punishment as a viable choice, but <u>choose</u> some other option to correct inappropriate student behavior. Teachers who use any form of corporal punishment against their students risk possible civil lawsuits by the student's family. Depending on the seriousness of the offense, the school district may take action against the teacher by issuing a reprimand, requiring counseling, or even terminating the teacher's employment in the district. In severe cases, the teacher may face criminal charges and could also lose her/his teaching certification.

**Limit your complaining.** Complaining is a habit and it can develop quickly, especially if one listens to others who are in that "rut." The faculty room is a great place for teachers to "vent", but do not complain every time you are in the faculty room.

**Give every student a chance.** Do not accept other teachers' opinions of particular students as proven fact. Students mature and improve over time and they need teachers who will give them an opportunity to prove themselves. When students who have previously been problematic appear in your classroom, give them a chance to adjust to you as a classroom teacher and to your overall teaching methods and practices.

**Establish and hold to high standards for your students.** Do not lower standards because of students' lack of productivity. Remember: many students will thrive when high standards are established, especially if they sense you have significant expectations for them to achieve those standards and you display a willingness to work with them.

**Flexibility is necessary**. Teachers should be flexible in the classroom methods used. Some techniques which work well in one class may not work well in another class. Students have different learning styles and a good teacher attempts to accommodate those differences. Students appreciate a teacher who is adaptable and open to suggestions.

**Keep your sense of humor**. Teachers should not only keep their sense of humor, but they should use it often for it can increase the productivity as well as the pleasure of the classroom experience for both the teacher and the students. Remember, too, humor should always be guided by a sensitivity to the feelings and diversities of others.

**Show your humanity**. Although a teacher needs to keep a professional distance, it is important to allow your students the opportunity to learn you are a caring human being. Your students need to know you have a strong desire to help them improve their lives. Students appreciate a teacher's willingness to listen to them, and students need their teacher's time and attention.

**Promote positive change**. Do not waste time criticizing what exists within your school without first investing time to create improvements.

**Students' moods and behaviors**. Teachers must understand that students' moods and behaviors are caused by many different factors. If you are concerned about the health, well-being, or negativism of a student, consult your principal or other professional staff members.

**Listen to your students**. Students have valid ideas and opinions and they often have interesting or unique ways of interpreting situations. Sharing ideas and opinions helps students expand their knowledge and understanding. The sharing of ideas also keeps the teacher excited and responsive in the classroom and in touch with fresh viewpoints and changing times. This interaction between the students and their teacher is what transforms a humdrum class into a potent learning experience.

**Personal professional growth**. Take advantage of in-service workshops (courses offered by local school districts or regional educational groups). Workshops offer opportunities to learn something new in a relaxed, non-competitive atmosphere; they also provide occasions to meet people and form new friendships.

**Maintaining discipline**. Maintain a sense of control in the classroom and consistently follow through on all "directives" you make concerning discipline. Students may resist a teacher's directions and test that person's resolve, but they dislike an inconsistent teacher far more.

**Applying discipline**.  Remember, strict discipline can be applied gently and with much consideration for the students.  A teacher maintains classroom control by establishing firm yet reasonable rules, by consistently enforcing them, and by refusing to allow students to disrupt a class.  A teacher need not be domineering - just firm, fair, and consistent.

**The fine art of disciplining**.  Whenever possible, discipline on an individual basis.  The entire class should never be punished for the offense of one student, nor does the entire class membership want to be included in a discussion (lecture) about a particular individual's offense.  Problems with an individual student should be solved with that individual; problems involving many students (e.g. many coming to class late, widespread cheating) can be openly discussed in class.

**Always be well-prepared**.  Thorough preparation of subject material is absolutely necessary.  To be adequately prepared for class presentations takes time, thoughtful planning, and personal motivation.  It also requires a genuine interest in course curriculum and successful student learning.  It may be understandable, yet it is unacceptable, for teachers to enter their classroom unprepared; not only are they wasting their own time, they are wasting their students' time - and everyone knows it.

**Invest time thinking about your teaching practice**.  Decide what you want to accomplish with your students, and then design a plan to achieve those goals.  Review how you interact with your students and colleagues for this greatly impacts how cooperatively others will work with you.  Critique the processes you employ in the delivery of academic content and the supervision of student behavior, and review the efficiency of classroom and time management techniques. In relation to your goals, are your practices effective?

**A word of encouragement**.  Stay with the profession for a minimum of three years unless you detest almost everything about your job.  The first year is the most difficult because everything is new to you:  the students, the school system, the faculty, and the curriculum.  Many times the new teacher in the department is assigned all the courses no one else wants to teach.  As a result, the new teacher may have a wide range of course preparations as well as the classes with the most serious discipline problems. This first year of teaching can provide a tough introduction to a teaching career, but succeeding years are somewhat easier as experience increases.

**More words of encouragement**.  The second year of teaching is bound to be better than the first, for you have gained valuable experience.  Do not be discouraged if your students tested your determination, even veteran teachers are so tested by their students.

**Your career choice**. Remember, you chose to enter into this profession. You have invested time, energy, and money preparing to become a teacher. Be proud of your accomplishments. Be happy about your career choice. Be confident and enthusiastic in your professionalism.


## OPPORTUNITIES FOR REFLECTION

1. **With which of the above reviewed ideas do you most agree? Most disagree?**

2. **Which aspects of your teaching style and your personality will be most identifiable in the classroom?**

3. **Which ideas presented in this reading challenged you to consider modifying your teaching style?**

4. **What additional teacher impacting ideas have you gained from discussing this chapter with your professor or mentor?**

# PART III

# OH, TO BE ORGANIZED!

**(IT IS POSSIBLE)**

# Chapter 7

# A TEACHER'S CALENDAR

At the beginning of the school year, each teacher is given a most important book called a "Plan Book-Register". This book is used to document teacher and student activities. The first half of the book is for recording each day's planned activities, followed by notes related to actual accomplishments for each class. All assignments should be recorded in the plan book when assigned and reminder notes can be written in the box of the due date. The second half of the book, the register, is used for recording student grades and student absences. **Teachers should be methodical and meticulous when writing in both the plan book and register.**

After receiving a plan book, it is wise to write your name on the inside cover sheet. This identification is important for when it is misplaced (most teachers do this at least one time) it will, with a little bit of luck, be returned to a very relieved teacher! The plan book-register should be kept with the teacher at all times during the school day or it should be secured in a locked place. Teachers quickly understand the meaning of the word "panic" when this book is lost, and most especially if it is lost just prior to the end of a marking term! Teachers' plan books have been taken and destroyed by students, so the plan book-register should not be left where it presents an open invitation to a disappearance act.

There are a number of companies which sell plan book-registers. Most of the plan book-registers include some extra pages for special information such as the teacher's daily schedule, equipment inventory, seating charts, and textbook numbers. Some of those extra pages are found in the front of the plan book-register, some between the two sections or at the end of the book. Some of the pages are helpful, some are not.

Just inside the cover of this book, I always kept certain papers including several office referral forms for reporting disciplinary problems, several attendance sheets for daily reporting, seating charts for each class, and a Scan-A-Score sheet (described later). My daily class schedule - listing times, periods, room numbers, and any other assigned duties such as study hall supervision - was taped to the first page of my plan book where it was readily available to me. I usually taped a clear sheet of plastic (an unused transparency works well) over my class schedule to protect it from being torn.

# THE PLAN BOOK

The plan book is a valuable teacher tool - it is a working calendar which can, and often is, changed. When properly used, the plan book provides a place for the teacher to clearly describe each day's planned activities such as a lecture presentation, viewing a videotape, completing a reading assignment, preparing a lab report, or leading a discussion. Descriptions should include specific information such as outline topic, name of videotape, book and page numbers for a reading assignment, or the topic of a lab report or class discussion. The plan book also provides an organizational format in which to write long-range plans for unit presentations, ordering and using audio-visual media, testing, and scheduling special projects. Teachers should be careful to indicate actual accomplishments for each class and announced homework assignments. The plan book can also be useful for recording various required meetings and individual appointments.

Each class should be listed separately in the plan book because there are times when different sections of the same class preparation will not accomplish the stated assignment or when a class will be canceled, thus making separate entries a necessity.

Classes can be listed in the plan book in any order preferred by the teacher. Many teachers list classes according to their schedule while other teachers organize their plan books by grouping same class preparation courses together; both methods are workable and satisfactory. If there are sufficient slots left in the plan book after listing each class, label one slot "Notes." This category is especially useful for writing reminders about scheduled meetings, parental conferences, testing dates, picture days, planned assemblies, need for copying material, sick or personal days, end-of-the-marking-term dates, and faculty parties! Also, in the "Notes" section, teachers can list specific audio-visual equipment needed for classroom use. If equipment must be reserved prior to its use, a check mark can be placed next to the listed equipment after the reservation request has been approved.

Plan books are most useful to a teacher when written information is brief, descriptive, current, and professional. By using a self designed word abbreviation system, teachers can write complete descriptions of planned class activities and assignments within the small boxes provided in the plan book. On the next page, you will find a size reduced sample of an open plan book. As you review the pages, notice the overall page design, type of information included by the teacher, abbreviations used, and assignments listed.

| COURSE NAME | MONDAY | TUESDAY | WEDNESDAY | THURSDAY | FRIDAY | NOTES |
|---|---|---|---|---|---|---|
| Am. Hist. Period 1 | Forms of Govt Mon, Democ, Parl, Dict. - define, adv, disadv-chart | World map- id countries by govt type Allies-diff forms | US govt-VT 5Br worksheet p. 215-221 | Rev. hw Candidates duties and qualifica-tions | Essay: You-a gov't official which count, position (why) duties, | Call L. Cook |
| Economics Period 2 | Intro Ch. 4 3 forms bus org - def, adv, disadv, #W read p. 48-56 | VT Hist of Free Enterprise #W read p 56-66 | Rev. history of corp devel Read pg 68 - 2 charts #W Ques.3,4 p. 75 | Govt / Bus. relationship control cooperation #W - Sum News articles | Stocks/invest Read exch quotes Intro project | |
| Am. Hist. Period 5/6 | Same as above | SAS | SAS | SAS distribute essay assign. | No class - pep rally | |
| Am. Hist. Period 7/8 | SAS | SAS | SAS | SAS | SAS | |
| Economics Period 10 | SAS | SAS | SAS | SAS | SAS | |
| Notes | | Fac. mgt 2:20 | Extra Help Day | Detention B. Smith R. Sloan | | |

Sample Plan Book Entries

# THE TEACHER'S GRADE REGISTER

The second half of the plan book-register is for recording students' grades and absences. Grades are very important, for they are the accepted measure of a student's success in learning content and completing work assignments in a course. There should be an adequate number of grades recorded in the register which realistically reflect the students' efforts and accomplishments (or lack thereof). Some school districts have stated policies related to grading, teachers should be aware of those policies and incorporate them within their grading standards.

Accurate attendance records are important since many school districts are now requiring their students to attend a certain percentage of all classes in order to obtain course credit towards graduation. In addition, attendance records are often important to the school district in determining state and other financial aid received by the school district. Also, in many states teachers' attendance records for their students are admissible evidence in expulsion hearings or in family court cases.

Three general but important rules about student grades are: 1) teachers must be able to justify all grades to students, their parents, and to school administrators, 2) teachers must know and follow all school regulations concerning grades, and 3) students should be allowed to review their grades at a time convenient to both the teacher and the student.

As part of my introduction to each course all of my students were given a copy of my "Requirement Sheet" (described later). The requirement sheet clearly described student behavior guidelines, assignment categories, and grade averaging method. At the end of each marking term, after the students had received their report cards, I would again take a few minutes in class to explain my grading system. Then, after giving an in-class assignment, I informed my students that if they did not understand the grade they received they were free to come to my desk right then for an explanation or see me after class. Often, many students came to my desk for an explanation - some to learn how they could improve, some to discover why they had done so poorly, and some just to admire their good work!

When parents come to a teacher to review their daughter's or son's grade, they usually are most interested in the areas in which the student is doing poorly and what can be done to improve the situation. Many parents are struggling with their teenagers over school work, so when discussing the strengths and weaknesses of their student, try to be encouraging without offering false reassurances or expectations. Suggest areas for improvement and ways the parents can continue checking on the student's status. Teachers can encourage parents to call them at school every two weeks for an update and return calls should be placed promptly. Returning a telephone call and talking with parents is an effective, efficient method for maintaining continued parental involvement and support.

There are times when a teacher must explain or justify a student's grade to the principal. This most often occurs when a student fails a course and will not graduate or will be required to attend summer school. Many times the high school principal is the person who calls the parents and informs them that their teenager will not be graduating. Since this is a rather unpleasant job, every principal wants to know that the teacher has recorded a sufficient number of grades to justify the failing average and has sent warning notices to the parents. It is important to assist your principal by maintaining all the necessary documentation and contact information.

Frequently, school districts will establish guidelines for teachers regarding grades. Such guidelines, stated in the handbook, can greatly assist the teacher if they clearly state or explain the number of grades required as a minimum, the types of grades to be included (e.g., tests, writing assignments, homework, special project), grade weighting, and a letter-to-number conversion chart. One of the schools in which I taught required a minimum of ten grades per student per marking term (ten weeks), not a difficult number of grades to have recorded per term.

Some school districts require teachers to return their plan book-registers to department chairmen or to the building principal at the end of the school year. Occasionally, during the summer vacation, a student's grade may be checked at the request of a parent. District administrators may also review the plan book-registers to ascertain that teachers have adequately recorded lesson descriptions, grades, and student absences. After the summer vacation, many school administrators will make those used plan book-registers available to teachers when they return to school in the fall. Whenever possible, "repossess" the plan book for it can be very helpful during the next year. I have often referred to a retired plan book to remind myself of past lesson plans, to find the name of a useful video tape, or just to compare the present year's progress with that of the previous year.

# GRADE AVERAGING METHODS

It is very important for a teacher to decide before the beginning of the school year how each grade earned by a student will relate to the term average. The term averaging method should be explained to students at the beginning of the course by distributing a requirement sheet or a course and grading description sheet. Assignment variety, which provides different opportunities for students to expand their knowledge, develop their skills, and earn a satisfactory grade, are important aspects which teachers should include in their grading decisions. After teachers have defined types of assignments, and their grade value, they must inform students of the grade earning plan.

Teachers are usually free to determine the different categories to be included within their course assignments and the percentage of the term average each category will represent. After careful consideration, I chose to use four main categories: homework / class work / quizzes, notebook, project(s), and tests. Each category counted 25% of the term average because each seemed equal to the others in importance, educational value, and time requirements. I categorized all my grades as I wrote them in my register so all homework, class work, and quizzes were listed together and in a separate section. The same procedure was used for notebook, project, and test grades.

Once I had all the planned grades for a particular category, whenever I had extra time near the end of the marking term, I calculated category averages. After calculating the averages, I highlighted each column using a brightly-colored marker. When the time came to average the four categories for the final term grade, the four category averages were easily found, totaled and divided by four. The term average was entered in the register on the right-hand side of the grade sheet and on a summary sheet if one was provided in the register. The last step was to mark report cards or computer sheets.

A number of my colleagues were asked to describe their grading system, including types of assignments, number of grades, grade categories, and weighting of various items. Listed below are some of their descriptions:

I collect one or two homework assignments or quizzes each week to record in my register (twenty grades). Every three weeks I give a unit test (three tests per term), and all test grades are doubled. All grades are then added together and divided by the number of grades (twenty-six) for the term average. Students are not required to keep a notebook and there are no large projects or other requirements.

I grade papers by giving a raw score on each paper (sixteen responses equals sixteen possible points; if a student answers three questions incorrectly, the score is thirteen). I collect and grade approximately thirty items per term: four to six tests (which are doubled), two to four in-class projects, and twenty to thirty homework assignments or quizzes. The term average is calculated by adding all points earned and dividing that sum by the total points possible.

I have far too many grades! I usually have thirty to forty grades in my register for each student. Single grades are given to weekly spelling tests, vocabulary quizzes, literature check-tests, grammar quizzes, and journals. Grades on major compositions are doubled, and unit tests are tripled.

I have three categories in my grading system. They are: unit tests (50% of term average), quizzes (25%), and homework (25%). Tests and quizzes are straightforward averages. In the homework category, students begin the marking term with 100 points. Every assignment not submitted subtracts four points from this 100 point homework total. Every assignment turned in late subtracts two points. All homework assignments are checked and are scored either satisfactory or unsatisfactory. When an assignment is unsatisfactory, it must be re-done and re-submitted.

I have twenty to twenty-five grades for each marking term. Homework and current events summaries count once each, tests are doubled, and special projects are tripled.

I have five categories of grades: homework and quizzes, class work, tests, notebook, and term project or term paper. In addition to these categories, I weighted quite heavily each student's participation in class discussions. After computing a student's final term average, I reviewed my seating chart and totaled the number of check marks I had placed beside the student's name. Each check mark indicated an important contribution to class discussions. Depending on the number of check marks assigned to each student, I would increase a student's term average up to an additional five points.

It is easy to see that teachers design their marking systems to measure items they believe are important. Tests, homework assignments, and a wide variety of special projects are common to most teachers. Teachers should design all work assignments so they encourage students to think and expand their understanding; thus diversified assignments are encouraged. Teachers should also recognize the importance and the effect of each grade on a student's term average. When designing a grading system, teachers should provide students with a variety of different opportunities in which to earn a grade, determine the importance of each assignment in relation to other assignments, and fully inform students of the grading system.

# RECORDING GRADES

All grades in the register must be accurately recorded, neatly written, and appropriately labeled. Teachers should record the grades as students earn them, and never change a student's grade to accomplish the passing or failing of an individual. Students have an entire marking term to establish an average, so let them live with the results of their work.

When writing grades in a register, teachers should use a fine-tip ball-point pen. If you are highly organized, use blue ink for passing grades and red ink for failing grades. When both colors are used consistently, one can immediately recognize the students who are having academic problems in each class. Pencils should not be used for writing grades in a register; they smear from frequent handling and become illegible. Also, avoid felt-tip pens because the ink may bleed through the paper or the color may run if it ever gets wet from spilled coffee, tea, or other beverage. If writing small enough to fit number grades into the little boxes provided in the register is difficult, use two boxes, and change the headings to meet your needs. Grades must be entered into the register neatly so they can be easily read and averaged. There is no substitute for this requirement! If letter grades are written on student assignments and they must eventually be converted into number grades for averaging purposes, it is best to complete the conversion chore promptly while the assignment and each student's work is fresh in your mind.

Each entered grade should be adequately labeled. Over a period of time, teachers develop an abbreviation system for writing descriptions of assignments. Each entry should include a complete description of the assignment, the due date, and the grading system. Listed below are some examples of my register entries, followed by an explanation of each:

HW-MC, pp. 217-8, # 1-9, 15, 18-21. 10/15. Base 14.

This first entry describes a homework assignment of multiple choice questions from pages 217 and 218; selected question numbers were listed, and work was collected on October 15. This type of assignment was usually corrected in class then given to me for scoring. I used the "Scan-A-Score" sheet to figure the score for each paper, based on fourteen available correct answers. If the student missed two questions, the score would be 86.

NB check. 10/16. Base -10/item.

The second entry refers to an October 16th check of student notebooks. There was a ten-point deduction for each required item which was missing or incomplete.

TEST, Chap. 4-5. 10/18. Base 68.

The last entry describes a test on chapters four and five given on October 18. There were sixty-eight responses, each weighted equally.

Most registers combine grade and attendance records by providing spaces for both items according to a weekly reporting system. This system has been used by teachers for many years, but it is flawed and inefficient. By combining two different types of information the teacher's ability to quickly recognize particular academic or attendance problems of students is reduced. It also reduces the teacher's ability to readily explain grades and list absences, and it takes time to label the date on the column headings in the register. Using a two-page spread which combines grades and attendance records makes grades more difficult to interpret, more time-consuming to record (since all grades on the right-hand page are far away from the student name list on the left-hand page), and more difficult to average for a term grade. It is also more difficult for the teacher to easily notice attendance problems of students when attendance information is combined with grades and spread out over two pages.

To separate student grades from attendance records is not a difficult task; you simply modify your register in this way:

1. Open your register and totally ignore all labels in the weekly evaluation columns.
2. Label the page on the left "GRADES" and the page to the right "ABSENCES."
3. Decide what types of assignments will be given to the students such as: tests, quizzes, objective or essay type homework assignments, projects, labs, abstracts, term paper(s), notebook, class work, demonstrations, designs, experiments, folders, book reports, etc.
4. Decide grade categories and which assignments will be included in each category. For example, my four different grade categories were: 1) homework / class work / quizzes, 2) notebooks, 3) tests, and 4) projects.
5. Decide what percentage of the final term grade each category will represent. Write the percentage figures in your grade register. I counted each category as 25% of the term average.
6. Decide approximately how many items there will be in each category and draw lines in the register to separate those different sections. I usually needed ten to fifteen spaces for the homework / class work / quiz category, three spaces for notebooks, one to four spaces for projects, and four to six spaces for tests. When writing grades in the register, group

43

them according to your chosen categories; this makes it easier to average them later as a group. When the marking term ends, compute an average for each category; then use those category averages to calculate the final term average. Remember to save one column in each category for writing the category average (included in the spacing counts listed above). Save the last usable column on the right-hand side of the "Grades" page for listing the term average.

You may wish to consider using an accounting journal as your grade register. Accounting journals offer larger-sized boxes for recording grades and absences and they contain fewer column titles. If you choose to use an accounting journal, it may be a good idea to place it in a report cover that firmly holds the journal binding. Accounting journals of varying design are available at an office supply store.

# RECORDING STUDENT ABSENCES

If you have chosen to record student grades and student absences on separate pages, the student absences sheet would appear as the right-hand page of an open register. Number each line in the first column consecutively to correspond with student names and numbers on the facing page. Every time a student is absent, enter the date (month and day) in the box provided. This system makes it very easy both to read the specific date(s) of absences and to quickly count the total number of days absent for each student. I usually took attendance at the end of the class period, and I did not keep a record of tardiness. When students came into my classroom after one-half of the class period was over, whether or not they had a pass, I marked them absent in my records. If tardiness became a habit for a particular student, that problem was discussed between the two of us until a course of action or solution was found.

It is important to stress the necessity of regular class attendance and to inform students of their attendance records. I usually did this every five weeks. It only took a few minutes of class time to inform each student of the total number of days absent from my class. This is an opportunity to verbally warn those who have been absent many days, and it shows the students that you are aware of and seriously concerned about any attendance problems.

# NEW REGISTER DESIGN

The next two pages of this chapter illustrate my method of categorizing student grades and separating student grades from attendance records.

The process described can be adapted to most class registers simply by changing column headings. The "GRADES" sheet would always be on the left-hand side of an open register, and the "ABSENCES" sheet would be on the right-hand side. The pattern for page usage is repeated for each marking term.

Teachers may include additional notations in their registers. On the sample register page, for example, look at the test grades for Student Q. During the last test the student was caught cheating. A grade of zero was assigned with a "C" written inside to indicate cheating. By writing inside the zero the teacher can more accurately explain the grade at a later time, if necessary. The dot placed in the box for the last test of Student W indicates the student completed the make-up exam and the teacher has the paper to grade. Depending on available space, textbook numbers and notations about warning notices or other communications with parents can be listed in either the grades or absences section of the register.

After reviewing the illustrated "Grade and Absences Register" on the next two pages, you may turn to the final page of this chapter for "Opportunities for Reflection."

# GRADES . . .

**Grade Descriptions →**

W/S - worksheet
(26) - basis for grade
HW/CW/Q - homework, classwork + quizzes
NB - Notebook

| Student Names | Quiz EL legal terms 9/5 (6x=26) | MC 1-15 T/F 1-10 p.23 9/28 (25) | W/S-Wills 9/30 (10) | L/T p.23 1-4 p.31 2-8 10/2 (11) | L/T p.49 2-5 p.56 1-3 10/5 (17) | C/N W/S 10/16 (16) | C/N Quiz terms 10/17 (15) | SL p.56 MC 1-16 MAT 1-12 10/23 (26) | SL W/S 10/26 (12) | SL p.72 MC 1-12 MAT 1-13 10/29 (24) | AVERAGE - HW/CW/Q | Family Law 9/23 (56) | Wills 10/1 (41) | Landlord/Tenant 10/9 (36) | Contract/Negligence 10/23 (42) | School Law 11/4 (59) | AVERAGE - TESTS | Newspaper articles 10/21 | Reading Day Reports 10/30 | AVERAGE - PROJECTS | NB Check 10/7 (-10/item) | NB Check 11/2 (-10/item) | AVERAGE - NOTEBOOKS | Warning Notice Sent | Final Term Average |
|---|---|---|---|---|---|---|---|---|---|---|---|---|---|---|---|---|---|---|---|---|---|---|---|---|---|
| 1. Student A | 92 | 96 | 80 | 100 | 86 | 100 | 93 | 92 | 92 | 96 | 93 | 91 | 90 | 92 | 95 | 88 | 91 | 90 | 80 | 85 | 100 | 100 | 100 | | 92 |
| 2. B | 96 | 88 | 80 | 82 | 71 | 94 | 87 | 92 | 83 | 92 | 87 | 89 | 85 | 78 | 90 | 97 | 88 | 95 | 90 | 93 | 95 | 80 | 88 | | 89 |
| 3. C | 73 | 81 | 80 | 91 | 100 | 88 | 80 | 73 | 92 | 88 | 85 | 93 | 83 | 86 | 88 | 76 | 85 | 100 | 80 | 90 | 85 | 95 | 90 | | 88 |
| 4. D | 88 | 92 | 70 | 91 | 86 | 100 | 73 | 88 | 67 | 83 | 84 | 88 | 78 | 81 | 83 | 95 | 85 | 80 | 80 | 80 | 100 | 90 | 95 | | 86 |
| 5. E | 77 | 69 | 80 | 82 | 86 | 94 | 87 | 73 | 83 | 79 | 81 | 82 | 71 | 75 | 79 | 83 | 78 | 75 | 60 | 68 | 80 | 85 | 83 | | 78 |
| 6. F | 69 | 81 | 70 | 82 | 86 | 81 | 80 | 85 | 75 | 75 | 78 | 79 | 73 | 69 | 79 | 76 | 75 | 90 | 90 | 85 | 75 | 90 | 83 | | 80 |
| 7. G | 81 | 73 | 70 | 82 | 86 | 81 | 73 | 69 | 67 | 71 | 75 | 82 | 76 | 83 | 76 | 88 | 81 | 80 | 70 | 75 | 85 | 95 | 90 | | 80 |
| 8. H | 73 | 77 | 80 | 73 | 86 | 75 | 67 | 85 | 83 | 67 | 76 | 73 | 61 | 75 | 81 | 75 | 73 | 80 | 80 | 80 | 80 | 100 | 90 | | 80 |
| 9. I | 77 | 85 | 80 | 73 | 86 | 81 | 80 | 69 | 67 | 92 | 79 | 86 | 83 | 78 | 71 | 75 | 79 | 90 | 70 | 80 | 100 | 100 | 100 | | 85 |
| 10. J | 92 | 96 | 80 | 82 | 100 | 100 | 80 | 88 | 75 | 88 | 88 | 71 | 68 | 81 | 67 | 80 | 73 | 90 | 90 | 90 | 100 | 95 | 98 | | 87 |
| 11. K | 54 | 58 | 50 | 73 | 71 | 50 | 67 | 65 | 58 | 63 | 61 | 57 | 61 | 67 | 62 | 59 | 61 | 50 | 70 | 60 | 50 | 80 | 65 | 10/5 | 60 |
| 12. L | 65 | 81 | 70 | 73 | 86 | 81 | 73 | 81 | 83 | 88 | 78 | 82 | 76 | 81 | 90 | 80 | 82 | 85 | 90 | 88 | 70 | 90 | 80 | | 82 |
| 13. M | 81 | 77 | 80 | 73 | 71 | 88 | 87 | 81 | 92 | 83 | 81 | 84 | 76 | 78 | 90 | 80 | 82 | 100 | 90 | 95 | 100 | 100 | 100 | | 90 |
| 14. N | 73 | 77 | 80 | 73 | 71 | 81 | 80 | 73 | 67 | 79 | 75 | 77 | 71 | 81 | 88 | 83 | 80 | 95 | 80 | 88 | 85 | 95 | 90 | | 83 |
| 15. O | 96 | 92 | 80 | 82 | 100 | 94 | 87 | 85 | 83 | 75 | 87 | 88 | 83 | 81 | 88 | 80 | 84 | 100 | 90 | 95 | 95 | 95 | 95 | | 90 |
| 16. P | 81 | 73 | 70 | 91 | 86 | 88 | 60 | 69 | 83 | 71 | 77 | 79 | 80 | 72 | 74 | 81 | 77 | 80 | 70 | 75 | 95 | 100 | 98 | | 82 |
| 17. Q | 58 | 50 | 60 | 73 | 71 | 94 | 53 | 69 | 50 | 63 | 64 | 52 | 56 | 53 | 52 | 61 | 55 | 0 | 50 | 25 | 65 | 50 | 58 | 10/5 | 51 |
| 18. R | 77 | 69 | 70 | 82 | 86 | 88 | 87 | 77 | 92 | 83 | 81 | 84 | 71 | 81 | 76 | 81 | 79 | 80 | 80 | 80 | 100 | 90 | 95 | | 84 |
| 19. S | 65 | 77 | 70 | 73 | 86 | 94 | 80 | 73 | 75 | 79 | 77 | 79 | 76 | 83 | 86 | 78 | 80 | 80 | 70 | 75 | 90 | 100 | 95 | | 82 |
| 20. T | 73 | 85 | 70 | 82 | 86 | 88 | 80 | 88 | 83 | 75 | 81 | 75 | 71 | 81 | 83 | 81 | 78 | 90 | 80 | 85 | 95 | 100 | 98 | | 86 |
| 21. U | 92 | 96 | 80 | 91 | 100 | 94 | 73 | 81 | 75 | 71 | 85 | 82 | 80 | 89 | 86 | 81 | 84 | 90 | 90 | 90 | 100 | 90 | 95 | | 89 |
| 22. V | 92 | 96 | 90 | 91 | 100 | 100 | 87 | 85 | 83 | 67 | 89 | 86 | 78 | 89 | 90 | 86 | 86 | 100 | 90 | 95 | 90 | 90 | 90 | | 90 |
| 23. W | 77 | 81 | 80 | 82 | 86 | 94 | 87 | 77 | 75 | 75 | 81 | 77 | 68 | 81 | 76 | 81 | 77 | 90 | 80 | 85 | 85 | 100 | 93 | | 84 |
| 24. | | | | | | | | | | | | | | | | | | | | | | | | | |
| 25. | | | | | | | | | | | | | | | | | | | | | | | | | |
| 26. | | | | | | | | | | | | | | | | | | | | | | | | | |
| 27. | | | | | | | | | | | | | | | | | | | | | | | | | |
| 28. | | | | | | | | | | | | | | | | | | | | | | | | | |
| 29. | | | | | | | | | | | | | | | | | | | | | | | | | |
| 30. | | | | | | | | | | | | | | | | | | | | | | | | | |
| 31. | | | | | | | | | | | | | | | | | | | | | | | | | |
| 32. | | | | | | | | | | | | | | | | | | | | | | | | | |
| 33. | | | | | | | | | | | | | | | | | | | | | | | | | |

| Student Number | Absences | | | | | | | | | | | | Student Number | Total Absences |
|---|---|---|---|---|---|---|---|---|---|---|---|---|---|---|
| 1 | 9/10 | 10/14 | 10/23 | | | | | | | | | | 1 | 3 |
| 2 | 10/19 | 10/20 | 10/21 | | | | | | | | | | 2 | 3 |
| 3 | 9/10 | 10/5 | 10/15 | 10/19 | 11/3 | | | | | | | | 3 | 5 |
| 4 | 10/5 | 10/16 | 10/19 | 11/2 | | | | | | | | | 4 | 4 |
| 5 | 9/10 | 9/15 | 9/23 | | | | | | | | | | 5 | 3 |
| 6 | 9/29 | 10/9 | | | | | | | | | | | 6 | 2 |
| 7 | | | | | | | | | | | | | 7 | 0 |
| 8 | 10/1 | 10/2 | 10/4 | 10/5 | | | | | | | | | 8 | 4 |
| 9 | 10/16 | 10/28 | 10/29 | | | | | | | | | | 9 | 3 |
| 10 | 10/1 | 10/2 | 10/13 | 10/14 | 10/19 | | | | | | | | 10 | 5 |
| 11 | 10/5 | 10/28 | | | | | | | | | | | 11 | 2 |
| 12 | 10/8 | 10/13 | 11/2 | 11/3 | | | | | | | | | 12 | 4 |
| 13 | 9/23 | 10/5 | 10/19 | | | | | | | | | | 13 | 3 |
| 14 | 9/10 | 9/11 | 9/27 | 10/21 | | | | | | | | | 14 | 4 |
| 15 | 9/8 | | | | | | | | | | | | 15 | 1 |
| 16 | 10/28 | | | | | | | | | | | | 16 | 1 |
| 17 | 9/5 | 9/1 | 10/2 | 10/13 | 10/14 | 10/15 | 10/16 | 10/19 | 10/20 | 10/28 | 10/29 | 11/2 | 17 | 12 |
| 18 | | | | | | | | | | | | | 18 | 0 |
| 19 | | | | | | | | | | | | | 19 | 0 |
| 20 | 10/1 | 10/28 | | | | | | | | | | | 20 | 2 |
| 21 | 9/5 | 9/28 | 10/23 | 11/3 | | | | | | | | | 21 | 4 |
| 22 | 9/16 | 9/28 | 10/2 | | | | | | | | | | 22 | 3 |
| 23 | 9/15 | 10/6 | | | | | | | | | | | 23 | 2 |
| 24 | | | | | | | | | | | | | 24 | |
| 25 | | | | | | | | | | | | | 25 | |
| 26 | | | | | | | | | | | | | 26 | |
| 27 | | | | | | | | | | | | | 27 | |
| 28 | | | | | | | | | | | | | 28 | |
| 29 | | | | | | | | | | | | | 29 | |
| 30 | | | | | | | | | | | | | 30 | |
| 31 | | | | | | | | | | | | | 31 | |
| 32 | | | | | | | | | | | | | 32 | |
| 33 | | | | | | | | | | | | | 33 | |

NOTES:

```
     1                    81
      81                  
      77              84    8.25
      85          4)336    40 5
      93              32   16.20
     ----              76  20.2 5
      336
```

47

## OPPORTUNITIES FOR REFLECTION

1. Why is it important to use a plan book and to keep it current?

2. What types of information will be included in your plan book?

3. List the types of student work assignments to be included in each of your instructional courses.

4. What is the comparative value of the different assignments?

5. Critique the suggested student grade and absence recording system previously described - can it work for you?

6. Is it important to you to inform your students of the grade calculating method you have designed? If so, how will you inform your students of the methods used?

# Chapter 8

# THE TEACHER'S HANDBOOK

In many schools, the administrators prepare a teacher's handbook. The purpose of the handbook is to inform teachers of school procedures, events, rules, regulations, and policies along with answering as many questions as possible before the school year begins.

All teachers within the school should review the handbook for important information such as end of marking-term dates, extra-duty schedules, homeroom duties, emergency building exit instructions, and, of course, the school calendar (paying close attention to all vacation days!). After reading and marking highlights of each of those "most important pages," turn to the table of contents and circle the page numbers. Those important pages are then noted and much easier to find when needed.

A teacher's handbook is informative; however, once read, one may not need to refer to it often. The information is most useful to first-year teachers or newcomers to a school district for it provides basic, school specific information and it makes the process of transitioning into the school community much easier. Information contained within a handbook can include directions for student assemblies, a map of the school facilities, a list identifying teachers and staff members working in the building, descriptions of student clubs, sports schedules, and directions for ordering multimedia. While some of the information in the handbook is most helpful for new teachers, there are some sections in the handbook which should be carefully reviewed by all teachers each year. All teachers should be aware of scheduled (required) meetings, testing dates, homework requirements, all aspects of academic grading (report card schedule, minimum number of student grades required per marking period, grade averaging requirements, letter-grade-to-number conversion chart), and fire drill or other emergency building evacuation or lock down plans.

All of the items included in a handbook have a purpose and teachers are required to know and follow stated directions, procedures, and policies. During one school year, our district administrators very quickly formulated building evacuation plans because several bomb threats were received within a few weeks time. Every time a bomb threat was received, the building was quickly emptied and searched, with only one exception. On that occasion, a letter was sent to the principal stating a bomb had been left in the building during the weekend and it was set to explode on

Monday. Since the letter was not received by the principal until Tuesday, no classes were disturbed!

Since the 1990's, and especially after the Columbine tragedy, school personnel are increasingly security conscious. Teachers must continually be aware of safety concerns and proper practice to insure the safety of their students, other staff members, and themselves. School personnel must take all building evacuation plans and practices very seriously. As a teacher, you must efficiently empty your classroom and leave it in the required condition (for example: windows closed, lights off). You must make sure all students leave the room and the building as required or directed. Some school districts require teachers to take attendance at an appointed gathering point. All of the school district's requirements regarding this topic must be met quickly and accurately.

Teachers should also be aware of state laws or board of education policies related to them and their numerous responsibilities. Laws exist which require teachers to report any case of suspected child abuse or maltreatment. Teachers also need to be aware of policies developed by their school district on such items as corporal punishment, the student disciplinary code, maintenance of public order, and teacher observations including the written report itself along with the teacher's right to review the report and respond to it. Since many important regulations and policies are periodically revised or clarified, teachers must take time each new school year to review the handbook. Sometimes it is difficult to remember all of the items included in the handbook, so keep the handbook in your desk or file cabinet and refer to it whenever a particular question or problem occurs.

The handbook can keep one from making embarrassing errors. Our high school building had three wings, all floors on ground level. Most of the classrooms were numbered in the 100's, but for some unique, unknown reason, the classrooms in the senior wing were numbered in the 300's. One new teacher was on her way to meet with her first class in the senior wing. Since the room was numbered in the 300's, she incorrectly presumed that the classroom was located on the third floor. The new teacher asked several students where the stairs were located. She then received strange looks from the students, followed by the comment "I do not know." Time was passing quickly and the teacher, not wanting to be late for her first class, was becoming upset. Finally, in desperation, she asked a student where room 322 was located, and she received simple, clear directions to the 300 wing. A quick look at the building layout plan provided in the handbook could have solved this problem before it began!

## OPPORTUNITIES FOR REFLECTION:

1. What board of education policies exist in your school which are related to writing lesson plans, teacher observations, grading practices, class attendance requirements for students, homework assignments, and testing requirements?

2. Have you reviewed the student discipline code for your school? Do you have any questions related to it?

3. Are you aware of school safety plans for exiting the building (fire drills, bomb threats)? Do "lock down" directions exist?

4. What student health information is available to teachers? Have you been informed of serious student health conditions? Also, have you been instructed as to any actions you should take to assist a student experiencing a health crisis?

5. What computer access is available for your use? If you need additional training for computer use, is it provided to you?

**Chapter 9**

# THE NEW SCHOOL YEAR

"I've had a great summer and I think I'm ready for another year to begin." "My new textbooks finally arrived!" "Are the class lists ready yet?" "My class schedule is workable and best of all, no lunch duty!" "When is the first payday? - I'm broke!" "Oh, no, the bell's ringing, I'm not looking forward to this year." "My first year - I hope it goes well." Each new school year brings with it a wide range of emotions for teachers - and for students.

## What lies ahead?

## What must I do to make this year successful for my students and for myself?

The importance of the teacher to the success of a student's academic year cannot be overstated. Most of the ground work for a successful classroom experience will be established during the first few days of the new school year, and the teacher must assume the leadership position from the very beginning.

# THE FIRST WEEK

The first week of school is exciting, challenging, nerve-racking, and exhausting. During the first day or two of the new school year, the teacher usually attends a wide variety of meetings such as a district-wide meeting, building and department meetings, and a teachers' association (union) meeting. Those meetings are intended to introduce new teachers and programs, give instructions for the first week of classes, inform teachers of present building concerns and conditions, and update past situations. One year, during the opening faculty meeting, we were told the fresh coat of paint on the student lockers was not expected to be dry by the day the students arrived. We were then asked to discourage students from investigating for themselves the truthfulness of the "Wet Paint" signs. What was so amusing about the request? We knew the request to be an enormous and impossible job. Human nature being what it is most of us already knew just how wet the paint was, as evidenced by the brightly colored enamel paint smudges on our own fingertips!

During those first few days of meetings many important papers are distributed: class schedules, extra duty assignments, payroll information, plan book-register, multimedia catalogs, teacher handbook, and student class lists. For the new teacher this is an especially overwhelming time, for everything is new. For returning teachers, those first few days are the calm before the storm! For everyone, the days of teacher meetings are a time to review paperwork and efficiently deal with it. The steady stream of paperwork for this year has already begun!

The key to surviving those first days is to get the paperwork organized as fast as it is received. It is advisable to take a few file folders to all teacher meetings. As papers are distributed, categorize and quickly place them in an appropriately titled file folder, then when you return to your desk, place the folders in a convenient place.

The next major challenge to be faced is the opening day of school when the students arrive! People who are new to the school or new to teaching are generally excited and somewhat nervous. Many of the veterans are a little apprehensive as well. The uncertainty comes from realizing that the first few days with the students set the tone for the entire year. Teachers know that students are forming opinions about course requirements, behavior expectations, and each of their teachers, so be as self-confident and business-like as possible.

For the first few days, all teachers should begin each class by naming the course and introducing themselves. Often, several students will make an error in reading their class schedule and they will need to go elsewhere. It is helpful to students when teachers pronounce their names and write them on the chalk or marker board, especially if their names are difficult to pronounce and spell.

After general introductions are complete, a teacher may explain the seating plan to be used in class and then take attendance. Many students' names are embarrassingly difficult to pronounce, so ask students for help in pronouncing those "impossible" names. After taking attendance, teachers should ask all students present whose names were not called to raise their hands. For clarification, teachers should review those students' class schedules to determine if they are in the correct class. Teachers should also announce the names of all unaccounted for students. Occasionally a student in the class can inform the teacher as to why some other student is not in class (still on family vacation, ill, or dropped out of school).

During the first day of class, the teacher should introduce the course by describing major topics and ideas to be studied. When helpful to the students' understanding of the course, the teacher should also describe some of the teaching methods to be used during class time along with types of student assignments.

I found the most efficient means for describing my general classroom rules and my grading method was to distribute a requirement sheet (see "Requirement Sheet," page 61). After each student had received the sheet, it was reviewed in class. While I was explaining the ground rules, I would add general comments and answer any student questions. Teachers should clearly explain their expectations, how problems will be handled, and what noise level will be tolerated. Teachers can require student signatures on the sheet indicating their complete understanding of all items listed. I did not require a student signature, but for some students it might have been a good idea! It is also a good idea to have extra requirement sheets available for parents to review when conferences are held.

Textbooks can be distributed to students during any of the first few days of classes. Teachers are usually required to record the textbook number assigned to each student. This information can be recorded in the class register. Also, students should be informed about the general care expected for textbooks and whether or not their textbooks are to be covered. Occasionally you may be able to obtain free book covers for student use from the guidance office or the main office (supplied by the armed services or a store). After distributing textbooks, teachers should check their students' ability to read the textbook (see "Textbooks and Reading Abilities." page 69").

One of the last activities of the "introductory" nature completed in my classes was to distribute a 3 X 5 index card to each student. I read several questions to my students and asked them to write their answers on the index card. Some of the information on those cards was reviewed in class, and some of the information was for my future use (see "Learning Names, Knowing Students," page 66).

After all the introductory and clerical work was completed, we quickly got to the course content. There are many different approaches which can be used to begin a course. At the very beginning of the course it is important to interest the students, so try some unique method to gain their attention. It is not enough just to say, "Read and outline chapter one." For many years I taught a Law Studies course. The course was divided into two parts: civil law and criminal law. I began the course by reading *It's Against the Law* by Dick Hyman (published by Reader's Digest). It is an illustrated collection of many strange or ridiculous laws still "on the books" in many different states. We would discuss some of those laws and speculate on the possible reasons for their existence. Then, we proceeded to discuss why laws are needed, how they are formed, and how they reflect the needs and wants of a society. This natural progression led into a variety of units related to civil law, followed by the students' favorite, criminal law.

In my geography course, I gave a "World Quiz." Students were asked to do their best on the quiz and were told no grade would be assigned to this quiz. I asked approximately forty-five questions about the earth, political events, societal issues, and environmental facts. A few examples of questions asked were: How many square miles of ocean exist on the earth's surface? Students were told to answer to the nearest million square miles. How many nations exist on earth? How many major language groups exist? How many countries have nuclear power plants? All of the questions asked were related to future units of study. Each year I reviewed the most current copy of The World Almanac to update the answers to some of the questions. After giving the quiz, we reviewed the answers in class. I allowed students to give their answers, followed by the correct information. Students were often surprised by their small view of the world. I believe using the quiz approach aroused the students' curiosity and they were then much more open to the beginning of course work.

During this first week of school all of the activities in my classes were teacher-controlled and directed. Time was well used. Students were given few liberties. My students were quickly introduced to the idea that inadequate student work and poor behavior would be immediately noticed and addressed. Yet, at the same time, I did my best to build the framework for a positive, successful classroom experience for my students. Some of my personal goals in teaching were to create an atmosphere in which my students enjoyed attending my class. It was important to increase student knowledge, understanding, and skills. It was also important to encourage students' positive efforts and assist them in experiencing success. Those are reachable goals for students and teachers alike.

# ESTABLISHING STUDENT BEHAVIOR STANDARDS

Everyone who has taken educational methods courses in a college or university has probably heard a statement about being tough during the first several weeks (or months) of school in order to get the students' attention and to set the tone for classroom standards for the entire year. That statement is partly true. I think the word "determined" rather than the word "tough" might be more accurate. However, before the first day in the classroom, the teacher must do some serious thinking about classroom standards. The teacher must decide what types of student actions will be

Limit the number of your stated rules.

Let "reasonableness" guide your classroom.

allowed, what actions will be corrected, and what actions will not be tolerated. Some specific guidelines should be considered and established then classroom standards will emerge from those guidelines over a period of time as situations develop.

## What do you consider as acceptable and unacceptable student behavior in your classroom?

Answering that question is essential for successful classroom management. It is one of the most significant questions which all teachers must answer for themselves then they must clearly communicate those expectations to their students.

Teachers are the individuals who establish guidelines for workable standards of behavior in the classroom and they are responsible for molding student actions and attitudes. I always tried to maintain a focused classroom, but not a silent one. Silence is not always good or even necessary (test periods excluded), for when there is silence there is no sharing of ideas or experiences. When surrounded by people, it is not in human nature to be silent; therefore, when designing the academic and social atmosphere within your classroom responsibilities, allow for intellectual and social exchanges.

Students must learn attendance and promptness to class are very important. Teachers can encourage this in several ways: by example (being in school except when absence is necessary and starting/ending class promptly), by instruction (stating to students they must attend and be on time), and by taking action when students are absent or late too often (detentions, telephone call to parents, warning notice). By encouraging attendance and promptness, the teacher will be helping the student with current school requirements. Equally important, the student may learn the value of those practices for future educational and employment pursuits.

Teachers should inform students as to what is needed for their next class and students must learn to come to class promptly, and prepared with the necessary course related tools. I often chided my students that if they could remember to come to my class, then they should remember to bring their textbook, notebook, pen or pencil, and completed homework assignment.

General courtesy must be observed in the classroom. Students must learn and practice good manners toward each other and toward teachers. Mutual respect and consideration for other students and for teachers should be a goal in each classroom. Whenever I had to interrupt the conversation of two students or refocus those who were not paying attention to classroom activities, I usually stated a somewhat mild comment. If a second statement to the students was necessary, it was brief and more directive. It is important to quickly change the undesired behavior and continue with planned classroom activities.

Along with courtesy, I believe that in the classroom there is no reason for swearing or using obscenities. Some students (and teachers) are very loose with what they say. I never believed the classroom was the place for offensive language, and I stated those beliefs the very first day of class. Students can learn to control their comments, and when their language was offensive, I told them so.

Safety in the classroom and throughout the entire school must be a primary concern. Students should be reminded that accidents can happen in a school setting and they should be careful in their conduct. Sometimes even the obvious must be stated, so my students were told not to throw anything in class, including a pencil to another student who was borrowing it.

Care for textbooks and equipment should be a requirement. Inform students if they destroy books or equipment it will be their responsibility to pay for replacement items. Student replacement of damaged books or equipment is usually a school policy and students are generally well aware of those practices.

Students must learn to control their behavior. I like individual spunk and humor, I do not like meanness and defiance - there is a difference. A teacher should quickly respond to inappropriate student behavior; tell students when their behavior is not appreciated or acceptable. Many students will change their behavior once a teacher has spoken to them about it. However, there are also the times when a student will not heed the teacher's directions. The teacher must then work within stated classroom guidelines, disciplinary code, and school policies. When teacher action is necessary, the teacher must respond with authority. It comes down to this question: How much will you take, or put up with, from your students? Some teachers tolerate excessive amounts of poor behavior from their students; I do not think it is necessary, desirable, or healthy to do so.

Class time schedules vary from one school to another but every minute is important. Whatever time schedule is used in a school, time passes quickly. Teachers should be prepared to use the entire time allotted for each class. Planning the use of entire class periods may be difficult for the first-year teacher, but planning skills improve with experience. When planned classroom activities have ended and time remains, a teacher has options other than the chaos which can result when students are not focused. The teacher can discuss a current issue, remind students of due dates for projects, review totals of student absences, or check textbooks for book covers. Occasionally, after reminding some students several times to cover a textbook, I would give the students book covers and have them give an impromptu demonstration of "proper textbook covering methods." The demonstrations were generally light-hearted yet controlled and continued to reinforce the idea that textbooks were to be covered.

Much of what goes on in the classroom is the application of good common sense, mixed with a generous amount of flexibility, consideration, and humor. Teachers must be the primary controlling force in the classroom, yet at the same time, they are the person most responsible for creating a favorable atmosphere for learning. Generally speaking, the atmosphere you create at the beginning of the course, or the one you allow your students to create, will last throughout the course. During the first few weeks of school, make sure the directions being set are what you desire. Even though your students will test your authority and determination, most students are willing to work with a consistent, fair teacher. Teachers also must be prepared to address problems as they appear. They should respond quickly to any challenge presented by ill-behaved students. Most problems between teachers and students can be resolved. Although students may complain about the teaching methods used or the many assignments given by a teacher, they do respect the teachers from whom they learn. Students do appreciate a teacher-supplied balanced atmosphere conducive to learning; they can and should receive that opportunity, and it's the teacher's responsibility to provide it.

# REQUIREMENT SHEET

At the end of this reading, you will find a copy of my course requirement sheet. It generally described my rules, expectations, and grading system.

Each of my students received a copy of the requirement sheet. During one of the first days of class the sheet was totally reviewed and student questions were answered. Students were required to keep the sheet, and when notebooks were checked, I looked for it.

It is helpful to the students to have rules, expectations, and a written description of their teacher's grading system to which they can refer. A teacher should be able to complete a listing of those items on one sheet of paper; if you have more than one page of rules, you have too many!

Regular attendance, preparation for class, and participation in classroom activities are essential to being a successful student and I stressed those ideas when the requirement sheet was reviewed with my students.

While reviewing the requirement sheet on the next full page, notice in particular item number seven. When your classes are well-behaved for a substitute teacher, everyone benefits. You can have confidence in your students' behavior and in the fact that all is well even when you are not in school. Your students can complete assignments and learn during your absence, and the substitute teacher can also have a good day. When you review the requirement sheet with your students, stress the importance of good behavior. Start training your students early about their responsibility towards substitute teachers, and when you are absent from school the day will not be wasted. When a substitute teacher informs the classroom teacher of a discipline problem, the classroom teacher should discuss the report with the student(s) involved and take appropriate corrective action. Firm teacher action will quickly impress students about the value and importance of good behavior towards substitute teachers.

**AMERICAN HISTORY**
Requirement Sheet

Teacher:  Mrs. Johnson

Course Goals:  To increase student knowledge concerning the historical events in the development of the United States of America and to understand the many challenges and changes which have occurred in our society

## Student requirements:

1. Attendance.  You are expected to come to class regularly, be on time, and be attentive during the entire class period.
2. Preparation.  You are expected to come to class prepared -- bring your textbook, pen, notebook, and completed assignments.
3. Textbooks are to be covered and well cared for at all times.
4. Participation in classroom activities is expected and encouraged.
5. Respectful, reasonable, responsible, and honest behavior is necessary.
6. Fire drills / emergency exit drills - leave the building near the gym doors and go into the south parking lot.  I must take attendance there so be sure you stay together as a group and remain quiet.
7. Cooperative behavior is expected whenever a substitute teacher is in this classroom.

## Grading standards:

Each category represents 25% of the marking term grade:

1. Homework / class work / and quizzes.  All work is to be completed on time.  If you are absent from school, you must talk with me on your first day back in class to learn of required assignments and new due dates.

2. Notebooks.  Bring your notebook to class every day and keep it up-to-date. Every entry in your notebook is to be dated.  The notebook is to contain class notes, photocopied sheets, and uncollected, completed assignments (a folder may be used for the additional papers).  Items contained in the notebook must be placed in order by date.

3. Projects.  Projects of various types are required each marking term.  Projects are completed outside of class and are in addition to classroom activities.

4. Tests.  Tests are given on major units and are both objective and subjective in design.  Tests are given every 2-3 weeks.  If a test is missed due to absence, it must be made-up within one week of original given date.

**If you are having difficulty in this course, or if I can be of additional assistance to you, please let me know.**

# GAINING CONTROL IN THE CLASSROOM

The first few days in the classroom each year are very important. Most teachers are trying to evaluate their classes, learn their students' names, recognize students with special needs, identify potential problem students, and make some progress toward a normal day. Meanwhile, the students are analyzing their teachers to determine which ones will be an easy mark and which ones not to challenge! It is important for the teacher to quickly claim the place of authority in the classroom.

There are a number of actions the teacher can take which will aid in gaining and keeping control in the classroom. Many teachers have stated they have much better control in the classroom when they are standing up. They can readily involve students in class activities and can easily observe student behavior. I usually stood in my classroom, paced back and forth in the front of the room, walked between the rows of student desks, or leaned against my desk. (Women wearing short dresses should not sit on desktops, not ever!) If you choose to sit on the top of a desk, make sure the desk can adequately support your weight, for it can be extremely embarrassing to be dumped on the floor as the desk collapses under you. Although I never had this happen to me, I do remember one very red-faced teacher who endured this catastrophe. His conclusion: student desks with adjustable legs are most untrustworthy!

It is important to quickly establish the understanding that time will not be wasted in your classroom. Teachers who end their lessons a few minutes before the class is scheduled to stop are actually training their students to cease class work early. If the teacher has no planned use for the time, students will devise a way to pass the time: talking, getting up and heading for the door, or other more imaginative exploits. Teachers must plan to use time effectively and completely. Have work assignments designed so students can complete class work or begin homework assignments during unclaimed time. During the first weeks of school, give little or no time to students for relaxing. Students must learn to follow your directions, and keeping students occupied aids in this process.

As quickly as possible develop routines for collecting homework, returning papers, distributing quizzes or tests, and other regular classroom activities. When students know the procedures used by their teachers they can be more self-directing and helpful. To assist students, teachers should keep extra copies of worksheets, handouts, and readings (to replace lost ones) and an ample supply of pencils.

After carefully and completely reviewing your class policies related to behavior, you must start enforcing those rules early. From the very first day you must be consistent and constant in the application of the rules, and that explains why you do not want to have too long a list of "class rules." Do not be afraid to insist that your students obey your directions.

Teachers must require students to pay attention to them from the very first day. Whenever you see or hear something you do not appreciate, inform the student(s). If students are busy with their own conversations instead of being attentive in class, interrupt their conversation and direct their attention to class activities. When a student does something you do not like, explain to the student why it is important for her/him to act properly. Positive phrasing is important. Instead of saying "stop talking" say "pay attention please." Tell students what you want them to do, rather than what you do not want them to do.

It is very important to face your students when conducting class. I have never enjoyed writing on the chalkboard - it breaks eye contact, reduces ease of conversation, decreases control, is tiring, and chalk dust is difficult to endure. The chalkboard is acceptable for listing assignments, short word lists, or short outlines; but when planning to give more extensive notes, it might be best to use an overhead projector.

During the first few days of classes, after distributing textbooks, reviewing requirement sheets, and completing name cards, I often started my geography-world issues course with a "How much do you know?" quiz. This was a fun, non-threatening way to introduce the course content and a beginning point for the course work which was to follow. This introductory method encouraged a team building approach and allowed me to become acquainted with my students before I began to give course work assignments. Some teachers distribute textbooks as soon as class begins on the first day, followed by a sizable assignment. This is often done as a control method to create an impression of teacher toughness, but many times that course of action only succeeds in irritating the students and creating discomfort and conflict. An assignment on the first day is not the best possible way to start a good working relationship with students, and I see no reason for antagonizing students during the first few days of a new course.

Once you feel you have gained control in a classroom (an awareness which may take several weeks to recognize) you must maintain it. There are times when a problem will simply start for no apparent reason. At first, it may not even be recognized as a problem, but it grows and eventually it must be corrected. Occasionally, the students in my classroom would gather near the door and wait for the bell to ring. Since their actions bothered me, I told the students to please sit down. Often as they started to return to their desks, the bell would ring and everyone turned and left the room. Each day a few more students would go to the door and wait for the bell to ring. I grew tired of telling the students to return to their desks so I went to the closed door and stood in front of it. I then made the announcement that no one was leaving my room until every student was seated in a chair. Peer pressure took over, and everyone "rushed" for a chair. (It appeared to be a disorganized game of musical chairs, and I had a great deal of difficulty containing my laughter.) The bell rang before everyone had found a chair, but since I was standing in front of the door insisting that all students return to their seat, no one could leave. Once everyone was in "their" chair, I dismissed them. The next day, as the class was about to end, I walked to the corner of the room near the doorway and stood there to finish my comments. I noticed that all students remained seated until the bell rang and they were dismissed. The students had learned to wait and the problem was solved without further teacher action.

Firmness, control, and direction are all needed during the first week of school and those features will set a good foundation for the entire school year. Gaining and keeping control in the classroom is not too difficult as long as you determine beforehand that you will be listened to and obeyed. You do not need to make a long list of rules for students to follow; "reasonableness" covers many situations. As problems arise (and they will), identify them, think about them, then design solutions which are easy to put into practice, effective, and do not create extra work for you, the teacher. When trying to change certain student behaviors, simply make the desired behavior more attractive than the unwanted behavior with its undesirable consequences for the student (see "Student Tardiness," page 234). Enjoy your students, work with them, and encourage them, and they will respond to you; do not underestimate the importance of the human "care" factor in maintaining classroom control.

# SEATING CHARTS

Teachers need an easy method for learning students' names. It is difficult to meet and learn the names of approximately one hundred twenty-five students in one day! Many teachers use seating charts in an attempt to memorize students' names, although I think there is an easier way which is described in the next unit entitled "Learning Names, Knowing Students."

Seating charts serve several purposes. First, they increase the teacher's opportunity to call students by name which, in turn, requires a more immediate student response. Seating charts can simplify the attendance-taking process, especially if the teacher requires students to sit in alphabetical order. Current seating charts will also assist substitute teachers in both controlling the classroom and taking attendance accurately, thereby greatly increasing their effectiveness during the day.

There are several different approaches a teacher can use when forming seating plans. The most commonly used seating plan is an alphabetical arrangement according to the students' last names. When the seating charts and register are both in alphabetical order, they complement each other and make the recording of absences easier. When students are seated alphabetically, papers can be collected easily in alphabetical order, thus assisting the teacher who uses a computer spreadsheet for recording grades (see "Collecting / Returning Assignments," page 81). However, students generally dislike an alphabetical seating arrangement, especially those who are constantly assigned seats in the front of the classroom. This system is viewed by many students as arbitrary, inconsiderate of their feelings, and totally unnecessary. Some teachers insist alphabetical seating plans aid them in learning their students' names; I question this, but if it helps, use it.

Some teachers use a seating plan as a first means of introducing the students to the idea that the teacher is "the boss." Seating plans based on that rationale can set the stage for teacher/student conflicts, since students immediately feel they are being told what to do in a manner unpleasant to them. At this point, some students will openly challenge the teacher's authority, so the teacher must be firm and definite when making seating assignments.

There are some variations to alphabetical seating plans which can be used. Teachers can assign boys to the first row, girls to the second, and so on. Still other teachers may try a "randomly arranged" seating plan which can, in effect, allow the teacher to place poorly behaving students near the front of the room without bringing excessive attention to that fact; however, the students will very quickly recognize that arrangement.

Before making seating plans for their classes, teachers should be informed of student health conditions (such as poor eyesight, deafness, or other handicaps) which require special placement of a student in a particular part of the room. The information can be obtained by reviewing a confidential student health information sheet provided by the school district or by your students telling you (verbally or in a note) of their special needs.

The seating arrangement of a classroom can be a positive event if a teacher chooses to make it so. I allowed my students to choose where they would sit. I asked them to stay in the same location for a week or two until I could easily identify them, then they were free to change their location. Students were informed that they were expected to behave and if a problem occurred, I would permanently assign the student to a "nice spot in the front of the room near my desk!"

Regardless of the seating arrangement chosen, there is no obligation to explain to students the reason for it unless the teacher thinks it will add to a more productive classroom atmosphere. Remember, too, seating charts and the physical arrangements of desks can be changed whenever necessary.

Often, the main office will supply seating chart forms; they are sheets of paper with approximately thirty little squares printed on them. Each square represents a student's desk, and teachers write the names of students who occupy the desk in the boxes. A common practice of school administrators is to require teachers to submit a copy of their seating charts to the main office for a substitute teacher folder. Write students' names on your charts then photocopy the seating charts for the office copy. If you use a pen, your copy will be neat until it needs to be changed. If you use pencil your copy may smear, but it will be much easier to change. Decisions, decisions!

Some teachers choose to use the class seating charts which are printed in the plan book-register. Those charts are usually found near the beginning of the plan book or between the plan book and the register. If you use the seating charts in the plan book-register, place a tab on the first page of the seating charts for easy reference. The advantage of using those printed seating charts is their inclusion in the plan book-register; they are not as easily misplaced as are separate seating charts. The disadvantage with many of the seating charts included in a plan book-register is the small space provided for writing your students' names.

Whether you use the school supplied seating charts or those printed in the plan book-register, or some other system, be sure to adequately label each seating chart. It will be helpful to you and to a substitute teacher if you include all of the following items: teacher name, course title, period and times the class meets, room number, and total number of students in the class.

# LEARN NAMES AND KNOW STUDENTS

Elementary teachers generally have twenty to thirty students for whom they are primarily responsible, and they are with those students most of the day. Since they work with the same students all day long, it may be easier to learn the students' names quickly. However, secondary teachers might have as many as one hundred fifty classroom students (thirty per class times five classes), plus study hall and homeroom students. Learning names quickly is necessary for classroom control. So, how does one learn to accurately pronounce one hundred fifty names and then correctly match them to the right students?

Learning individual student names seems to be much easier if you learn something about each student as a person. In addition, this personal insight can help get your year-long association off to a good start. Here's how I began to learn the students' names and to know them as people.

After some introductory procedures I gave each student a 3 X 5 index card and asked them to write the following information on the card:

**Name**: Written as the student wanted me to learn it - no need to write last name first.
**Parent(s) or Guardian(s) names**: Listed as Mr. and Mrs., or Mr. only, or Mrs. only.
**Mailing address**:
**Telephone number**: Listed correctly!
**Student age**: (This helped me to remember how young my students were. One year while discussing the JFK assassination, I asked, "Do any of you remember watching the funeral on TV?" The students replied: "No, we had not yet been born." I still remember how their reply brought me back to the realization that time marches on!).
**Employment**: Past or present.
**List of sports, hobbies, or special interests**: Items of interest the student would like me to know, excluding dating, partying, etc.
**Travel experiences**:

The above-mentioned items may be adjusted to suit individual group needs and teacher preference.

After collecting the cards, I spent a few minutes talking about the responses with each student, starting with the topic of student employment. There was no need to discuss parents, or addresses (those facts were to assist me if I needed to contact parents). If I had taught older brothers or sisters of present students, I often inquired about them. The purpose of this introductory method is to establish human contact and discover common ground between the student and the teacher. Since many interests of the students overlap with one's own experience, it is easy to make quick conversation. If you can find no similarities, just ask some questions about students' responses. As the other students in the class listen to the conversation they become interested in what is being said and eager for their turn to talk. This is an especially effective method for creating an attitude of class togetherness. Students who have never really met each other or students who are new to the school begin immediately to know each other and the foundation for working together is formed.

I have had some interesting student-to-teacher exchanges. One student wrote "summers on Cape Cod" as a travel experience. I asked where he stayed on Cape Cod and what he liked about the Cape. After he answered, I told the class that I lived on Cape Cod for seven years and had graduated from a high school there.

Another student listed a special interest in moto-cross. He told of races he had entered and how well he had done. I then described my experiences in learning to drive a motorcycle and why I gave it up - the tree refused to move!

Yet another student told of working in a printing shop. Since no one knew much about that topic, I asked the girl to tell us what she did and how she liked it. Her response was informative and of interest to students.

Keep each conversation brief. Try to interview one-half of the class the first day and the remaining half the next day. If those discussions are held during two different class periods the interest of most students is sustained and class control is maintained.

By using the introduction card method, I quickly became acquainted with my students and they learned about me. We established a friendly, working relationship and yet had a controlled classroom atmosphere even in those first hectic days of the new school year.

In all honesty, I must say that my name-learning system is not totally foolproof. After teaching in the same school district for a few years, one is apt to have the younger siblings of former students. It is usually a nice experience to meet and work with several members of one family. During my ten years of teaching I had three boys from the same family, and they all looked alike. Wayne's name was easy to remember, for he was the first brother. Then came Roger, and I learned his name, but often thought of Wayne. When Larry came along, my mind struggled at times to keep up with the changing faces and names, and I kept calling him Roger. The class enjoyed my confusion (they were very understanding!), but Larry and I were getting somewhat frustrated. I offered Larry a deal; every time I called him Roger and he caught me, I owed him a dime. I paid several times as I was "re-programming" and eventually the problem was overcome - until now. I think the birth order of brothers was Wayne, Roger, and Larry, but it could have been Wayne, Larry, and Roger!

Knowing your students for the purpose of helping them to learn and grow as individuals is one of the highest professional goals which a teacher can reach; however, knowing your students and their abilities has its "fringe benefits" too. One day, being somewhat behind schedule and in a great hurry, I locked my keys inside my car. I needed those keys to unlock my classroom, my file cabinet, my closet, and later in the day to travel home and enter my house - so it was most frustrating to see my keys on the front seat of my car. I did not know the first thing about unlocking a car door from the outside with a coat hanger, but I knew from a previous conversation that one of my student's knew how to do it! I simply had to find that young man. After finding him and explaining my predicament, I gave him the coat hanger, and within fifteen seconds (on his second try) the car door was unlocked and I had my keys!

# TEXTBOOKS AND READING ABILITIES

Many school teachers make the disappointing and troublesome assumption that their students can read well. In heterogeneously grouped classes, it is critical that teachers learn of their students' reading abilities or deficiencies in the first few days of a new school year. A discussion with previous teachers, guidance counselors, or a review of student folders can provide teachers with valuable insight into their students' reading abilities or needs; however, that type of search is very time consuming especially at the start of a new school year. Teachers need to develop an "early warning system" to identify students who have reading problems and this evaluation system must be dependable, practical, and time efficient

To quickly determine the basic reading ability of my students, I decided to have the students read aloud a small portion of their textbook to me. This reading exercise was done immediately after textbooks were distributed. My students were informed of the oral reading activity and its purpose. Students were told that each one would read several sentences (usually three to five sentences) and the students would be randomly called upon to read. Everyone was encouraged to be attentive to the text. Many students dislike reading aloud, so I purposely limited each student's reading to a minimum - that seemed to alleviate most students' apprehensions. Students were also told that if reading aloud was difficult or a great source of stress for them, once their name was called, they simply had to say "pass" and I would call the next student. Once the students began reading, it was very easy to recognize their basic reading abilities. Students who chose to pass or who had difficulty were noted. After completing the oral reading activity an assignment, along with class time to work on it, was given to the students. Then I invited students who had noticeable difficulty reading the text or those who chose to "pass", to come to my desk (one at a time) for their private reading opportunity.

There are several ideas to keep in mind when determining basic reading abilities of students. Some students who appear to have a reading problem are simply very nervous at the prospect of having to read aloud in the classroom. Each teacher should consider the oral reading option, and adapt it as necessary. If many students seem to be embarrassed about participating in an oral reading (as it often is with lower ability students), the teacher can give the entire class membership an assignment. Then, while the students are quietly working, the teacher can go to each student and have the student read aloud a short passage from the textbook. Whatever method is used, all teachers should evaluate at the beginning of the school year their students' ability to read the textbook. Often, in heterogeneously grouped classrooms, many of the students do not know each other and in a new setting they may be more tolerant of each other, so a quick oral reading experience may be acceptable. You may also decide to review the academic files of students who had difficulty reading so that you learn of any other deficiencies which may impact the student's performance in your class.

All teachers should learn about the remedial reading programs available to students in their school district. Once teachers identify a student who has great difficulty reading the textbook, they should take the initiative and privately discuss the problem and reading assistance programs with the student and/or parents. It is also important to inform other professionals from the reading department or guidance personnel and seek their assistance. The importance of the teacher's role in identifying and referring a student to a reading assistance program cannot be overstated; for without the ability to read a student will continue to be very disadvantaged. After referring the student, occasionally ask the student about his progress and talk with those providing services. It is encouraging to learn of a student's improvement and your colleague(s) will appreciate your interest.

The one year I neglected to check my students' reading abilities was the year I should not have failed to do so. The school year started quickly and seemed to be moving along nicely. My students appeared to be successful in their studies. In October, my students were presenting oral reports on the contributions made to our society by specific immigrants. One student was having a terrible time reading his own report. The student was very embarrassed and kept commenting that he could not read his own handwriting. Some of the other students began to snicker and the situation was quickly becoming embarrassing for the reporting student. Another five minutes remained before the class was to end. I knew I had to rescue my student, so I interrupted him and asked if I could use the remaining class time for announcements. He very gladly let me take over.

At the end of the class period I requested the young man to stay and talk with me for a few minutes. I asked to see his report; his writing was poor but legible. It was becoming evident to me that this student could copy, but he could not read very well. There was a Reader's Digest on my desk, and I knew it was basically written on a fifth-grade reading level. I opened the book and asked the student to read a paragraph to me. He read approximately twenty lines and made innumerable mistakes - major mistakes. This was a serious situation. I was somewhat surprised by his now-obvious problem, for he was one of the most knowledgeable students in this Regents class. We talked about his ability to keep up with the workload in my class. He stated he very much wanted to stay in my class and he promised to do his best. I agreed to allow him to stay in the class as long as he wanted to stay. We talked a little longer and then agreed that he should go to the reading specialist in our school and see if she could help him improve his reading skills.

Occasionally I talked with the reading specialist; first to verify if the student met with her and later to learn of his progress. I have great respect for that young man. The very day we discussed his reading problem he went to the reading specialist for help. Within a short time he was tested to establish his reading level (he was reading on a fourth-grade level). This student had attended many different schools; however, he had never successfully been taught phonetic reading skills. After his evaluation was completed he was enrolled in an individual reading program. He continued working with the reading specialist for the entire school year and made good progress. By the end of the school year he was reading on an eighth-grade level. This student's reading abilities improved so much that he took and passed the Regents Exam in social studies at the end of the school year. The reading specialist, the student, and I were all delighted by his success.

This student could have been one of those people who graduate from high school but who cannot read adequately. In eleventh grade he was reading on a fourth-grade level. Why did it happen? He had lost so much time in his moves from school to school. As an eleventh and twelfth grade social studies teacher, I lacked both the experience and time to teach a student to read. However, as teachers, we all need to take the time to learn of the abilities or lack of abilities of our students, to help them where possible, and to refer them to other in-school or out-of-school professionals who can provide additional assistance. We must assist our students so they acquire the basic skills needed for learning and for life.

There's always more work to do!

# Chapter 10

# INFORMATION OVERLOAD

The flood of information generated within a school system not only seems endless - it is! The messages received by teachers can be written on paper, announced over the public address system, or delivered by email. Whatever system is used, the stream of information begins long before the school year starts, and it does not end until a week or so after the last students have left for their summer vacation, at which point another new cycle has already begun.

Every teacher must create a process for efficiently dealing with the incoming information. Developing and maintaining this processing skill is one of the "life saving" practices necessary for survival in the teaching profession. Every time a teacher receives a message from the main office, central administration, or any other person, the message must be read then categorized according to its importance or relevance to the teacher. Some messages are simply informative (sport's schedule) or unrelated to the teacher reading the message (9th grade field trip schedule - not related to 12th grade teachers). Once those messages are read, if they are of no interest, they may be discarded. Some of the information requires a response by a certain date or an appearance at a meeting. Those items should be recorded in the plan book or on a personal calendar to which one often refers. If a written response is required, write the reply as soon as possible for there will be additional required responses by the end of the week - if not sooner!

Teachers not only receive notices, they also contribute to the flow of information when they share ideas with colleagues, send a message to administrators, and communicate with parents. This teacher generated contact can occur by written expression or via computer generated methods. Whatever method is used, teachers need to be concise and deliberate in their communications.

# DISCIPLINARY REFERRAL FORM

The disciplinary referral form is the general name given to a preprinted form or a computer based communication system used between teachers and administrators when dealing with a troublesome student. Teachers complete the form by describing student behavior which was a violation of the school's discipline code. Once the teacher has written the information describing the student's unacceptable behavior, the message is sent to the building administrator for disciplinary action. Teachers should always keep a copy of any office referrals they send to the main office for administrative action. Once the referral is received by the main office, the principal is expected to "visit" with the student and determine a corrective course of action. Disciplinary referral forms usually include space for the administrator to inform the teacher of the discussion held with the student and any disciplinary action taken.

When completing a disciplinary referral form, teachers are wise to clearly describe the problem in a factual, non-emotional manner. If the administrator receiving the referral has questions or needs further clarification, s/he can contact the reporting teacher. Disciplinary referrals can be used in superintendent's hearings or in some court cases, so teachers should clearly and carefully state all pertinent information.

# RECOMMENDATIONS FOR STUDENTS

As a teacher, you may be asked to write recommendations for students for a variety of situations such as college entrance, employment, and honor society consideration. If you agree to write a recommendation, complete the job as quickly as possible because your prompt reply is important to the student's future.

When you agree to write a recommendation for a student or a colleague, it is important to describe known strengths. If teachers comment about personal or academic areas in need of improvement, they should suggest how the improvement can be accomplished and whether or not the improvement is likely to occur. By writing a balanced response, the recommendation is more complete, and perhaps, a stronger evaluation. I once recommended a girl for acceptance into a nursing school. The girl was having a difficult time in my course, but she was a very responsible and hard-working student. I believed, if she could get through the academic courses, she would become a good nurse. I acknowledged in my recommendation that even though academically this student was not maintaining a high average in my course, I thought she had sufficient ability and incentive to become a nurse. Years later, I learned she had successfully complete nursing school and had become a registered nurse.

Recommendation forms often have two sections - one part being a check-off list and the second part requiring a written statement. The check-off part is easy to complete, but the written part requires thoughtful planning and time for completion. Always write a rough draft on separate paper or on a computer; then, when all comments are clearly stated and you are satisfied with your statement, copy it onto the form provided.

After completing the recommendation form, make sure to photocopy it for your records. Then, if asked to complete a second or third recommendation for the same student, your work time will be reduced. Also, check with guidance office personnel to learn if they compile a college admissions folder for each student, and if so, you should forward a copy of the recommendation to them.

Teachers should inform each student of the approximate date when the recommendation will be completed. Then, as a "completion check" teachers may suggest that their students inquire whether or not the recommendation was written according to the planned date. For me, those student reminders were very helpful, and after the first reminder, sufficiently embarrassing to cause me to "get the job done" before receiving yet another student reminder.

There may be times when you are asked by a student to complete a recommendation form and you cannot honestly give the student a better-than-average recommendation. If that situation presents itself to you and you would rather not write the recommendation, simply decline to do so. Teachers are not duty bound to endorse every student who requests a recommendation. I have never dishonestly recommended anyone; however, there have been times when I have refused to complete recommendation forms for students. When refusing to write a recommendation for a student, the teacher should explain why the request cannot be granted (the teacher lacks the necessary time, does not sufficiently know the student, or cannot highly recommend the student), then suggest that the student ask another teacher.

The writing of recommendations for students is occasionally a necessary part of a teacher's job and it is time consuming - often requiring an hour or more per recommendation. Teachers should carefully consider their commitments and time availability before agreeing to write recommendations or reference letters.

# COMMUNICATIONS WITH PARENTS

Communication between parents and teachers is often touted by educational experts as vital to the academic success of students. However, for a variety of reasons, there seems to be little communication between parents and secondary level teachers beyond the general introductions at "back to school" night or as a result of negative academic or behavioral situations which develop during the school year.

Occasionally one finds an example of positive teacher contact with parents in order to build a supportive, pro-student relationship. At the beginning of each school year, one of my colleagues called the parents of each of his classroom students. After introducing himself, he stated a few positive comments about the parent's daughter or son and encouraged the parent to contact him with questions or concerns. This quick telephone call was unusual and pleasant for parents and it established a positive working relationship between the two adults. Although this can be a time consuming activity, it is an effective means of building communication between parent and teacher.

Most of the teacher to parent communication occurs to insure parental awareness and responsibility. For example, in one school system teachers have computerized their class lists. Each Friday the teachers print a letter to parents informing them as to whether or not their child is up-to-date with all assignments. If all assigned work has been completed, parents are so notified. When a student has not completed all assignments, parents are informed as to which assignments are missing along with new due dates. The letter is to be signed by parents and returned to the teacher on the following Monday. Clearly, teachers are making an attempt to regularly inform parents of the academic status of their children and overall, the system appears to work well.

Many teachers inform parents of major student assignments. A project description sheet which defines the project, states due dates and presents the grading rubric, is sent to the home. Often these project description sheets must be signed by a parent and the student as proof that everyone understands the assignment (again, this is about parents being informed and sharing accountability - not communication related to the needs of the student). Often, when a parental signature is required, a teacher will build into the rubric and point or two for the returned, signed requirement sheet.

# RESPONDING TO PARENTAL CONCERNS

Many parents are concerned about their daughter or son's academic progress and behavior in school. When a noticeable negative change occurs, parents do contact the guidance office to arrange for a conference with teachers and other school support personnel. Since the parents are seeking explanations for the change in their child's behavior, guidance office personnel usually contact all of the student's teachers and request those teachers to evaluate the student's academic performance, behavior, attitude, and recent noticeable changes in any of those categories.

Teachers should promptly and carefully reply to any inquiry from the guidance department. When teachers are asked to report observations, they are not requested to give a complete psychological profile of the student - they should just report observed changes. Teachers may also take the opportunity to suggest possible actions the student may take which would improve the overall academic or behavioral situation. When completing a written report, teachers should be mindful that written material may become part of a court record or Superintendent's Hearing, so plan your response then write comments carefully and specifically.

If possible, all of the troubled student's teachers should attend the parental conference. This meeting is important because it begins a combined effort between the parents and the school to meet the needs of a particular student. During the conference, parents, teachers, and guidance personnel or administrators should review their concerns and observations in a candid discussion. Teacher input in the meeting is most useful when brief and to the point; but remember that while being truthful, it is also necessary to be tactful. Sometimes these meetings are very stressful for everyone involved especially if everyone focuses only on the student's problems. So, whenever possible, teachers should be prepared to offer both practical and useful solutions, and if possible, encourage the parents in their efforts with their children.

Many times, a contributing factor to a student's academic problem is alcohol or drug abuse - it is usually not the total problem, but it can definitely be a factor. Although public schools are generally not equipped to supply the types of assistance which many students need, school personnel (other than teachers) can assist students and their families by recommending available social service providers and programs.

Since parental support is often vital to the success of a student, it is very important to establish a parent-teacher team approach when dealing with a student's serious academic problem. Teachers should encourage parents to call them at school for academic updates and when a return call is requested, it should be placed as soon as possible. It takes extra effort and time on the teacher's part to be involved in parental conferences and further follow-up, but when a student becomes successful, it is professionally and personally rewarding for each teacher.

Teachers should consistently practice the parental contact methods established and/or required by the school in which they work. It is not only vital for parents to be informed about their children's academic status, it is their right and responsibility. Teachers should encourage parents to actively monitor their child's academic progress and teachers should carefully and promptly respond to parental requests for information;

however, teachers should be cautious about taking on additional reporting or supportive responsibilities.

# PROGRESS REPORTS / WARNING NOTICES

Administrators in most school districts encourage communication between teachers and parents. It is important to keep parents informed about academic requirements and their child's progress (of lack of it). Often, the teacher-to-parent contact is beneficial because it builds parental support and confidence.

School districts and/or teachers have developed a number of different methods to increase contact with parents in order to keep parents informed about class requirements and their child's performance. Report cards are usually sent to parents anywhere from four to six times per school year. Progress reports and/or warning notices are often sent at the midpoint of each marking term. Warning notices inform parents of the possibility of an academic failure by their child. A progress report is often seen by parents and teachers to be more positive in its approach for it documents the successes as well as deficiencies of each student. Although the forms are generated from different viewpoints, they both require the identification of the student, parent, teacher, and course name. Teachers then inform parents of academic successes or need for improvement, evaluate of the student's work ethic, possibly request a conference, and welcome a parental response.

Teachers must be careful when addressing warning notices or progress reports; the reports must be sent to the correct parent(s) or guardian(s) at the most current known address. In each of my courses at the beginning of the school year, for my quick reference, I always had my students write the names of their parent(s), current mailing address, and telephone number on a 3 X 5 file card. I clearly stated I wanted correct information but some students do think ahead. One year, a girl in my course had listed a last name on her 3 X 5 card for her parent which was different from her last name. This was not unusual, except for the fact that I knew the girl lived at home with her two parents. This girl had decided to have any mail that would create problems at home sent to her boyfriend. It was a good plan on her part, but in this case it did not work (she did not know I knew her parents). The address on her card was "updated" by me and the notice was sent to her parents!

Many, if not all, school districts require teachers to send warning notices to all parents when a student is in danger of failing a course. Administrators want parents warned of impending student failure, especially when a student may not advance into the next grade or graduate from high school. When it is necessary to send a warning notice, it should be sent early enough during the marking term so that the student has an opportunity to improve if s/he so desires. Parents also need the warning notice in a timely manner so they may engage in corrective action at home. If a parent places a telephone call to the teacher for clarification or discussion, a return telephone call should be made as soon as possible.

In order to individualize the progress report of warning notice, many teachers devote hours of time completing the descriptive "Teacher Comments" section. Often, it seems this extra effort elicits little parental concern or response, and teachers become discouraged. It is important to individualize the report, yet not to waste one's time. I seldom wrote lengthy comments in the "Teacher Comments" section, yet I tried to individualize each notice by changing a word or two or adding specific information on the preprinted comments. The notice then informed the parents more precisely while encumbering less of my time.

A teacher places additional pressure on the parents by requesting a conference – this I did often. If a meeting is scheduled, the teacher can stress student and parental responsibility, design an improvement plan, and offer additional teacher assistance. All of these suggestions are most easily developed during a personal meeting and once the parents and teacher are working together, the student frequently improves.

Often, parents do not respond to warning notices or progress reports. During an average year I sent approximately forty to fifty warning notices to parents (4 marking terms, 10-12 warning notices per term, on average two warning notices per class); if I received ten responses from parents I would have been pleased. Some parents discuss the notice with their daughter or son and feel that is sufficient while a few others place a telephone call to the teacher. Some parents will never receive a warning notice because their children pre-sort the parents' mail and discard such problem creating letters from the school! Still, teachers have an obligation to send the notices to parents and attempt to collect signed ones if so required by school policy.

It is advisable for teachers to keep copies of all communication with parents related to grades or other difficulties. Often, warning notices or progress reports are preprinted forms and a teacher copy is included, but if not, photocopy a teacher copy before mailing the report to parents. The teacher copies should be placed in a folder and kept in a file cabinet or desk drawer. It is not necessary to spend time organizing the contents of the folder by class or alphabetizing students by last name, for seldom will a teacher need to retrieve the actual notice. Once a teacher has completed writing warning notices, a notation should be entered in the grade register.

A most efficient method for recording this information is to mark one column in the grade register and entitle it "Warning Notice Sent". Then, next to the name of each student who was sent a warning notice, write the date in the titled column to record when the notice was sent.

# STUDENT PASSES

Most schools use a student pass system as a means of controlling the number of students roaming hallways and loitering in rest rooms. To be valid, some or all of the following information is usually required: student name, date, time of day, point of departure and/or destination, and teacher signature. Some school systems require the use of a preprinted form, while other school systems accept passes written on scraps of paper, a book cover, or even on a student's hand!

When giving a student a pass for use later in the day, teachers should take the time to write it properly. A pass does not take long to write, but stopping class activities to write a pass can be very disruptive. Whenever possible, write passes at the beginning or at the end of the class period.

When issuing a pass for a quick student trip to a locker, rest room, or another classroom to deliver or retrieve something for the teacher, a teacher can write a pass or use a "class pass". While searching through some school supply catalogs I noticed manufactured plastic passes approximately 4" X 5" in size. Those plastic passes provide space for a teacher to write the required information with a marker. In practice, those plastic passes may be more bother than they are worth for they must be cleaned after each student use. However, the idea of a permanent pass is valid. One of my colleagues had a large board (approximately one square foot in size) which was painted white. Using large black letters, he wrote "Hall Pass" and his last name on both sides of the board. He then drilled a hole in one corner of the board so it could be hung on a hook in his classroom. When a student requested and received permission to go to the rest room or locker, the student simply took the "class pass" and left. Upon returning to the classroom, the student hung the pass on the hook. The teacher used the same pass for many years with few problems. His system worked well since the pass was large, recognizable, and acceptable to other faculty members. Since teachers in the building knew students using this pass were monitored by the issuing teacher and a quick comment to the teacher about student misbehavior when using the pass would be dealt with, students were not required to have an individual pass.

Teachers should choose one particular way to sign their names on a pass, use it consistently, and eventually the entire faculty will recognize each signature style. Some teachers sign only their initials while others write their entire last name.  Once in a while a student will try to forge a pass by signing a teacher's name on it, but it is more difficult to accomplish when teachers use a distinctive or fancy signature.  One time a colleague of mine told me he always clearly wrote out his entire last name.  He went on to explain that students never forged his name on a pass because none of them could correctly spell it!

# COLLECTING / RETURNING ASSIGNMENTS

Collecting student assignments and returning graded papers in an efficient manner is possible with some organization and consistency in the methods used.  One might ask why this topic is even being mentioned in this book, for collecting and distributing paperwork seems to be quite a simple task.  It is simple, but it can also be an incredible time wasting experience.  If teachers are not careful, it is easy to waste five to ten minutes per class completing this job.  Consider this scenario: A bell signals the beginning of class and the teacher informs students to give their latest homework assignment to the teacher.  Several students complain that they could not complete the work and therefore do not have their papers, several more students have left their work in their lockers by mistake - can they go to their lockers and get the papers?  The teacher must then sign a few student passes.  Time is passing.  After most of the papers have been collected, one student asks the teacher to check through the papers to make sure the student had written his name on his paper - so the teacher looks through the stack of papers and finds the student did write his name on his paper.  Since the teacher is involved with collecting papers and class work has not begun, some students become engrossed in conversations.  The clock continues to show the passage of time.  Students return to the room at different times after going to their lockers and this is disruptive to the teacher who is trying to begin class work.  Finally, five to ten minutes after the class was scheduled to begin, a frustrated teacher begins the lesson presentation.

If the previously described events occur four to five times every two weeks, the teacher would have lost about one class period (40-50 minutes) in those two weeks to paper collecting - projected over a school year equals twenty classes devoted to paper collecting (1 class period every 2 weeks for 40 weeks).  If you accept that collecting papers can involve too much time, think about the time impact of returning papers to students - the need for efficiency when returning papers is more obvious since it consumes even more time.  When teachers understand and accept this explanation, they realize the importance of efficiency in this process.

Collecting completed papers from students is an easy job - and it can be done in a number of ways. Students can place their ungraded papers on a table or desk as they enter the classroom or quickly pass papers to the front of the room for the teacher to collect. The teacher can be in the process of introducing the next work assignment while collecting papers which have been passed to the front of the room. Once a collection method has been determined and explained to the students, the collection routine can quickly be established.

The perfect plan for efficient collection of papers is totally interrupted when students leave their assignments in their locker! If teachers do not allow students to go to their lockers and retrieve their papers, the students will not have their papers for review, may disrupt the class in anger, and may never submit the papers. If teachers allow the student to go to their lockers without penalty, this will be a continuing problem. The teacher needs to develop a plan to make the student come to class prepared. If your school has an after school detention policy, use it. Turn to page 235 and begin reading at the first new paragraph in the section entitled "Student Tardiness". A teacher may adapt the tardiness plan so students accumulate "late minutes" when they leave the classroom to get papers or a textbook from their locker. Students may get creative in this process, and ask for a pass to the rest room, then stop at their locker for needed items on their way back to the classroom - so be ready for this situation - and give late minutes to students who take advantage of a rest room pass.

Collecting tests can also be done using several methods. Students can be told to bring their completed tests to the teacher. This process can cause some disruption in the classroom during the testing period, but it can also allow students who have complete taking the test some time to work on other assignments or rest. Another test collection method is to instruct students to raise their hand when they have completed taking the test, thus requesting the teacher to come to them and collect the test. This is a quieter method and allows the teacher to circulate throughout the classroom monitoring students during the testing period. Still another method for collecting test papers is to have all students keep their papers until the testing period is over, then students are instructed to stop writing and quickly hand their papers to the front of the room where the teacher collects them. The advantage to this system is that students are required to remain quiet for the entire testing period. The disadvantage is wasted time for those students who finish the test quickly.

After student papers are collected and graded, teachers must enter the grades into a grade register or computer program. If student grades are recorded on a computer program, it may be easier to place student names in alphabetical order, then number the students chronologically, and assign the number to each student. From that point in time students must write both their name and their number on all papers given to the teacher. It is faster to put the student papers in alphabetical order using the number system rather than according to the student's last name.

Student papers should be promptly graded and returned to students. Grading papers quickly was not particularly a problem for me but, I must confess, I was often delinquent in returning homework and class work assignments. Most students are interested in knowing their earned grade on assignments, and if papers are returned quickly, students may learn from their mistakes or be encouraged by their good work.

Eventually, I determined to review homework and class work assignments during class time so students would receive the benefit of learning. After objective answer sheets were exchanged among students, correct answers were stated for grading purposes, and grade computation was accomplished. Once the papers were returned to their owners, students were given an opportunity to ask questions related to their responses. The assignments were then given to me so grades could be recorded then the papers were discarded.

Some assignments which I graded needed to be returned to students for inclusion in their notebooks. There was a shelf in the back of my classroom over which I hung signs naming each of the classes I taught. When I had less important papers to return to students, I placed the papers on the shelf at the appropriately listed class name. Students were free to sort through the papers and reclaim their own papers - this was usually done near the end of class time. After a week or so, all remaining papers were discarded.

Students were reminded to discard unwanted papers in the wastebasket, not in student desks. Although I never did this, some teachers, in an attempt to encourage students to use the wastebasket, deducted points from student papers found in a desk. When such a plan is followed consistently, it can produce good housekeeping results in a short time, but in most cases it becomes just another "job" for teachers. I found a kind reminder referring to the circular file accomplished the same housekeeping results.

The third part of my plan for efficiently returning those "most important" papers (tests and projects) to students was to personally deliver them. It is important to protect the students' privacy and to be personable at this time. Rather than call one student to me and wait until the student received his paper before calling another name, I would read aloud several students' names at one time. As those students returned to their seats, I called several more names until all of the papers were distributed. After all students received their papers, I took time to review the tests or projects, answer student questions, and explain the grading process. If a student wanted further review of her/his paper, we would talk later and I would listen to, and consider, their comments. It was always important to me, and should be to you, to be able to explain and justify any grade to any student.

Whatever methods are chosen for the collection and distribution of papers, teachers should use time efficiently, protect student privacy, and maintain order within the classroom.

# CLASSROOM ATTENDANCE

The responsibility for recording student attendance belongs to the classroom teacher and accuracy in this duty is of utmost importance for several reasons. School systems are dependent on accurate attendance records for the purpose of financial aid. Also, many school districts require students to attend a percentage of the total number of class periods in order to receive course credit toward graduation. Accurate attendance records may assist the teacher to quickly recognize students who may need extra help or encouragement. Finally, student attendance records may occasionally be used as legal evidence in an expulsion hearing or in other legal settings. It is easy to understand why attendance records are so important, and since they are important, students should not be allowed to complete this activity in place of the teacher.

Once a teacher has recorded the names of absent students, those names should be announced. It is easy to miss seeing a student in the classroom, especially if a seating plan is not enforced. Simply announce: "The following people have been marked absent" then read the list of absent students' names. Often, a student would respond: "I'm here!" or a student may inform the teacher where an absent student could be found.

Teachers can use five or more minutes of valuable class time with attendance related duties which include checking passes of late-arriving students, learning the whereabouts of several unaccounted-for students, checking the absentee list, writing the names of "missing" students on a daily attendance sheet, and marking the attendance register. In order to save time, teachers use various methods for taking attendance in their classrooms. Some teachers will read through the list of students found in their register and search the classroom until each student is found while other teachers will review their seating charts to discover missing students. The problem with both of those methods is a teacher must look for present as well as absent students, and that takes time. All the teacher really wants is an accurate list of absent students. There is a faster method to accomplish the attendance taking task.

At the beginning of the school year, after enrollment in each class has stabilized, teachers should count the number of students in each class and write the total number of enrolled students in the attendance register or on the seating charts. Then, each day when taking attendance, simply count the number of present students and subtract this number from the total enrollment; the difference tells how many students are absent. The teacher then informs the class membership how many students are absent and asks students for the names of absent students. At the beginning of the school year, students are not very helpful because they do not know or remember all of the other students in the class, so the teacher must rely on a seating chart or the register until class members become acquainted with each other. Another problem at the beginning stages of implementing this system of taking attendance is the general feeling held by the students that giving the teacher the names of absent students is being disloyal to fellow classmates (and most especially to anyone who is skipping the class). This problem is overcome by taking attendance at the end rather than at the beginning of class. I found my students much more willing to tell me the names of missing students once they learned the class would not be dismissed until attendance taking was complete! Teacher consistency in taking attendance and reporting absent, unaccounted for, students is important in this process as well. Students quickly learned that all absent students would be identified and without their assistance, the process would just take longer. So, in order to be dismissed on time, students cooperate with the teacher and name absent students. Trust me, it works!

Teachers should learn to end classes one or two minutes before the dismissal bell rings. This allows plenty of time to take attendance and sign passes. One advantage of taking attendance at the end of class is that all latecomers have arrived and changes will not have to be recorded in the attendance register. I generally did not mark student tardiness in my attendance records. When students arrived more than ten minutes late for my class, they needed an excellent excuse and a pass. When tardiness became habitual, it would be noted in my register and discussed with the student. If tardiness continued to be a problem, I would contact attendance personnel, a guidance counselor, and a parent.

Another important advantage of taking attendance at the end of class is being able to begin class work promptly, thus encouraging students to be on time and to quickly focus their attention.

One obvious difficulty in using this attendance-taking method is learning to end class activities one or two minutes early in order to take attendance. It is quite difficult to take attendance by memory after the students have left the room. Believe me, I know! A second difficulty in using this method is the requirement of some school systems that attendance be taken at the beginning of the class period and be immediately reported to an attendance officer. The motivation for student cooperation in naming absent students is often reduced.

Once this new attendance taking method is mastered by both the teacher and students, the system works well. The teacher can take attendance accurately and quickly, and the students are able to use the minute before class ends to collect their belongings and get ready to move to their next class.

# STUDY HALL ATTENDANCE

Generally speaking, monitoring a study hall "is the pits" however, it is preferable to a lunch duty assignment! Study halls are usually over-crowded, under-staffed, and contain a mixed combination of different grade level students - many of whom the teacher does not know. Those factors equate a troublesome combination from a teacher's point of view. Added to the difficulties of monitoring a study hall are the possible requirements of taking attendance, designing and enforcing a seating plan for 50-100 students, and maintaining a quiet atmosphere while meeting in an auditorium or cafeteria. Is it any wonder why teachers find it difficult to arouse personal enthusiasm for such non-academic duties? (I believe my personal bias is conspicuous - experience is my excuse!) Even when opposed to this type of duty, teachers must when required, complete them - or at least attempt to complete them - in a responsible, timely manner.

One year, I had three consecutive twenty-five minute study halls scheduled during the lunch periods. Since there was a general lack of space in our building, the study halls were meeting in the auditorium. This room lacked proper lighting and had no desks or tables for student use. There were three teachers scheduled for the first and second study halls, and a fourth teacher joined us for the last study hall (he objected to being assigned to a study hall and announced he would attend as required, would sit in the back of the auditorium, and not be involved with the attendance "game"). The first study hall had eighty-six students, the second study hall had one hundred forty-one students, and the last study hall had one hundred ninety-seven students. Some students attended only one study hall while other students attended two or more of the study halls. Some students attended the first and third study halls while others attended the second and third study halls. Some students were assigned to the study hall on Monday, Wednesday, and Friday, some students were there every day, and some only on Tuesdays and Thursdays. Some of the teachers assigned to this block of study halls were on a rotating basis and some were there every day. Additional confusion and frustration was caused by inaccurate class lists, students who obtained passes to other locations, students who were absent from school, and students who decided to skip the study hall. Remember, the study hall periods were only twenty-five minutes long and we were expected to accurately take attendance, keep students relatively quiet, and prevent vandalism in this poorly lit room. If you think this situation was a nightmare, you are absolutely right! I never before (or since) experienced such a terrible duty. One of the teachers assigned to the study hall stated his main goal for the year: "I want to avoid getting an ulcer!"

All of the teachers monitoring study halls in the auditorium were given a special memo from the building administrator regarding proper care for the auditorium. We were told to make seating plans and enforce them strictly. Students were to sit in the front third of the auditorium and use every seat. We were also told to accurately take attendance (even though no one could assure the teachers that the student list was accurate) and report all absent students. Several of the teachers assigned to this study hall met to design the seating plan - it took hours to organize this plan and it never was completely reliable. About a month into the new school year, the process looked somewhat successful and the students were beginning to remember where their assigned seats were located!

Then, all teachers who monitored a study hall in the auditorium were given new instructions from the administration. Students were complaining because they lacked space for their books and the close seating arrangement made it difficult to work. We were instructed to make another seating plan and assign the students to every other seat. We complained, but complied. The new seating plan was written and put into effect in spite of student groaning and teacher headaches. Another month passed and, again, the students were beginning to adjust when the main office came through with its third directive for teachers monitoring auditorium study halls. Since the custodial staff was reporting extensive damage being done to the auditorium, the administration told study hall teachers to form another seating plan and assign students seats in every other row - this was to improve teacher surveillance of students, but for us, it was the last straw! We simply chose to ignore the memo. Thankfully, that study hall assignment lasted only twenty weeks; we all had a reason to celebrate when the semester was over!

Yes, the previously described situation was as difficult as described; however, it happened only one time to me in eleven years of teaching. Teachers usually find that taking attendance and establishing seating plans for study halls are not so overwhelming. I have had many study halls in which I was able to complete some school work while keeping tabs on the students. Also, once students clearly know their attendance in study halls is required, most students comply without protest. Teachers who consistently record and report student absences in study halls, and who are supported by building administrators, provide an important incentive for students to attend. Remember, too, attendance taking is more important than seating plans, since disruptive students can be relocated to a seat near the teacher.

There are several methods which can be used by teachers when they are required to write seating plans (for their classrooms as well as for study halls). One can institute an alphabetical plan or assign seats according to some other random method such as the order in which students arrive in the room, alternating boy/girl, etc. Often it seems that instituting a seating plan begins a negative process which sets the stage for a power struggle between the teacher and students. I had a personal distaste for implementing seating plans; they were not necessary, took valuable time to write, and were often aggravating to students at the beginning of the year when I wanted to establish a positive atmosphere. I preferred to allow students to choose where they would like to sit, and their choice became the basic seating plan. Students were told that if they could not behave where they chose to sit, then I would assign them a seat in the front of the room - the system worked well.

During the last few years of my teaching career, I used another method for taking attendance in study halls. Most of my study halls were held in the cafeteria. The students were allowed to choose the place where they wanted to sit. I had an alphabetical list of the names of all students assigned to the study hall. I photocopied the list so each day when I took attendance I used an unmarked sheet. To take attendance, I simply walked around the room, stopped at the different tables, and asked the students for their last name. As students stated their last names, I repeated them and crossed the names off my list. After deleting the names of additional students who had signed out of the study hall or who were absent from school, the remaining names represented the "unaccounted-for students". I announced the names of all missing students, and sent the list to the main office. The entire process of taking attendance for sixty to seventy students usually took no more than ten or fifteen minutes - and it was a painless as possible for both students and teacher.

There were some definite advantages to the attendance taking system just described. I especially appreciated not having to waste my time writing a seating plan, and I soon discovered that by walking around the room to take attendance I was able to quickly settle students into the study hall routine. Students appreciated the opportunity to choose where in the room they would sit and with whom. Students were also encouraged to be responsible for good behavior and most were successful. If there was a problem with a student's behavior, the student was required to sit at a table near me for one week. After the week passed the student was allowed to return to his regular spot, and with good behavior he could remain there.

Study halls should provide a quiet time in which students may complete homework assignments, study for a test, read for enjoyment, rest, or conduct a subdued conversation. Students can learn to be quiet, if not for their own sake, then for the benefit of others. Study halls should not be a stressful time for teachers or students, and taking attendance should be an easy task involving little time and effort. Inform students at the beginning of the school year or semester of your expectations, enforce your rules from the very first day, and the study hall duty will not be difficult.

# ORDERING TEXTBOOKS AND SUPPLIES

A yearly task for teachers is to order textbooks, resource materials, and supplies. Many catalogs are sent to teachers for review thus providing an opportunity to discover course related new materials and support resources. While reviewing catalogs teachers evaluate the materials, determine which materials are best for their students, and project what is actually needed for the next year. Before searching through catalogs, teachers should know the amount of money which is available for ordering resources and supplies. It is disappointing to compile a long list of needed items, only to learn there is little money available - and it must be shared among all member of the department. There are two overall ideas to keep in mind when ordering resources and supplies. First, a teacher may choose to order a few items for each course taught and build resources over a period of time. A second ordering method is to concentrate on the needs of only one course during a budget cycle, thus securing more resources for instructional purposes in one particular area and excluding others. The purchasing plan is dependent on identified needs, resources offered by publishing companies, and available funding.

Of the three types of ordering listed above, the most difficult to order are textbooks. There is a wide variety of textbooks available for most courses and since textbooks are usually expensive, they must be chosen carefully. Frequently, publishing companies (if requested) will send teachers complimentary preview copies of textbooks which are seriously being considered for purchase in class sets. Complimentary textbooks should be carefully reviewed and compared for content, writing style, readability, illustrations, end-of-chapter assignments and reviews, ability to meet curriculum goals, and available teacher aids. Before choosing a textbook, teachers should become familiar with several possible textbooks by reading and outlining several chapters in each book and then writing lesson plans based on those chapters. After becoming familiar with several textbooks, compare answers to some of the following questions related to those books. Was the information clearly presented? Were explanations sufficient? Were illustrations meaningfully related to content? Were assignments given so students would be challenged to learn and then apply their learning, or were the assignments merely recall? If a teacher does not like the textbook after it has been purchased, it's too late to make changes. The teacher and students are then simply "stuck" with the textbook and it will probably have to be used for several years. So, when you are given the opportunity to choose a new textbook for your students, take the time to thoroughly review several possible textbooks before writing a purchase order.

Ordering resource materials can be the most enjoyable part of the ordering responsibilities. When ordering resources the teacher has the opportunity to select items which would be "nice to have" for enriching the topics discussed in class, for increasing materials available to students, or for expanding the teaching methods used. While teaching a law studies course I maintained a library of books containing many interesting short stories related to law enforcement and criminal cases. Each year I tried to add ten to fifteen new titles to that library. The library was used by students to read individually selected articles during a "reading day" which occurred once every two weeks. The students wrote brief summaries of the articles for an earned grade. For another course, I ordered project-related resource materials designed to increase life skills of my lower-ability students. Other types of resource materials ordered included prepared worksheets for several different courses, transparency sets, and prepared tests (from which I chose questions to incorporate into my tests). The range of available resource materials is extensive; choose them carefully, use them often, take care of them, and expand your collection whenever possible. In a short time, you will have many useful and varied aids which will greatly increase the knowledge and understanding of your students and your impact as a teacher.

School budgets do affect and limit what a teacher may order; however, there are some other avenues open to teachers for securing desired resource materials even when there are no available funds in the department budget. Teachers can request free items from banks, insurance companies, government agencies, museums, research foundations, or professional organizations (described in the next topic section). Teachers can request their school librarian to order desired books and audio-visual media. Many times a school librarian will ask teachers to submit a list of specific items desired, or to list general topics to include or upgrade in the school library. This is a golden opportunity for teachers to submit requests and receive additional items. Another source of funding resource material purchases is to write a grant requesting special funding for a "new" activity or idea. Sometimes the school district itself will offer "mini-grants" to encourage teachers to expand their programs; at other times grants may be available through government funding programs or educational foundations.

Ordering general supplies and equipment for classroom use is rather mundane but necessary. Frequently, the department chairman orders items such as pens, pencils, paper, chalk or markers, tape, paper clips (etc.) for all teachers in the department. It is then up to the individual teacher to order specific items needed but not included in the department's general supply order. Some items, which always appeared on my "shopping list" and are mentioned in this book, were:

- pens in colors other than red for grading papers (I used marking pens in bright colors such as green, purple, or orange just for variety).

- large envelopes for student readings and other handouts (see "Student Readings Packet," page 95).

- 3" X 5" index cards and Post-It pads are great for reminder notes, passes, and student information.

- transparencies along with a variety of colored pens for writing on the transparencies.

- a selection of twenty to thirty pocketed folders in a variety of different colors.

- several legal-sized pads of paper (helpful when developing a chart for grading student projects, writing tests, or outlines).

- one can of desk cleaner spray.

The job of reviewing catalogs, evaluating materials, and completing requisition forms is easier when done methodically. Label a file folder "Requisitions," "Wanted/Ordered Items," or any other title you may wish to use. As you receive catalogs, look through them and circle all textbooks and resource materials you believe would be valuable to your students or yourself, as well as items you wish to further evaluate. Then write the page number for each item on the catalog cover where it can be clearly observed. Store those current catalogs in which you have indicated items of interest in the requisitions folder. Discard catalogs which contain nothing related to your course needs. Maintain a list of wanted or needed general supplies in the requisitions folder as well; then, when general supplies are ordered, you will be able to quickly include desired items. Complete your ordering a little ahead of the due date and remember to give the requisitions to your department chairman. Keep copies of all submitted purchase requests and order forms in your requisitions folder. After each item is delivered, mark your purchase order form to indicate the item was received. It is fun to receive items which were ordered and then to begin plan for their use.

There are several ideas to keep in mind when ordering textbooks, resource materials, supplies, and equipment. First, the ordered items must be reasonable in relation to desired quantity, price, and usefulness to the course of instruction. Second, there is a limit to the amount of money available so teachers must often prioritize their purchases. Third, recognize the difference between "would be nice to have" and "absolutely necessary and vital to the course." Fourth, consider options other than direct department purchase. Those options include requisitioning through the library, increasing your use of regional media service organizations, or searching for available free materials.

As new items are received, attentively examine them to learn how and when to use them in the courses you teach. Teachers should be willing to share purchased items with colleagues; remember, the resource materials are not "yours" and they were purchased to increase the quality of education in your school. When possible, order some new items each year for your classes. It is not necessary to order many or expensive items, but you should look for new methods and sources of information to enrich your instruction. If, year after year you continue to teach the same courses using the same materials, you may then become stagnant and unable to challenge your students.

Once you have received requisitioned items make it your responsibility to care for them. Textbooks, resource materials, and supplies all cost money. If the items were important enough to order, they are important enough to be cared for properly. Store them in labeled closets whenever possible; they will then be secure and easy to find.

When ordering textbooks, resource materials, and supplies one must be an optimistic realist. Teachers should order items that are necessary for good classroom instruction; then order additional items which would be nice to receive. Some years you will receive all ordered items and at other times you will receive very little as a result of serious budget shortages. In either case, it is important to review catalogs and know of available educational resources.

# IF IT'S FREE, ORDER IT!

There are many organizations, corporations, government agencies, and special interest groups which make free information available to schools in the form of pamphlets, charts or graphs, educational portfolios, booklets, books, and video tapes. Those items may be given as a single copy or in class sets, or they may be available on a free loan basis. Class presentations can be greatly enhanced with much of the material offered by these special interest groups.

For the teacher, there are three major obstacles to obtaining the free teaching aids that are so readily available. First, the teacher must know what materials are available. Second, the teacher must have an address to which a request for material may be sent. Third, the teacher must find a means of requesting materials which does not require the investment of much time. A description of those problems and possible solutions follows.

## How does a teacher learn of the existence of free educational materials?

There are several ways a teacher may learn of the existence of free teaching materials. One way is to network with other teachers within your own school system or from other districts who teach similar courses. When I first began teaching, one of my colleagues gave me several boxes of course related materials. I spent a few hours sorting through those materials; some of the resources were useful, some were good but outdated, and some were useless. When a booklet or pamphlet looked promising, I usually found on it an address to which I could write or call for further information. I designed a form letter identifying myself and the purpose of the letter, then I stated my request for specific (and free) educational material. Many times a list of other available educational aids was sent along with the requested materials. Another means of obtaining free materials is to write a letter of inquiry to a corporation, embassy, governmental agency, museum, or organization. Yet another method of discovering free material is to talk with businessmen, such as bankers, insurance agents, or lawyers. Many of those individuals are connected with organizations which have educational departments on a state level. Another individual who may be of great help is the school librarian. The librarian may be willing to search for possible sources of free materials or to order certain materials for you which are not free and pay for them through library funds. Still other sources of information can be found in books which list free educational materials (however there is a charge for the book!). I have seen those books advertised in school supply catalogs and I have searched through and ordered items from one such book; however, I was generally unimpressed with my success in receiving the materials ordered. Many of the letters requesting information were returned to me stamped "addressee unknown." Last, but not least, a teacher can search for educational information on the Internet.

As a social studies teacher for senior elective courses, I sent many letters to corporations (Proctor & Gamble, Ford), government agencies (Federal Reserve System, Department of Education, Internal Revenue Service), embassies (Latin American, European, African, and Asian countries), the New York Stock Exchange, and the American Council of Life Insurance. Most of the educational materials I received from those groups were used as supplements to or in place of textbooks and they were re-ordered every year.

## What is an efficient method for writing letters to companies and agencies to request free educational materials?

It is very time consuming to write an individual letter to each addressee when requesting free educational materials. Since the type of letter written makes no difference to the mailroom clerk or the stockroom attendant, there is no need for a personal letter - although a professional letter is necessary. The solution, then, is to write a short form letter leaving blank spaces for the date, addressee, item(s) requested, and your signature. In the letter state that you are a teacher and list the courses you teach; then request information describing free educational materials available for those courses, or list specific items desired. After writing the form letter, photocopy it or keep it on your computer. Then, as you find desired materials, complete the form and mail it. Many companies and agencies supplying free materials require proof of teacher employment; therefore, be sure to print your form letter on paper with the school's letterhead. Requesting educational materials is not a difficult job; and it can easily be completed during a preparation period, a homeroom or study hall duty, or when a normally scheduled class is canceled - and you are not required to take a room full of rambunctious students to an assembly!

Both you and your students will be rewarded for your efforts since you will constantly be receiving packages of useful, informative, and interesting materials. Companies and organizations often send special teaching guides or supporting visual aids along with the student supplies. The teaching aids received will increase your knowledge and background in a specific area of study and enhance your classroom presentations. Your students receive the benefit of your efforts by being exposed to a wide variety of materials which can expand their knowledge. Often the change from a textbook to a booklet which will be used for a week or two rejuvenates student interest in a subject. So, send those letters!

Frequently, when unpacking a box of materials, the teacher finds an evaluation sheet to judge the effectiveness of the materials. After using the materials, be sure to complete the evaluation form and return it to the listed address. Evaluation reports submitted by teachers assist in the updating, improvement, and on-going availability of many free items.

# STUDENT READINGS PACKET

Each school year I spent many hours at the photocopy machine. As a social studies teacher it was personally very important to keep my students up-to-date, so I provided current information concerning topics being studied. Most of the readings I photocopied were several-to-many pages long. After spending hours photocopying interesting articles for students to read, it was discouraging to learn that some students had read and trashed, or just trashed, the papers. Sometimes photocopied articles can be used for several years before being outdated, so those articles ought to be saved. It is a waste of time, energy, and money to photocopy the same articles each year for several years. It is also time-consuming to distribute, record control numbers, and then collect those copied articles.

There had to be a process which could be developed to reduce the amount of time I spent with the photocopy machine and still have students return articles to me without using much class time to distribute and collect the articles. I wanted to be able to distribute the articles quickly, require the students to care for the articles, and collect them quickly at the end of the study unit, marking term, or course. The keys to this entire process were assigning a number to the students, giving students a means of protecting the articles, and informing students of the requirement of keeping then returning the copied articles.

At the beginning of each semester, I assigned each student a number. The number was the same as the student's line indicator number in the class register - I did not have to develop and keep another list. I also gave each student a large 9" X 12" envelope. The student's name and number were written on the outside of the envelope. Students were informed of the requirement to keep certain articles in the envelope and return the envelope and articles at the end of the course just as if it were a textbook. The contents of the envelope would be checked and if articles were not returned, students were required to borrow article(s) from me and photocopy them so that they returned a complete package of readings.

The first year I used this method all of the articles were new to the envelope. During one of the last days of class at the end of the course, I had the students discard certain outdated articles and place the remaining articles in a stated order for the following year's students. After I checked each student's stack of articles for completeness, the articles were placed in a new envelope and labeled with the same number. The following year, at the beginning of the course, I gave each student a "Readings Packet" which had the student's number at the top. For easy identification, students added their names on the envelope. When I wanted the students to read a certain article, I assigned it. If I wanted the students to read an article they did not have, I copied it, gave it to them, and it was to be kept in the envelope. At the end of the school year, the articles were sorted and made ready for the next year's students.

The "readings packet" system worked well for several reasons. The students were instructed to take care of the articles, and they were given an envelope in which to keep the articles. Students were informed of the necessity of having a complete set of articles at the end of the course. If an article was missing from their packet, they were to copy the article at their own expense. I considered the return of a complete set of articles as important as the return of a textbook, and grades were withheld if the articles packet was not returned intact. I saved myself large amounts of time at the photocopying machine and reduced photocopying expenses for the school district at the same time. Little class time was wasted with distributing and collecting photocopied articles. Finally, the extra reading assignments appeared neat, well-organized, and ready for future student use.

Using large envelopes as an organizational method can be successful for a variety of different course assignments such as worksheets, lab reports, practice sheets, and other projects. Student worksheets or special reading articles can be prepared for each unit (or for the entire course) and distributed to students at one time. The large envelopes give students a protected place in which to store their papers. New papers can be added to the packet at any time and outdated articles can be discarded. When first using this system, it probably would be most convenient to prepare papers by the unit. Then, in following years, the teacher can expand the number and types of papers included.

# A FOLDER FOR THE SUBSTITUTE TEACHER

When teachers are absent from school, they are expected to submit instructions for a substitute teacher to follow in each class. Some teachers will send in a current work assignment or a supplemental assignment using books or articles in the classroom related to current work. Still other teachers will send in "filler" material which may or may not be related to the current course topic (commonly known as busy-work) for students to complete. Other teachers simply inform the substitute to use "emergency lesson plans" which are available from the main office. Although unrelated to current course work, emergency lesson plans are designed to keep students working for an entire class period (see "Emergency Lesson Plans," page 98). Although it is usually best to send in current work assignments, there are times when it is impossible to do so. In any case, teachers should try to make the day's assignment worthwhile to the students as well as a plan which the substitute teacher can put into action.

Whatever the choice of lesson plans happens to be, the substitute teacher must have a number of other items to make the day pass smoothly. Teachers should maintain a file folder for substitute teachers to use in their absence. On the outside of a pocket folder, teachers should write their name and "Substitute Teacher Folder". If you have someone who will take your lesson plans to school when you are absent, then keep this folder with you so you can add necessary last-minute items to it. If you do not have a means of getting such a folder to school when you are absent, then leave it in your desk and show its location to several dependable students who have been appointed by you to assist substitute teachers.

You may include anything in this folder which you believe would be helpful to a substitute teacher. Some necessary items to include are:

1. A note informing the substitute teacher that your students have received clear instructions requiring good behavior toward substitute teachers and detentions will be given to any student reported for poor behavior.

2. In the note, ask the substitute teacher to write a description of the work accomplished in each class. Request the return of the folder and its contents to you; state that it may be left in your desk or in your mailbox.

3. A copy of your daily class schedule clearly listing class periods, times, room numbers, and all extra duties.

4. Current copies of seating plans for the purpose of student identification and accurate attendance-taking. Inform the substitute teacher if the seating charts are not closely followed. On each seating chart list the course name, times and periods when the class meets, total number of students enrolled in the class, and room number. Also indicate any exceptions to attendance regulations such as for Honor Society members (see item #7 below).

5. A daily attendance form on which absent student names are listed.

6. Several disciplinary referral forms for reporting to the main office any major problems with students.

7. A list of special class rules such as: "No passes to be issued from a particular class except for a clear emergency," or "Honor Society members can be excused from class after receiving assignments."

Sometimes building administrators require all teachers to submit a folder for substitute teachers, but they may not require all of the above listed items. Remember, too, the office folder may quickly become outdated due to the addition or deletion of students, changes in seating arrangements, or semester course changes. So, to assist the substitute teacher, classroom teachers should occasionally review the office file to update its contents or add helpful items. It is a very simple task to do and it is essential if you expect a substitute teacher and your students to have a successful day.

Whenever you are absent from school, plan to take a minimum of thirty minutes to write out instructions for the day; usually it will take longer. If you have the previously mentioned support papers gathered together in one place (with you, in your desk, or in the main office) then you will have to write only your lesson plans. This advanced preparation will save you much time; and early in the morning of the day you call in sick, you will definitely appreciate your ingenious foresight!

# EMERGENCY LESSON PLANS

Many school administrators require teachers to submit emergency lesson plans to the main office or to their department chairman. Those emergency lesson plans are kept for future use in the event the teacher is absent from school and unable to send current lesson plans to the school. An emergency lesson plan gives a substitute teacher specific, detailed plans for each class to be taught. Usually emergency lesson plans are very general, topic-related assignments which the students could complete any time during the school year. The assignment should be sufficient in content to keep the students working for an entire class period.

Some teachers write but do not use emergency lesson plans; some teachers write ten or twelve emergency lesson plans for each course early in the school year and those plans are used whenever the teacher is absent from school; and some teachers use both methods depending on the situation. Some teachers use emergency lesson plans because they have no means of delivering current lesson plans to the school, and some find it more convenient to use emergency lesson plans when an unexpected absence occurs. However, teacher convenience should not be the only concern when writing emergency lesson plans. Teachers should prepare valid work assignments for students which are sufficient in length to occupy the students' attention for an entire class period. The lesson plan should be designed so a substitute teacher can easily put it into action. Along with specific directions for each emergency lesson plan, teachers should include answer keys (where applicable) for use by the substitute teacher. Classroom teachers should prepare all papers necessary to the emergency lesson plan or be sure the substitute teacher will have the necessary time to photocopy the papers before the class is scheduled to meet.

After writing the required emergency lesson plans for each course, the teacher should number them and then list them by number and topic somewhere in their plan book-register. Then, whenever the teacher is absent from school and chooses to use an emergency lesson plan, it is a simple task to call school personnel and list lesson plan numbers for each class. Additionally, the teacher will know exactly what assignment was given to each class.

Many schools require emergency lesson plans as a protection against the teacher who calls in sick and fails to send in directions for a substitute teacher. Before I became a permanent teacher, I did some substitute teaching in a high school in Vermont. I was called to the school one day and a teacher's plan book was handed to me along with the statement, "The teacher did not send in any special lesson plans, so just follow the directions as given in the plan book for today." I opened the plan book and found nothing, absolutely nothing! This was in January, and the last time the teacher had entered lesson plans in his plan book was early in October. I went to the department chairman and asked what he wanted me to do. Since there were no emergency lesson plans on file from this teacher, I was given a stack of outdated, student magazines and told to create some assignments and collect the students' work at the end of each class period. The poor students had similar assignments for an entire week! This was difficult for me to cope with, boring for the students, and a terrible waste of everyone's time. Keep this example in mind, and when you design emergency lesson plans remember to make the assignment valid.

There are many different types of emergency lesson plans teachers can use. Here are some examples:

**English:**

1. Students read a short story in a literature book and then write answers to the textbook questions or teacher-formulated questions.
2. Students take a *Reader's Digest* vocabulary test entitled, "It Pays to Enrich Your Word Power." Include the answer key for use by the substitute teacher. Students may use a dictionary and are encouraged

to do well by having their work collected, corrected, and their grades recorded.

3. Students read a short story which has had the ending omitted. Students then write an appropriate ending.
4. Students are given a list of topics and are instructed to choose one topic and write a 150 or 200-word composition.
   Sample topics are:
   - During the Past Week...
   - Looking Outside the Window I See...
   - In Twenty Years I Hope To Be...

**Social Studies:**

1. Students are given a course-related article from *Time*, *Newsweek*, *U.S. News and World Report*, or *Reader's Digest*. They are instructed to read the article, then summarize the article or describe their reaction to the article, or both.
2. Students complete a teacher-designed worksheet based on the maps found in their textbook.
3. Students receive graph paper (with squares large enough for writing letters in them) and are instructed to make a crossword puzzle using new vocabulary words from the present textbook chapter. The crossword puzzle must include written definitions for all words used.
4. Students receive several political cartoons from newspapers or other sources and then:
   - write an explanation of the cartoon and
   - agree or disagree with the opinion shown in the cartoon and state the reasons for their viewpoint.

**Science:**

1. Students read copies of an article from a current magazine on a topic related to the course and write a summary of the article.
2. Students read a chapter in the textbook which is not a part of the regular course curriculum. After reading the chapter, students complete end-of-chapter questions or a worksheet.
3. Students complete one-day units developed by the teacher from science duplicating books or other science learning aids purchased from catalogs.

**Math:**

1. Students complete a teacher-prepared sheet of varied math problems.
2. Students solve several math puzzles appropriate to their grade level.

3. Students complete a teacher-developed crossword puzzle featuring math terms from the textbook used in the course.

**Health:**

1. Students read units from First Aid instruction booklets and answer related questions written by the teacher.
2. Students read articles from a health-related magazine, then write a summary of the article, or answer a list of teacher-prepared questions attached to the reading.

**Foreign Language:**

1. Students complete teacher-developed grammar review sheets correlated to their textbook.
2. Students read a story written in the foreign language and answer several teacher-prepared short essay questions. Depending on individual ability, students write essays in English or in the foreign language.
3. Students are given a picture from a book or magazine and are instructed to write (in the foreign language) words describing items seen in the picture. The more advanced students could write a description or what is seen in the picture or a story to accompany the picture.

It is important to design emergency lesson plans with student learning in mind. Students deserve the opportunity to invest their time in an academic pursuit even though their regular classroom teacher is absent and the class is directed by a substitute teacher.

# PACK IT IN!

Every morning when I went to school and every afternoon when I returned home from school, I carried papers: papers to grade, course outlines and class notes, my plan book-register, textbooks, office memos, and an assortment of other important papers. Somehow, those papers had to be taken to and from school safely.

I began to notice a wide variety of teacher styles in dealing with this situation. Some teachers simply "stuffed" all loose papers into their plan books and piled textbooks on top of the plan book. This kept the class papers together and gave limited protection to the papers, but that was all. The student papers were easily bent or torn and after a short time, the pages of the plan book were also ripped. One windy day, I saw a teacher who kept papers in his plan book slip on some ice, drop his plan book, and immediately the wind took over - papers went flying everywhere. The teacher got up quickly, and with the assistance of several students, began chasing after each paper. I was not at all interested in having a similar event happen to me.

Some teachers still use their plan book as the carry-all method, but others use a tote bag, backpack, portfolio, or attaché case. Tote bags and backpacks lack form thus allowing papers to fall out of folders and get bent. Since they may be open along the top, papers, books, and any other items in them are unprotected from rain and snow. Portfolios are often too small to contain the many papers and books teachers must carry. Many teachers, both women and men, now choose to use an attaché case and find a wide variety of attractive, useful styles from which to choose. An attaché case provides the necessary protection for papers and books, is convenient to use, and has sufficient space for teacher papers, books and supplies - and they can act as a portable workplace for teachers who travel to a number of different classrooms each day.

# PART IV

# EVERYONE WORKS!

**(TEACHERS AND STUDENTS)**

**Chapter 11**

# LESSON PLANS / TEACHER NOTES

Once teachers have been able to organize their class notes and resources, teaching a course becomes much easier. The challenge is to learn, and consistently practice, organizational skills; however, for some teachers this presents a major problem! During my ten years of teaching I tried several different systems for organizing my lesson plans, notes, and teaching aids - it was a long, arduous process.

## How do you rate your organizational skills?

I began my serious effort toward gaining organizational skills during my second year of teaching. My first year of teaching, simply stated, was spent trying to be well prepared for each day's activities and, in general, to survive! For me, being ready for each day's presentations was not only a requirement, but a true challenge as well.

# LESSON PLANS

Just as a carpenter needs a blueprint before he builds a house, a teacher needs a lesson plan to guide the design and presentation of an educational experience for students. When developing lesson plans, some teachers use a daily approach while others write unit lesson plans. Whichever method a teacher chooses to use, the lesson plan should be viewed as a tool which aids in the development and presentation of course content. In order to be a useful tool for the teacher, lesson plans should be concisely written - the thoughtful use of words is essential. Lesson plans should be no more than one page in length and written in list form - no paragraphs allowed! Bullets should be used to indicate different topics, ideas, or activities within each listed category on a lesson plan.

On the next page you will find a basic unit plan format which you may adopt or adapt to meet your needs.

**Lesson Topic:** (identify title / theme**) Unit:** (text reference)  **Date(s):**

**Goal(s)**: (Statement of topic, reason for lesson presentation, domains).

**State / District Curriculum Standards**: (knowledge and skill references).

**Objectives:** (Describe what a student should be able to do as a result of the lesson / how students will demonstrate increased knowledge / skills).

**Announcements, Assignments, Attendance:** (Stated at beginning or end of class time).

**Teacher / Student resources and materials needed:**

**Introduction:** (Topic, anticipatory set - list key descriptive words).

**Procedure:** (planned activities, information to be presented and instructional methods to be used).

**Closure:** (quick review of major ideas / concepts, summary, preview future lessons).

**Evaluation:** (list items which may need further review).

**Teacher reminder notes:** (things to do in preparation for next class).

The lesson plan format found on the previous page may be somewhat less specific than the format required during student teacher days; however, it contains the necessary elements for thorough lesson development. Once a teacher is familiar with a chosen format and uses it consistently, the process of writing lesson plans becomes less difficult. Often, unit lesson plans, which are topical rather than per day, seem to allow for a more cohesive plan and are more time efficient to write.

When developing lesson goals and objectives or student assignments, it is highly recommended that teachers refer to Bloom's Taxonomy of Educational Objectives. Information related to the Taxonomy can be found in many books related to teaching strategies or on the Internet.

# ORGANIZING TEACHER RESOURCES

For my first attempt at organizing my class notes and resources, I chose a large, three-ring binder with divided sections for each course. I had used a three-ring binder during my college years and thought it would work well for my teaching years too. There were several advantages to using the three-ring binder. All of my notes were in one, well-defined place and additional papers could be incorporated into the notebook rather easily. The binder was large and distinctive in appearance; therefore, it was easily found among all the other papers, books, and general clutter on my desk. The system worked well for about two months then it became very obvious that the system was breaking down. The rings from the binder were ripping the papers and many were falling out, it was inconvenient to punch holes in transparencies and other resources, and the binder was gaining weight rapidly.

By the time Thanksgiving arrived, I decided to quit using the three-ring binder and I purchased a spiral notebook for each course. The cover of each notebook had a different color for easy identification. The advantages of this system were a constant and large supply of paper, easy identification of course notebooks, and my papers stayed in the notebooks. This system did have its share of problems though. I still had no place for neatly incorporating handouts and transparencies where they could be kept in sequenced order with class notes. In order to protect those teaching aids, they were kept separately in a manila folder but that meant keeping track of two separate items for each class. As a teacher who was traveling to many different classrooms, I learned first-hand how difficult it was to keep track of numerous separate items. Also, I could not change the order of my notes, and the collection of notebooks was heavy from the start.

My search for the perfect system continued; there had to be a better way. I decided to use one manila folder for each course for it seemed to offer desired versatility. Using large letters I labeled each folder, added paper to it, and began another school year with yet another system. It was easy to combine worksheets, handouts, or transparencies to my notes, and all of the papers were kept in order. It was also easy to change the order of the papers in the folder when necessary. I tried using paper clips to hold the papers inside the folder, but rather quickly, the paper clips began falling everywhere (always order large paper clips). There were several serious disadvantages to this system as well. Manila folders are slippery inside and outside, thus allowing papers to slide out of the folder at any time, especially when the folders are dropped or placed on an inclined surface. The folders themselves did not stack well and often would slide all over my desk (I continue to have difficulty maintaining a neat desk!). Since the folders all looked alike, it was easy to grab the wrong one when in a hurry. I often wasted valuable time sorting through stacks of folders and papers to find a particular folder. Once again, my new system, which at one time appeared to be the "big improvement" over previous systems, failed. I still had more to learn about organizing my teaching materials.

Since I had been unable to devise my own ideal organizational method, I observed practices used by other teachers. Many of those teachers used file folders and simply put up with the inconveniences they presented. Other teachers stuffed their notes and teaching aids into their copy of the course textbook and packed papers to be graded into their class registers. Most of the methods I observed were not sufficiently useful, so I continued to experiment in the hope of designing an improved method.

I decided on one last attempt to organize my class papers and finally found all that I needed in the pocketed portfolio. The portfolio is a sturdy folder which comes in many colors, is approximately nine by twelve inches in size and has two inside pockets which hold papers securely. I chose a different colored portfolio for each of the five courses I taught, and another color for a portfolio which was labeled "Papers to Grade." I placed all ungraded papers in that folder along with answer keys. This system worked, and worked well - for the remainder of my teaching days!

The advantages of using pocket portfolios were many. The folders were easy to find and identify by class since they were different colors. I wasted little time looking for the needed folders. The portfolios were durable; each one usually lasted through a year of heavy use. These portfolios were large and the inside pockets securely held my class notes, worksheets, transparencies, readings, and tests. I was able to organize my papers according to my lesson plans, quickly insert additional material or delete outdated information, and rearrange the papers whenever necessary. When a portfolio was open, the pocket on the right side contained course work which was not yet completed, and the pocket on the left contained completed course work placed face down and in order. If two or more classes were involved with the same assignment, I kept the papers in the bend of the folder until all classes had completed the assignment; then the papers were put into the left pocket. When an entire unit was completed, the papers were removed from the left pocket and placed in a regular file folder, then into the file cabinet. The filed unit was then complete (teacher notes, worksheets, transparencies, readings, audio-visual information, quizzes, tests, and keys) and in order, ready for future reference or use. By filing the papers after completing each unit, the portfolios were seldom heavy.

I still use portfolios for organizing paperwork at home, and am still pleased with them. Maybe the pocket portfolio can provide the organizational system which would work well for you, too.


## OPPORTUNITIES FOR REFLECTION:

1. Identify your organizational needs and then list suggestions which may improve your practice.

2. Daily or unit lesson plan - which format will you use and why?

3. Review the lesson plan format presented. Can you identify any categories which should be added or deleted? Will this format work for you?

Inform and assist students.

**Chapter 12**

# STUDENT RESPONSIBILITIES

Although there are many different assignments and requirements associated with the wide variety of courses taught in secondary schools, the completion of those assignments must be the students' responsibility. It is important to design a course so the different assignments required of students complement each other and aid in the learning process, both of which will increase student interest and possibly a willingness to participate. To accomplish those goals, teachers must invest their time in thoughtful planning, experimentation, and constant updating of content and teaching methods employed.

After several years of teaching, I organized my course requirements into four separate categories: homework / class work / quizzes, notebook, projects, and tests. Each category represented 25% of a student's term grade. In each of the four categories the students had the opportunity to do well; it required personal effort but the opportunity was provided. The students were told, and occasionally reminded, of the four grading categories and what was required in each category. I was available to assist students with any assignment, but they were required to complete assignments and do them correctly. Students must learn the importance of producing high quality work for it increases knowledge and establishes a positive work ethic.

Throughout the remainder of this chapter, the four above mentioned grade categories will be described along with guidelines for establishing requirements and grading rubrics.

# HOMEWORK ASSIGNMENTS

Most teachers give homework assignments because it is difficult to adequately review an entire course curriculum if all assignments are to be completed within class time. If homework assignments are valid, and students put forth effort, students will learn from them. Homework assignments must have a definite purpose, such as aiding the student in developing subject area knowledge, providing an opportunity to practice a new method or concept, reinforcing an explained method or process, or monitoring the student's understanding of reviewed material. It is, therefore, both a practical necessity and an educationally acceptable concept that homework should be a required student activity in most courses.

Homework assignments, along with due dates, must be clearly stated to students. Before collecting homework assignments, teachers should review the assignments with the students and students should be given an opportunity to discuss problems they encountered with the assignment.

Homework should not be assigned as a punishment (although I must confess to having done this on occasion when I was teaching eighth grade). When an assignment is given in anger, students often feel it is unjust and they put forth little effort in its completion.

At times, I have questioned the validity of including homework assignment grades into the students' term averages. Ideally, students should complete homework assignments in order to increase their personal knowledge base. Since "learning" is the goal, students should complete homework assignments to the best of their ability. The accomplished learning would then be validated on tests, thus making homework grades unnecessary. The problem with the previously stated idea is, in reality, many students are not motivated to learn from homework assignments or the homework assignments lack true educational value. Another reason for questioning the validity of including homework grades (especially from objective assignments) in term averages is related to student cheating; it is a definite problem. With those ideas in mind, I still believe homework assignments are important to the learning process. Since homework assignments are a necessity and students need the encouragement provided by receiving a grade, in practice, the teacher must record some of the homework grades to insure student completion of homework assignments. I do not believe every assignment must be collected and graded by the teacher but all homework assignments should be reviewed for accuracy and student understanding. Students must be taught to meet requirements without having to receive a grade "reward" for every assignment. I usually collected, graded, and recorded one or two assignments (objective and subjective) per class, per week on an irregular basis.

The correcting process for objective assignments (homework and quizzes) can easily be done in class by the students. The students should exchange papers and sign their name on the bottom of the paper they will be grading. When students sign papers it tends to reduce cheating and, if there is an accuracy problem, the teacher can easily talk with the student who completed the grading process. To maintain uniformity, students should be told how to mark papers such as placing a "C" next to correct answers or an "X" next to incorrect answers. After reviewing the papers, the teacher should tell students how to calculate the grade or to total the number of correct or incorrect responses. The grades or totals should be clearly written at the top of the paper and then the papers should be returned to the owners.

After students have received their own papers, teachers should inform students of their willingness to discuss any question or answer which was not understood; however, reviewing an entire assignment when there are no student questions is an unnecessary waste of time. The review discussions can be very important to learning and can be completed in an organized way. For example, let's suppose a teacher assigned questions # 1-10, 15, 17, and 20-22. Rather than discuss those questions out of order and lose the attention of some of the students, the teacher announces each question number in chronological order. When students want the question or answer explained, they simply have to inform the teacher. The teacher says: "Question #1, #2, #3, #4," and if, at that point, a student said: "Yes," question #4 and its answer would be explained and discussed; then the next number is announced. By using this grading and review method papers were graded quickly and fairly, little cheating occurred, students were informed promptly of their success and score, and students' questions or mistakes were explained immediately. Students' papers were collected, the grades were recorded, and then papers could be returned or discarded. Students seldom review objective answer sheets, so I often discarded the papers after entering the grades in my register.

Sometimes teachers face a problem when accepting objective homework assignments from students. Clearly, students understand the importance of completing assignments, yet some students have little regard for how it is completed (i.e. sharing, copying). The fact that cheating occurs is of little concern to many students. For some students the only problem with cheating is occasionally being caught. I think all teachers should be aware of the cheating problems in schools and establish standards for the students to follow (see "Student Cheating: Suspected / Occurring, page 198"). One time when I was absent from school the substitute teacher gave my students an assignment of multiple choice questions as I had directed. The next day while grading those papers, I noticed nine of twenty-three papers were exactly the same. Not only did those nine students miss the same questions, but they missed the questions with all the same answers. I was very disappointed in those students. In class I returned the papers with the statement that nine papers were exactly the same, those papers had no grade written on them, and I believed those students owed me an explanation as to how the assignment was completed. I invited them to stay after class for a few minutes and discuss this matter with me, or a grade of zero would be assigned to their papers. Only one girl stayed and we discussed the method used for completing the assignment. She informed me that all nine students worked together. I asked: "Why?" for in many months of teaching her class I had never allowed students to complete an objective assignment using the "team approach." She stated simply: "We thought it was all right and we did not think you would notice." Translated, her statement meant the students questioned their work method but decided to take a chance and hoped I would not notice. All nine students received a zero for the assignment, none protested the grade.

At times, homework assignments become a mere game played between teachers and students. Over the years teachers have learned that "reading only" assignments are often ignored by many students. Teachers have, therefore, learned to increase the probability of a reading assignment being completed by requiring a written assignment based on the reading or posing the possibility of a short quiz. The increased assignment now requires more time and effort from both the student and the teacher, but students will have a more complete assignment (reading to gain information and writing to show evidence of interaction with, and understanding of, the reading assignment). Teachers have increased their workload as well for they must design an assignment and/or write a quiz then grade the students' work. This is not a pleasant process for students or teachers because it reduces the learning excitement in a course; however, there are times when a teacher must resort to giving quizzes as a means of motivating students. When quizzes are given they should be prepared before the class begins and they should be in written form, not given orally. If quizzes are given orally the questions often must be repeated many times to the students and the value of the quiz is lost. One of the best ways to avoid having to use read-and-quiz tactics is to be excited about what you are doing in class and provide many opportunities for student involvement in class activities. The teacher's enthusiasm and teaching methods can entice many students.

It is important and necessary for teachers to employ instructional methods which increase student participation in, and responsibility for, their own education without greatly increasing the teachers' workload. There are several methods by which this goal may be reached. First, teachers should require students to maintain a notebook. The notebook should contain class notes, completed worksheets (not always graded by the teacher but always reviewed), and any other materials the teacher chooses to require students to include. During a notebook check, teachers view the required items to determine if they were completed.

Teachers can write short quizzes related to assignments and give them on a regular basis. Quizzes reinforce the idea that students should complete reading assignments and any written work, then learn the information presented as well. Although they take more time to write, I found multiple choice questions preferable to true/false questions. True/false questions tend to be either very picky, too obvious, or provide a 50-50 guessing opportunity.

Another method used by teachers to increase students' responsibility for their own education is to give the students the opportunity to explain their answers on homework papers. It is not necessary for teachers to stand at the front of the room and read answers or offer explanations. Teachers should allow students the opportunity to explain why their answers or solutions are correct and other choices are incorrect. By using this method, students know they must be prepared to defend their work and many of the students will complete their assignments more carefully.

Teachers must always be aware of their educational rationale when designing a student assignment. Ask yourself: "What is the educational goal in this assignment?" "What should students learn from completing this assignment?" "Is the assignment tailored to the needs of the class membership?" "Are directions clearly stated?"

When learning is the goal of assignments, not all of the assignments will be objective in nature. Students desperately need to learn how to clearly express themselves in written form, and there is a growing public demand directed at teachers to stress writing skills. Writing clearly is a learned skill. Practice, effort, and time must be invested by teachers and students in order to develop and improve writing skills; however, teachers often prefer to give objective rather than subjective assignments simply because subjective assignments require so much more time to grade.

It is possible to give writing assignments which will not overly burden the teacher. One year I experimented with a new idea which worked very well. Before assigning a Regents Exam essay question as homework, I found a piece of paper and wrote an "impeccable" answer. I asked another teacher from my department to grade my essay using the Regents standards (but I did not inform him I had written the answer). He scored my essay and reported the answer received full credit. I reviewed the question and answer with my students and reported my grade. I then counted the number of lines it took me to write that "piece of perfection." I had used fourteen lines on regular sized paper. Since I was feeling very generous that day, I added eleven lines to my total and informed my students their written answer should not exceed twenty-five lines. At first, they were very appreciative for here was a teacher who was not making them write a long essay answer. Then they began to think about the assignment and one student asked, "What if we write on more than twenty-five lines?" I replied with a promise to stop reading their answer at the end of the twenty-fifth line. Students were encouraged to write a brief outline in order to organize their thoughts and specifically address all parts of the essay question. I sincerely believe a well-written short answer is far superior to a poorly-written long answer. Students can produce high quality work when they know it is expected and they have been taught how to accomplish the goal. I used this method many times after that first "limited" assignment, and I still believe it helps students to improve both their organizational and expressive skills.

In summary, teachers should be purposeful and creative when designing homework assignments and responsible in grading procedures. Students are to be held accountable for carefully completing their assignments and learning from them. Students also must know if their work was completed correctly and when a mistake was made, it must be explained and corrected. Clearly, homework assignments can provide useful learning experiences; they also require time and effort from both students and teachers.

# CLASS WORK

It is a known fact that people learn faster and more completely when they are actively involved in the learning process. Students also need the opportunity to attempt work assignments while their teacher's assistance and course related resources are readily available. Thus, class work assignments are an important part of the teacher's curriculum planning and students' activities.

Class work assignments should have a defined, definite purpose and should involve students in a wide variety of learning activities. Depending on the assignment, students may work alone or in groups. The important idea to keep in mind is the necessity of actively involving each student in the work assignment.

An important consideration in assigning class work is that teachers are allotted time to work with individual students within the time frame of the school's daily schedule. Class work assignments may be used to introduce new material, to review previously presented information, or to reinforce or expand acquired knowledge. Students may be required to read and write, or they may be more actively involved such as when completing a laboratory experiment. Students may be involved in researching a topic or discussing differing viewpoints. Sometimes class work is completed within the class period and other times the assignment must be completed after class has ended. Whatever the reason for class work and the method used, teachers must carefully plan the activity and be available to guide their students step-by-step, if necessary.

There are many different types of class work assignments available to teachers and students. At the beginning of each new chapter, the teacher could assign the reading of the chapter as homework. In class the next day students can be instructed to present a vocabulary list of new terms or an item list of new ideas. Students can suggest outline topics, headings, and supporting ideas. These assignments can be completed in a group work setting or in a discussion mode. Since students had an opportunity to read the chapter prior to the class work assignment, they should be able to discuss major ideas presented in the reading assignment.

Another type of class assignment is the completion of a worksheet which can be designed to complement a reading assignment, review or practice an explained process, or direct further study and student response. Worksheets provide an efficient means of introducing new material or reviewing past material. Worksheets can aid students and teachers in determining whether or not students gained an understanding and ability to work with new material or ideas which were presented. In each case the student must complete a work assignment and have teacher assistance available. Once students are familiar with new vocabulary and major concepts, supplement the course with activities which expand student understanding and experience.

Extra reading from resource books is another valuable class work assignment. While teaching a law studies course I ordered many books with short readings on law related issues, case studies, and individual reports from law enforcement personnel, victims, or criminals. I reviewed the books in class so students knew what types of articles were included in each book. Once every two weeks we had a reading day. Students were free to choose any of the available books and read for thirty to thirty-five minutes. They then wrote a short report on a 3 X 5 index card stating the main ideas of the article and their reaction to it. Once I learned which books were the most popular, I ordered extra copies so students were able to read the articles in which they were most interested. Students often engaged me in conversations related to the stories they read - it was wonderful - this clearly was a popular class activity.

Students can also be given time to work on individual projects, Internet or library searches, or experiments. By using some class time for lengthy student projects, teachers can work with all students and review their progress. For lower-ability students, teachers can design a project and then work through the project with the students.

Class time can also be used for planning group presentations. Extensive background preparation work by the teacher is vital to the success of those assignments. Teachers must carefully plan the project, gather a wide variety of resource materials for student use, thoroughly inform students of the requirements and goals of the project, work through the project with students, and then grade the finished product. Group projects require much teacher and student effort but when well-done, the projects can be impressive.

**OPPORTUNITIES FOR REFLECTION:**

1. **Define your student assignment policies related to over all appearance of the assignment, completeness, and quality.**

2. **How flexible will you be with due dates and late acceptance of homework or class work papers?**

3. **What are your "individually completed work" standards?**

# STUDENT NOTEBOOKS

According to many teachers, students and notebooks go together; however, many students do not readily agree! Often teachers expect their students will maintain a notebook based on a genuine interest in the course but this interest does not exist in every student. Many high school teachers assume their students know how to filter information received in class into useful notes which will assist them throughout the course but those student skills are in need of assistance.

I always required students to keep a notebook for the following reasons:

1. Students develop a method for recognizing and recording important ideas (items explained, stressed or expanded). Ideas are reinforced when written in an organized fashion.
2. Students have a means of gaining information about class work on days when absent from class.
3. Students' attention is centered on classroom instructional activities. I was determined that my students would do more than just sit in my class and listen, occasionally state an opinion, ask a question, or daydream! Requiring students to keep a notebook seems to be a sensible, practical method for directing students' attention.
4. Students learn organizational skills by managing notes and additional paperwork.
5. Students develop a study guide for tests.
6. Students are provided an opportunity to demonstrate effort and stabilize their average.
7. Requiring students to maintain a well defined notebook has an effect on students and teachers. A teacher who invests time preparing outlines and other class activities is encouraged to

continue presenting class work in a clear, precise manner. Students appreciate classes with defined, purposeful presentations from which they can obtain useful information. The notebook becomes a focal point for classroom activities.

Once a teacher determines students will be required to keep a notebook, there are several details which need to be completed. Teachers must inform students that maintaining a notebook is a requirement. I allowed my students the opportunity to choose whatever style of notebook or folder to use with one exception, no steno pads (spiral across the top of the pad) for they are too difficult to grade. Students must also be told what is to be included in the notebook, how the notebook will be graded, and what percentage of the marking term average the notebook represents.

When determining what is to be included in the notebook, remember: the notebook is supposed to be a helpful tool to the student, not a burden! During the first few days of school I informed my students of the required contents of their notebooks. The list of required items included a copy of my requirement sheet, class notes, handouts, worksheets (completed) and uncollected homework assignments (also completed). Graded objective papers which were returned to the students and tests were not required to be kept in the notebook, although some students kept those papers too. Students should be told that photocopies of another student's notes or other papers are not acceptable; all students are expected to write their own notes.

One time, a few days before I was to grade notebooks, a student came to me and claimed to have lost his notebook. He never asked what he should do about his loss; he simply announced to me that his notebook was gone. The student seldom wrote anything in his notebook during class, so it came as no great surprise to me when he "lost" his notebook. The story continues with a few interesting twists. I had misgivings a day or two later when he placed his "new" notebook on my desk for me to grade. As I opened the notebook and began to read the first entry, I shook my head in disbelief. My assuming student had simply borrowed another student's notebook and photocopied everything including notes, worksheets, and completed homework assignments; he never even bothered to delete the other student's name from the worksheets and homework assignments! Needless to say, the final surprise was experienced by my student for I refused to grade "his" notebook and he received a zero for twenty-five percent of his term average.

Another time I received two notebooks written by the same person, one belonged to a girl and the other belonged to her boyfriend. One of the duties of the girlfriend in this relationship was to maintain the boyfriend's notebook. Both notebooks were very well done; however, there was a previously explained requirement which stated each student was to write her/his own notebook. It was not difficult to determine the grades for those notebooks. The girl received a grade of one hundred for her well maintained, complete notebook. The boy received full credit for the two entries he had completed, earning a grade of twenty.

Grading notebooks can be a monumental job. When I first started teaching school, near the end of each marking term I used every possible minute in school for grading notebooks, then took the remaining notebooks home to complete the job. After carrying the notebooks out to my car and then into my apartment, I proceeded to ruin the evening by grading them! Then, the next morning I had to carry those notebooks back into my classroom. This process occupied four or five evenings at the end of the first marking term, and it was not an acceptable way to spend my time. I learned two valuable lessons from this experience. The practical lesson learned was to secure paperwork when transporting it. Notebooks should never be stacked on the back seat of the car - one sharp curve taken a little too fast and there can be an unbelievable mess! The second lesson was of great importance, but it was just beginning to evolve. I began to take time to think about process development. I recognized the necessity of having defined goals, but still needed to improve my ability to design efficient management methods.

By the time the second marking term was about to end I decided not to grade student notebooks at home. So, for several days, I stayed in my classroom grading notebooks until five or six o'clock in the evening. This method was an improvement only in that it reduced the time and inconvenience of carrying the notebooks home; grading student notebooks was still a long, boring job. I was still spending (wasting) an incredible amount of my time looking for items which were supposed to be in each student's notebook. There had to be a more efficient process for grading notebooks and I was determined to find it.

An improved notebook grading system emerged once I realized that the students should find the required items and show them to me. Since students were familiar with the organization of their own notebooks, they should be able to find the required papers faster than I could. I also realized the grading process would be much faster if I could review many notebooks at the same time, so student notebooks had to be similar in their organization. To help the students organize their notes, I decided students must date all of their notes. The date was to be clearly written on the left or right margin, followed by one or two blank lines, then the class notes. Some students circled or underlined the date as well. During each class in which notes were given, I announced the date to the students. Since I gave notes in an outline form, all students should have similar notes. When students were to take notes from audio-visuals, the notes would be different yet the date and general ideas should be the same.

Another advantage of the notebook requirement occurred after students were absent from class. Students were required to make up work missed while absent, and the acceptable method for obtaining teacher presented notes was to copy those notes from another student's notebook. This system worked well, for students could copy the notes when it was convenient for them and I did not have to loan my notes to students. If the students had any questions about the copied notes, we would review the work. Worksheets were to be made up as well, but not copied! To help the students organize their worksheets and handouts, I labeled and numbered consecutively each sheet distributed. Listed below, you will see several examples of worksheet and handout headings.

American Studies
Government Unit, #6
Worksheet, Pages 16O-164

American Studies
Government Unit, #7
Movie Review: The Federal Government

American Studies
Government Unit, #8
Chart: Three Branches of Government

Students were given the choice of keeping worksheets and other handouts in their notebooks according to the dates or in a separate envelope or folder.

Teachers can require students to divide their papers into different sections in a notebook. For example, an English teacher may require the following sections in a notebook: spelling/vocabulary, grammar activities, literature notes, and journal. A science teacher may require the following sections: vocabulary, labs, class notes, abstracts, and homework assignments.

Several days prior to the actual grading day, students should be informed as to when notebooks will be graded. Although it should not be necessary, some students need additional time to gather and organize their papers. When I called for a student's notebook to be checked it was due, failure to have it ready to be checked resulted in a ten-point deduction for each school day the notebook was unavailable.

A few days before I began to check notebooks, I reviewed my plan book and made a list of ten to fifteen items I wanted to see in the student notebooks. The items were listed by date and topic then I numbered them in chronological order. My list was written on the top half of a sheet of paper, the bottom half of the sheet of paper was to be used while grading the notebooks. I then placed the grading sheet on a clipboard and was ready to begin the grading process.

The day before I graded notebooks, I prepared a class work assignment for my students. On notebook grading day, I distributed a worksheet to all students and instructed them to complete it for the next day's class. The students were to work on the sheet during class time when not involved in the notebook check. If the worksheet was not completed by the end of class, it became homework. I found a worksheet assignment was more conducive to a quiet classroom than was a reading assignment. Students were also informed that if they disturbed the classroom while I was grading other students' notebooks, ten points would be deducted from their notebook grade.

The next day, as students entered the room they received the worksheet. I also had the first ten or twelve students who entered the room sit in the first two rows - the notebook grading check would begin quickly. Since each desk in the row was occupied, I graded two rows at a time. It was easy to grade ten to twelve notebooks every fifteen minutes. My prepared grading sheet had been attached to a clipboard and on the lower half of the grading sheet, I wrote the students' names in order of their seating arrangement. There is a sample notebook grading sheet at the end of this article. I would then call for a particular set of notes by date and topic or a worksheet by number and title, and the students would find the item. As I walked past each student, I reviewed the item in the notebook. Using a brightly colored marker, I placed a check-mark on the date indicating the beginning of a day's notes, or on the student's name on worksheets. Using a marker makes it impossible for students to loan or borrow notes or worksheets from each other for the notebook check. There was a ten-point deduction when most of the day's notes were missing or when a homework assignment or worksheet was lost or incomplete. If the work was partially completed it would mean a five-point deduction. On my grading sheet for each item missing or incomplete, I wrote the item number followed by the point deduction if other than ten points. After reviewing ten items in the students' notebooks, I calculated student grades. Students were told what items were missing and their earned grade. The notebook review was over for the first group of students and it was time to form another group.

Since notebook organization was standardized and students were informed about the requirement to maintain a notebook along with items to be included, most students only needed to open their notebook to begin the check. The entire plan for developing and maintaining the notebook was easy to put into practice. Grading sheets can be useful in many different grading instances, and they are easy to design.

Since the students found the required notes and other papers, I wasted no time searching for those items. I quickly reviewed the entire page and judged its completeness; I never read through all the notes a student wrote either before or after I developed this method. I know some teachers read everything in a student's notebook; I just do not believe it's necessary to do so. Since many notebooks were being graded at the same time, I was usually able to grade all the notebooks from an entire class within a forty-five minute period. It usually took about fifteen minutes to grade ten notebooks. The highest number of notebooks I graded in one day was one hundred twenty-eight, totally completed within class time yet without wasting the students' time. The classroom was quiet and controlled. At the end of the day I was tired but I did not have to grade any notebooks at home: a most delightful thought!

A correctly maintained notebook should contain all of the required papers and be a study aid to the student. Students received credit for the items they showed me; if they could not find an item, it probably was not there. By using a grading chart and reviewing one item at a time, I seldom missed items. Overall, the students seemed to like this system and judged it as fair to them.

When averaging marking term grades, I counted the notebook grade as 25% of the term average. The notebook was a very important part of my attempt to make the course meaningful; therefore, it was counted as an equal to three other categories: tests, project(s), and homework / class work / quizzes. Notebooks were graded twice during each marking term (ten weeks) for several reasons. First, I found there was too much material to check thoroughly if notebooks were only reviewed once per term. Second, I realized some students needed the extra incentive provided by a mid-term notebook check. Third, I noticed that a student who had one poor grade could still recover if improvement was made by the second notebook check. Students who maintain excellent notebooks were also encouraged to continue their good work.

All students who were absent during the notebook check were required to leave their notebooks on my desk the day they returned to class. I reviewed the notebooks during free time and returned them the next day.

After grading all the notebooks in one class, I entered the grades into my class register. I saved the marking sheets until several weeks after report cards had been sent to parents. Thus, if a parent wanted to review a student's grade, I had all of the information needed. Job complete!

123

The methods described above work well for both the students and the teacher. It is also great to know that approximately one hundred twenty-five notebooks graded eight times per year do not have to ruin a teacher's life!

## OPPORTUNITIES FOR REFLECTION:

1. Is it necessary for your students to maintain a notebook? If you require students to maintain a notebook, what items must be included?

2. What process will you use in order to grade notebooks? Should grading notebooks be a teacher activity completed outside of regular class time?

3. What percentage of the student's term grade will be determined by the notebook grade?

On the next page you will see an example of a notebook grading sheet. The top portion of the sheet lists items to be checked. The items were numbered, listed by date, and described. I usually checked ten items. There was a ten-point deduction for each item missing, with a five-point deduction for incomplete items. On the second half of the grading sheet I listed the students' names according to where they were seated in the classroom. I wrote the students' names on my sheet just before starting the grading process. After the student's name is a list by number of missing item(s), followed by the grade earned for the notebook.

# SAMPLE NOTEBOOK GRADING SHEET

Choose any 10 items to review:

| | | |
|---|---|---|
| 1. | 9/10 | Course Requirement Sheet |
| 2. | 11/17 | Worksheet # 1 - Intro to Governments |
| 3. | 11/20 | Notes - Declaration of Independence |
| 4. | 11/24 | Notes - Articles of Confederation, Introduction to US Constitution |
| 5. | 11/30 | Worksheet #2 - Constitutional Compromises |
| 6. | 12/1 | Notes - Types of Powers |
| 7. | 12/3 | Worksheet #3 - Checks and Balances |
| 8. | 12/4 | Student List - Strengths and Weaknesses of Checks and Balances |
| 9. | 12/8 | Homework Assignment - Essay, Page 164 # 1, 2, or 4 |
| 10. | 12/9 | Worksheet #4 - Government Chart |
| 11. | 12/17 | Comparison - House of Repr and Senate |
| 12. | 12/21 | Notes - How a Bill Becomes a Law |
| 13. | 1/5 | Notes - Congressional Committees |
| 14. | 1/6 | HW - Pg 179, Ident. # 1-8 and MC # 1-10 |

GRADING SHEET:

| Name: | Items Missing: | Grade: |
|---|---|---|
| SMITH | 1, 4, 7, 1O, 11 | 5O |
| WHEELER | | 1OO |
| ALLEN | RS | 9O |
| WHITE | 9 (-5) | 95 |
| HAYES | 13 | 9O |
| PETERSON | | 1OO |
| JONES | 11 | 9O |
| DANIELS | 4 (-5), 9 | 85 |
| DAY | | 1OO |
| DOUGLAS | 1 | 9O |
| ARNOLD | | 1OO |
| JOHNSON | | 1OO |

Another set of names:

# PROJECTS

It is most important to combine course content with current or past events in our real world. One method for accomplishing this goal is to develop a newspaper project. Newspaper projects can be designed for almost any curriculum by using a topical approach or a weekly reporting system. Teacher inventiveness, especially in the area of topic development and definition, is vital. Projects can be organized in many ways. Students may be offered a wide range of topics or limited to a few, selected topics. The projects can be a presentation of articles with or without student summaries. The projects can be an individual or group effort and the information gathered can be presented through a wide variety of methods.

# PROJECTS USING NEWSPAPERS

The first step toward successfully using newspapers as a basis for a student project is for teachers to clearly define the project. Second, teachers must list the project directions and specify the types of articles students should find, clip, and save. Third, teachers must inform students of all requirements for correctly completing the project. Fourth, teachers should remind students of their willingness to assist them upon request. Careful teacher planning is a prerequisite and the project must be presented early enough in the term so students have sufficient time to find the required articles and complete the project.

When I was teaching American History, a project using the newspapers was especially useful when we were studying the United States Government unit. Students were given the task of finding approximately twenty-two newspaper articles which illustrated the workings of government or defined governmental terms. Required articles included the following:

3 articles describing Presidential use of different executive powers
1 article describing the action of the Vice President
2 articles describing actions of the Senate
2 articles describing actions of the House of Representatives
1 article about a New York Senator
1 article about a New York Representative
2 articles describing actions or decisions of the Supreme Court
2 articles describing actions of lower federal courts
3 articles describing the actions of political parties: one article about the Democrats, the Republicans, and a third party
5 articles, one each defining or illustrating any of the following terms: quorum, bipartisan, log-rolling, filibuster, pork barrel legislation, veto power, checks and balances (students had to know the meaning of each term in order to find a correct newspaper article)

Students were instructed to underline parts of the article which explained the action being reported and information which qualified the article for each category. This requirement made it necessary for students to read some of the article instead of simply relying on the article title. I kept a project requirement sheet at home and checked off articles as I found them to fit each category. I informed the students that if I was unable to find an example of a required article, then they would not be required to have it either.

To encourage neatness, students were to carefully clip their newspaper articles and attach each article to a separate sheet of plain white paper. Students were to list the date and the name of the newspaper from which the article was taken, thus reinforcing the idea of source documentation. Articles were to be placed in the order listed on the requirement sheet, a requirement which made grading easier for me to accomplish (grading process explained later). Finally, students were to create a title page on which they listed the project title, their name, and the due date. The project was to be stapled or clipped together with all papers in correct order. Students were informed of the due date, reminded often about the project, and encouraged to search the newspapers on a daily basis. This was a difficult assignment to complete in one night, so said several students!

One time, after assigning a newspaper project, some of my students regretfully informed me that they would not be able to do this project since they did not receive a newspaper in their home on a regular basis. I felt so badly for those students that I made arrangements with the school librarian to have the school's newspapers sent to my classroom once they were "day-old." The students were then free to take those newspapers home, search through them, cut desired articles then discard the newspapers. As a result, all of my students had the opportunity to complete the project!

In order to grade the projects quickly, I made a chart which listed the required articles across the top of a sheet of lined paper, and student names in the left margin in grading order. I did not bother to list the names in alphabetical order, for then I would have had to either alphabetize all the projects or work all over the grading sheet; both of those efforts were a waste of time. When grading the projects, I placed a check mark on the designated space on my grading sheet as I saw each of the required articles. Point deductions for incorrect articles were written on my grading sheet. Point deductions and the reason for them were written on individual pages of the student's project. After the project grade was determined, it was written, along with some teacher comments, on the student's title page. The grade was listed on the grading sheet and eventually in my register. A recommended practice is to save the grading charts until several weeks after report cards are sent to parents, just in case a grade review is requested.

After I returned the projects to the students, I offered to further explain to anyone the grade assigned to the project. Since comments were written on the projects, few students needed or wanted further explanations. After stating an in-class assignment for my students, I invited anyone with project questions to come to my desk one at a time for the additional review. Since all the students had an assignment to complete, they were quiet and controlled while I met with individual students.

I found there were several advantages to assigning a newspaper project. First, the newspaper project reinforced and enhanced class work by providing current examples of items being studied in class. Second, while students were searching the newspapers, the titles of other articles would catch their attention and many of those articles were read. Third, the very nature of this project was attractive to many students, for it offered a challenge and it was different from the common research project. Fourth, grading the project was a pleasant change for me because the students often found extremely interesting articles some of which I had missed. Fifth, due to purposeful planning (the articles were to be in a pre-determined order and underlined items should quickly indicate whether or not the article fit the category) and the use of a grading chart, the newspaper project was quite easy to grade. The grading chart was similar to the one shown as an example at the end of the next unit entitled "Projects Using Magazines."

One additional comment: teachers must clearly instruct students that only newspaper articles are allowed and that no magazine or photocopied articles will be accepted. By refusing to accept magazine articles teachers protect the library's stack magazines from being destroyed, and by not accepting photocopied articles teachers encourage individually completed projects.

On the next page you will find a newspaper project description sheet which I used in a Law Studies course. It is easily adaptable to other courses once a teacher has decided what types of articles are suitable for a project. The page after the description sheet lists ideas for using a newspaper project in a variety of other disciplines.

# LAW STUDIES PROJECT

COLLECTION OF NEWSPAPER ARTICLES ILLUSTRATING CIVIL LAW

Directions: You are to find ten newspaper articles illustrating some aspect of civil law. Cut the articles out of the newspaper, and neatly trim them. At the top of each newspaper article write the date and the name of the newspaper from which the article was taken. Place each article on a sheet of 8 ½" X 11" white paper. Use one sheet of paper per article. Place articles in order by date.

Underline the following information in each article:
1. Names of people or companies involved in the case.
2. Description of civil action being taken.
3. Name the court in which the case will appear. If the case is out-of-state, then name the court in New York State which would hear the case. Check the diagram of the New York State Court System in your notebook if you have any questions - the diagram was discussed in class on December 9th.

Write a title page - include the following information:
1. Your name.
2. Due date - February 11, (year)
3. Title - "Collection of Newspaper Articles Illustrating Civil Law"

Put all sheets together and in order by dates. Place the title page on top of the sheets and staple all pages together.

Other General Guidelines:
1. No photocopied articles are acceptable.
2. No magazine articles are acceptable.
3. **If you have questions about your newspaper articles, discuss them with your teacher.**
4. Include at least five different types of cases. You are to have newspaper articles, not court actions as reported in the legal posting called "Public Notices."

Grading: There is a ten-point loss for every incorrect newspaper article and partial point loss if instructions are not followed. Late projects will have a ten-point deduction per school day for every day late after the due date.

This is an important assignment. Please follow all of the directions and complete the project by (due date).

# SUGGESTED NEWSPAPER PROJECTS

A newspaper project can be designed for almost any course. There are four major components: project definition (what is to be done and how), collection of articles, student interaction (underlines, write a summary or conclusion), and project presentation (to teacher only or an oral class presentation).

Listed below are suggested newspaper projects and possible student assignments for a variety of disciplines:

**MATH** - Collect articles or advertisements which:
1. Use statistics to demonstrate changes (in crime rates, in salaries of members of professional sports teams, in gasoline prices) then students should summarize information presented.
2. Use graphs to compare different items (purchase of a stereo, computer, cell phone), then have students summarize information presented and develop a "best purchase recommendation".
3. To all math teachers: please forward additional ideas!

**SCIENCE** - Collect articles related to:
1. New medical research or findings then summarize the findings.
2. Volcanoes, earthquakes, or an aspect of meteorology, then state some predictions and the rationale for them.
3. Special interest areas such as space exploration, oceanography, or environmental problems, then present a list of recent discoveries.

**ART** - collect articles which:
1. Display artistic techniques used in advertisements and then explain the use of color and other techniques included.
2. Examine different lettering styles then define the perspective.
3. Display different companies' logos and then explain their meaning.
4. Compare different architectural styles in homes, high rises, or bridges, then identify by time period or architect.

**MUSIC** -Collect articles which
1. Review different types of local musical programs, then interview one of the participants and report the interview results.
2. Define or review varying styles of musical performers, then describe one's own personal choice.

**ENGLISH** - Collect articles which:
1. Define a specific author's writing styles or topics, and write a summary of one of her/his works.
2. Present an individual point of view (editorial) then write a letter of support or disagreement for each editorial included in the assignment.

3. Choose one topic, expanded topics, or opposite topics. Find several newspaper articles related to the topic, then relate those articles to some of the literature read during the year. Topics could include: war/peace, success/failure, life/death, or love/family.

**SOCIAL STUDIES** - Collect articles which:
1. Describe a specific country or geographical area then write a summary essay about the area.
2. Describe a particular country's leader, the leader's political points of view and leadership style, and then write your own news report about the leader.
3. Present a cultural study of a particular group of people, then compare and contrast those cultural practices to those of the American society.
4. Define specific terms or describe specific situations.

# PROJECTS USING MAGAZINES

It is possible to use magazines as well as newspapers for special projects. The entire magazine may be used or only a single, specific article. Magazines can greatly increase the general or specific knowledge of a student, and they add a wonderful variety to the general learning tool called the textbook.

Current, weekly magazines are great for students to receive and read. Each week teachers can assign the reading of certain articles related to the course curriculum. Publishing companies for magazines such as *Time* and *Newsweek* offer special rates on large bulk orders from schools. Although there is a financial cost involved when purchasing the magazines, it is not an expensive program. As an extra incentive those companies also offer a wide range of multimedia teaching resources.

Magazines can be used successfully in any discipline; it simply depends on the teacher's imagination and determination. When using entire magazines in a general way, such as collecting advertisements, teachers should collect as many magazines as possible from friends and relatives, store them in the classroom, and inform students of their availability. When magazines are made available to students for use in completing projects, little damage is done to magazines from the library. Students should be warned against cutting magazines which belong in the library, and teachers should inform the librarian of the project so protective measures can be taken.

During most of my teaching years I taught a consumer economics course. Each year we studied advertisements to learn of some of the techniques used to influence consumers. One project required students to collect examples of different types of advertisements and classify them according to the varying approaches used in the advertisement. Before starting the project, each student received a project description sheet which was reviewed in class. The sheet clearly stated the directions and listed the different types of advertisements required. Since the project was done during class time, the students had many opportunities to discuss the advertisements among themselves and with me. Those discussions reinforced the students' ability to decipher some of the many approaches displayed.

Grading the projects was completed quickly and without difficulty since I made a check-off chart. On the grading sheet I filled in a small circle to indicate items which I had looked for but could not find. The circles were easily seen and counted. After counting the number of missing items, I wrote the score in the "grade" column on the grading chart. On the student's project cover I wrote the description number of any missing item followed by the student's grade. After grading all the projects, the marks from the grading sheet were entered into my register and the projects were returned to the students. At the end of this reading section, you will find the consumer economics project description sheet followed by a sample grading chart.

Teachers can incorporate magazine articles into their curriculum development plans. Students can be required to read specific articles selected by the teacher or students may be assigned the reading of a certain number of articles of the student's choice on a particular topic. Frequently science, English, health, and social studies teachers will require all students to read a specific article, then write an outline or abstract of the article, present an oral summary, create a display for a bulletin board, or create some other type of presentation. Sometimes, teachers require students to submit a copy of all magazine articles read for the project. Whenever possible, it is important for students to be required to submit photocopies of articles rather than an original copy from a magazine. This requirement will save many of the magazines in a library from being destroyed.

When assigning a specific article to be read by all students the teacher can make a copy for each student, make several copies of the article and loan them out, or submit several copies to the school librarian for student use. The students may ask the librarian about sign-out procedures.

There is no reason for requiring a written report on every reading assignment given to the entire class membership. However, it is important for students to be held responsible for the information gathered as a result of the reading assignment, and there ought to be a method for monitoring the students' success in completing the assignment. It is very easy to include several questions on a unit test related to any reading assignment. The questions should be specific enough so that only the students who read the article would know the answer. By including several questions on a test, students realize it is necessary to complete all reading assignments.

One of the senior courses I taught was named "Law Studies." During the first ten weeks of the course we studied civil law, and during the last ten weeks we studied criminal law. For most of my teaching career, I was a collector of unique stories or articles having to do with the law. Many of the short articles were from *Time* or *Newsweek,* and some of the longer articles were from *Reader's Digest* and *Life*. There was a wide range of topics from strange lawsuits and wills, to a description of proper dress for a court appearance, and the problem of battered husbands. I included many of those articles in my class presentations while other articles were given to the students to read for themselves. One day, every two weeks, was set aside for reading magazine articles or short (true) stories from books about legal cases. One year, after sorting through my collection, I chose twenty-two short articles for my students to read. The articles were photocopied and made available to the students to be read during class time. Each student was given several sheets of paper which were divided into eight equal sections. Each section had the title of one of the articles followed by the words "Main points." After reading each article, the student wrote a short description of it. Students were told to write about the main idea of the article or their reaction to it. I wanted some proof that they had read the article, yet I did not want to read twenty-two long summaries from each of twenty-three students. After the project was completed, we usually took a few minutes to review any of the articles about which the students had questions or comments. The students very much enjoyed the reading days and it increased their awareness of the world around them.

Another Law Studies project I devised involved longer articles from various magazines. Three articles were photocopied and circulated among the students. The original articles were made available to the students so they could view the pictures (pictures often do not photocopy well, especially if in color). To accompany the articles, I made a list of objective questions which could be answered easily after reading the articles. At the bottom of the question sheet was this one last question: "Which reading did you like best, and why?" When answering this question many students indicated they generally liked all the articles. The students had obviously paid close attention to their reading assignment for they satisfactorily compared the three articles. It was enlightening for me to read their reaction to the different stories and to learn how they preferred one article over the other two.

Still another option for magazine use is available to teachers. Magazines like *National Geographic, Time, U.S. News and World Report,* and

*Newsweek*, publish special reports which can be of great value in the classroom. Those special reports can be an in-depth study of a topic included within their usual publication, or the reports can be a special edition. In either case the reports contain quality, up-to-date information.

There are many special interest magazines which offer useful information that can greatly enhance a course. Review the *Reader's Guide to Periodicals* and note the magazines which might be useful to incorporate within your course curriculum. For your review, several unique magazine titles are listed below followed by the listing of possible related courses.

*Architectural Digest* - art or design courses
*Art in America* - art courses
*Astronomy* - science courses
*Consumer Reports* - life skills or math courses
*Earth Science* - science courses
*Environment* - science courses
*Gourmet* - cooking for pleasure, life skills courses
*Psychology Today* - health courses
*The New York Times Book Review* - English courses
*The Reader's Digest* - informational, related to many courses

Those listed magazines represent only a few of the wide variety of special interest magazines available; the list is by no means complete.

Generally, high school libraries have a limited number of specialty subscriptions. If there is a specific magazine or two you would like the library to purchase, discuss the subscription request with the librarian. If there are a number of specific articles you wish to obtain but do not necessarily feel a subscription is desirable, request the librarian to secure those articles for you.

Before requiring students to read articles in any magazine, teachers should be familiar with the types of articles included, the general reading level, and the availability of the magazines to students.

Magazines provide a great source of information on many topics. They can be used to supplement a textbook (or to escape from it). Magazines are generally well received by students, and often they will read additional articles which attract their attention. Teachers should include magazine articles whenever possible for enriching their course curriculum; textbooks have a purpose within the classroom, so do magazines!

On the next several pages you will find a project description sheet which was used in one of my consumer economics courses. Students were to collect and classify certain magazine advertisements and organize them according to stated directions.  Following the project description sheet, you will find an example of my grading sheet for the project.

# CONSUMER ECONOMICS PROJECT

## COLLECTION AND CLASSIFICATION OF ADVERTISEMENTS

**Directions**: Find an example of each advertisement listed below. No photocopied advertisements allowed. Place the advertisement on a sheet of plain white paper, then identify the advertisement by name and number as listed below. Place the advertisements in the order listed below. Staple all the sheets together. Write a title page and attach it to the front of your project. On the title page state the following information: "ADVERTISING PROJECT" followed by your name and the due date. The due date for the project is January 5, (year), but it may be given to your teacher before the due date. Projects given to your teacher after January 5th will lose ten points per school day after January 5. **If you have any questions about your advertisement selections or how to complete the project, please discuss them with your teacher.**

**Find an example of each of the advertisements listed below**:
1. A new product (advertisement must use the word "new").
2. An improved product (advertisement must use the word "improved").
3. An advertisement offering a service.
4. An advertisement encouraging travel.
5. An advertisement directed toward youth.
6. An advertisement directed toward women.
7. An advertisement directed toward men.
8. An advertisement using the "family" idea.
9. A public service advertisement.
10. A testimonial (famous person likes the product).
11. An advertisement based on a caution or a warning.
12. An advertisement attempting to gain contributions for a worthy cause (money, time, action).
13. An advertisement comparing like products (example: several types of toothpaste, spaghetti).
14. An advertisement using patriotism or an early American theme.
15. An advertisement using prestige appeal (be important).
16. An advertisement offering a recipe for additional use of the product.
17 An advertisement using a well-known slogan.
18. An advertisement encouraging purchase of the product by offering a coupon.
19. An advertisement based on a trademark or brand name.
20. An advertisement based on "love for your animal."
21. An advertisement based on numerical claims.
22. An advertisement using a chart or graph to show advantages of a particular product.
23. An advertisement based on a "scientific" claim.

| Project | Smith | Peterson | Jones | Rogers | Douglas | White |
|---|---|---|---|---|---|---|
| 1. "New" | ✓ | ✓ | ✓ | ✓ | ✓ | |
| 2. "Improved" | ✓ | ✓ | ✓ | ✓ | ✓ | |
| 3. Service | ✓ | ✓ | ✓ | • | ✓ | |
| 4. Travel | ✓ | ✓ | ✓ | ✓ | ✓ | |
| 5. Youth | ✓ | ✓ | ✓ | • | ✓ | |
| 6. Women | ✓ | ✓ | ✓ | ✓ | ✓ | |
| 7. Men | ✓ | ✓ | ✓ | ✓ | ✓ | |
| 8. Family | ✓ | ✓ | ✓ | • | ✓ | |
| 9. Public Service | ✓ | ✓ | ✓ | • | ✓ | |
| 10. Testimonial | • | ✓ | ✓ | ✓ | ✓ | |
| 11. Caution/Warning | ✓ | ✓ | ✓ | ✓ | ✓ | |
| 12. Contribution | ✓ | ✓ | • | • | ✓ | |
| 13. Like products | ✓ | ✓ | • | ✓ | ✓ | |
| 14. Patriotic/Early American | ✓ | ✓ | ✓ | ✓ | ✓ | |
| 15. Prestige | ✓ | ✓ | ✓ | ✓ | ✓ | |
| 16. Ad. with recipe | ✓ | ✓ | • | ✓ | ✓ | |
| 17. Slogan | ✓ | ✓ | ✓ | ✓ | ✓ | |
| 18. Ad. with coupon | ✓ | ✓ | ✓ | ✓ | ✓ | |
| 19. Trademark/Name Brand | ✓ | ✓ | ✓ | ✓ | ✓ | |
| 20. Love of animal | ✓ | ✓ | ✓ | • | ✓ | |
| 21. Numerical Claim | ✓ | ✓ | ✓ | • | ✓ | |
| 22. Chart/Graph | ✓ | ✓ | ✓ | • | ✓ | |
| 23. Scientific Claim | ✓ | ✓ | ✓ | • | ✓ | |
| Grade | 96 | 100 | 87 | 61 | 100 | |

Consumer Economics

137

# PROJECTS UTILIZE STUDENT CREATIVITY

Wonderful projects can be developed by the individual classroom teacher or in conjunction with teachers from other disciplines. Students can illustrate concepts (political cartoons), display or classify information and designs (insects or architectural styles), build models (feudal castle or solar system), create a story or play, design an advertisement - the list is almost endless! Teachers should develop opportunities for students to expand their knowledge and understanding of course content through creative, student centered projects. Just as with other project development ideas presented in this unit, teachers should clearly define the project parameters, write then distribute to students the project requirement sheet and grading rubric.

# STUDENT ORAL REPORTS / PROJECTS

Although the announcement of an oral report requirement may not be well received by students, it is not "Mission: Impossible." Oral reports are important for several reasons. Preparing an oral report helps students to organize information into a meaningful report and present their findings in an interesting manner. Presenting an oral report gives the student an opportunity to develop, increase, or refine speaking skills. Also, an oral report requirement offers the students a challenge. Students are required to face a difficult situation and they learn that they can succeed. When my students were required to give an oral book report within the first few weeks of the school year, I noticed that a bonding occurred between the students. They were all facing the same adversary (the oral report not the teacher!). They encouraged and sympathized with each other, and together they prevailed. Through this assignment the students became better acquainted with each other and they began working together as a group.

Each year my eleventh grade American Studies students were required to give an oral book report as the term project. The assignment was given during the first week of school, and the oral reports began about five weeks later. Although students complained "loud and long," they usually succeeded in meeting the requirement. The unit topic was American People and it included a study of immigration and minorities. The students were instructed to choose a book about a recent immigrant (since 1940) or a person who was a member of one of the following minority groups: Native Americans, African Americans, Hispanic Americans, Women, or Handicapped Americans.

When assigning an oral book report (or any other oral report or project), teachers must take the time to establish guidelines for students. Before making the assignment the teacher should determine exactly what the students are to do, how it is to be done, and when it is due. Then, teachers must clearly state those instructions to the students. It is essential for teachers to write the instructions on a sheet of paper and distribute a copy of the instructions to each student. Students must have this guidance and direction.

It is very important to give the students a complete list of all requirements, including a description of how the oral reports are to be graded. Then teachers should grade the student reports according to the listed requirements. In order to be successful, the entire process requires careful planning by the teacher.

Teachers ought to check with the school librarian to learn of available books housed in the library which could assist students in completing their projects. School librarians find it helpful when they are informed of the students' projects and given a copy of the requirement sheet. When requested to do so, some librarians will compile a list of available books from the school library which fit the project requirements. Many librarians are also willing to assist students in locating needed books through an interlibrary loan system. Librarians can also assist teachers by informing them of other classes working on similar projects (an event which can quickly reduce the availability of needed books).

Once the background work has been completed by the teacher, it is time to present the requirements to the students. Teachers ought to take time to review the requirement sheet with the students and answer any of their questions.

My students were free to choose the topic of their report, but the book they chose to read required teacher approval. I wanted to take a look at the book to make sure it was an appropriate grade level book and it was consistent with the stated category. Since the students were given a due date for teacher approval of their book, the students were compelled to obtain a book and could then start the project. The students could obtain teacher approval for their book any time prior to the stated teacher approval date. If a student failed to obtain a book with the teacher's approval by the due date, there would be a five-point deduction on the oral report grade. Students were encouraged to obtain teacher approval for their book as soon as they chose one, for I allowed only one report to be given about a particular individual. When seeking my approval for their book, students wrote their name, the book's title, and the author's name on a 3 X 5 index card. After approving their selection, I kept the card. Students were given one week after the book approval date to decide whether or not to keep the book they had chosen (sometimes students did not like their book after they began to read it). After that time period expired, students were not allowed to change their topic or book. Students were expected to read the entire book; many did, some did not. It is difficult to determine how much of a book a student did read, and I did not try to make that determination. However, I found it was generally very difficult for a student to meet the requirements of my scoring method without having read most of the book.

Many times, I gave a short lesson on how to write an outline. Students were encouraged to work on their outlines as they read their book, and they were often reminded to record page numbers for every item included in their outline. The outline served three purposes. First, it aided the students in organizing their notes. Second, it helped the students to include a sufficient amount of material so they could meet the three-minute minimum presentation time requirement. Third, it aided the students when they were giving their report. Students were allowed to have an outline with them when they gave their oral report, but they were not allowed to read their report from a prepared essay.

In attempting to justify a scoring method, I devised a point system for grading the oral reports. The available points were related to content, mechanics, and presentation. The scoring rubric is described below:

5 points: Book approval requirement met.
25 points: Biographical description, important contributions.
20 points: Describe two examples of discrimination faced by this person, then tell how the problems were overcome.
20 points: Outline form, informative, includes page numbers for each item listed
10 points: Page numbers on outline correctly correspond to the pages in the book.
10 points: Presentation: well-planned and organized. Minimum of three minutes presentation time required.
10 points: Evaluate the book by describing its strengths and weaknesses. Do you recommend the book? Why or why not?

Each day when the students presented their oral reports, I reserved the last five minutes of class time for reviewing the outlines and matching the page numbers listed on the outline to an idea in the book (similar to checking footnotes). I chose an item from the student's outline and told the student to turn to the listed page number and show me the source of the information. If the information was found as listed, the check was over and the student gave me the outline. If there was an item which did not match, then I would check more items before accepting the outline. I kept the outlines overnight so I could review them, write a few comments concerning the report, and state the grade. The outlines were returned to the students the following day.

One year, a student chose a very long book and within a short time claimed he had read it and written his report. I had my doubts, but said nothing. He was one of the first students who volunteered to give his report. The report was poorly written, disorganized, and somewhat strange. When I checked the page numbers, I learned why the report was so substandard. The first item I called for was on a page which had only pictures, so I decided to call for another item. It, too, was from a page of pictures, so I requested a third item. Same results. I asked the student why all of his information seemed to be taken from the picture descriptions. He admitted taking his outlined information only from the descriptions of important event pictures included in the book. I asked the student if he read the book. He said, "No, I just did not have enough time, so I read the picture captions and wrote my outline from that information." I thought to myself, "This report might be 'in the ballpark' as far as he was concerned, but it was 'the third strike' as far as I was concerned." The grade received by this student was not one he would willingly show his parents just before asking to use the family car!

How successful was the oral book report project? Some students enjoyed learning of another person's accomplishments by reading a well-written book, while other students seemed to enjoy meeting the challenge of giving an oral book report. Some students detested the entire project. One girl almost fainted, and another girl continually asked "Have my three minutes gone by yet?" Some of the reports were very well done, some were not. We all survived.

Many of the students discovered unique facts about the person they were studying and shared those ideas with all of us. Sometimes students would ask questions of the reporting student. Occasionally, something wonderful would happen: a student from the "audience" who was knowledgeable about the person being described would volunteer additional information. When questions were asked and comments were added I was really pleased; obviously, the students were listening and learning. The students were receiving the benefits of being introduced to approximately twenty-five people who had overcome major difficulties, succeeded in their own lives, and who were then able to make contributions to society.

Some students find it quite entertaining to watch other students give an oral report but boring to listen to them. I wanted to increase the value of the oral book reports to all of my students, so it was necessary to make listening to the reports worthwhile to my students. Here is how I accomplished my goal.

The students were told to write notes about the individuals described during the oral book reports. Students should pay close attention to the person discussed and why the person was important. After all the oral book reports had been presented, there was to be an open-notebook test. I wrote a short description about every person included in the oral reports. The descriptions were based totally on the information heard in class and included in my notes. The descriptions included a number of specific items of information which allowed for easy identification of the individual (if the student listened to the report and wrote adequate notes). Here are two examples of items on the test:

> Women's rights advocate, teacher, lecturer, well-known for her work for the passage of the 19th Amendment to the U.S. Constitution. (Susan B. Anthony)

> A physically handicapped person who is an artist, writer, and speaker. She works to encourage other physically handicapped people by sharing her religious faith and by showing them it is possible to enjoy life and learn new skills after becoming handicapped. (Joni Eareckson-Tada)

Most of the students did quite well on the open-notebook test. The test was entered in my grade register and counted as a regular test grade. The open-notebook test idea motivated many students to listen to the reports and they began to understand and appreciate many other people.

When a teacher requires students to give an oral report of any kind, it should not be viewed simply as a means of reducing grading time or eliminating class preparation requirements for the teacher. Reduced grading time may be a benefit since the teacher does not have to read long, written reports. However, oral reports do require many hours of work from the teacher. A considerable amount of background planning must be done by teachers before assigning oral reports to students. Teachers must organize the entire process making sure materials are available for students, requirements are clearly stated, a fair grading system is established, and due dates are scheduled. It may be necessary for teachers to assist students who are having a difficult time while preparing their reports. A high degree of concentration by the teacher is necessary when students are presenting their oral reports so accurate note taking and grading are possible. While oral reports are being given, the teacher also must be aware of the behavior of the other students in the classroom. The teacher should develop some means of involving the entire class membership so oral reports are not a waste of time for the "audience" students. Depending on the type of report, the teacher may have to summarize or highlight student presentations so the reports have educational value to everyone in the class. Finally, the teacher still must grade the oral reports and have some written justification for the grades assigned.

On the following pages you will find a copy of my oral book report requirement sheet followed by a copy of the grading sheet used to evaluate each student's report and to justify the student's grade. The project requirement sheet was given to students to provide directional guidelines and to describe the project grading process. This requirement sheet and the grading rubric are easily adaptable to other types of reports, both oral and written.

The grading sheet was completed in three different stages - during the student's presentation, while checking the student's outline, and at the end of the day when I reviewed my notes and the student's outline. After totaling the points, the student's grade was entered in my register. Since the oral presentation was a major term grade category, I photocopied the completed grading sheet. The photocopied sheets were kept for a month or two after the marking term closed. The original grading sheet was attached to the student's outline and the papers were returned to the student the next day.

# ORAL BOOK REPORT REQUIREMENT SHEET

The project assignment for this marking term is an oral book report. You may choose to read a biography or an autobiography of a person identified as a member of one of the following minority groups: Native American, Women (American), African American, Hispanic American, Handicapped American, or a recent immigrant (since 1940) to the United States. Many books are available in the school library or you may choose a book from another library. If you have difficulty finding a book, discuss this with the librarian or your teacher. This project constitutes 25% of your term grade. Book report requirements include:

1. Choose a book from one of the above-mentioned categories.
2. On a 3 X 5 index card, write your name, the name of the book and the name of the author (index cards are available from your teacher).
3. Bring the index card and the book to your teacher for review and approval by (date). After the book is approved, your teacher will keep the index card.
4. After receiving your teacher's approval, **read the entire book!**
5. Prepare your report in outline form as you read the book. For each item listed in your outline, list the page number on which the information was found.
6. You may use your outline when giving your oral report. Be sure it is only an outline; you will not be allowed to read an essay.
7. Score card for this assignment is as follows:
   - 5 points: Book approval requirement met.
   - 25 points: Biographical description, important contributions.
   - 20 points: Describe two examples of discrimination faced by this person, then tell how the problems were overcome.
   - 20 points: Outline form, informative, includes page numbers for each item listed
   - 10 points: Page numbers on outline correctly correspond to the pages in the book.
   - 10 points: Presentation: well-planned and organized. Minimum of three minutes presentation time required.
   - 10 points: Evaluate the book by describing its strengths and weaknesses. Do you recommend the book? Why or why not?
8. Oral reports are to be ready for presentation on (date). Volunteers will be allowed to give their reports first and then students will be chosen in alphabetical order. There will be a ten-point penalty for anyone who is unprepared to give their report when called upon to do so. Bring the book you read to class each day until you present your report. After presenting your report, give your outline and the book to your teacher.

# ORAL BOOK REPORT GRADING SHEET

Student name: _____

Title of book and author: _____

Subject of report: _____

| Points available | Description: | Points earned |
|---|---|---|
| 5 points | Book approval requirement met. Yes/No | _____ |
| 25 points | Biographical description, important contributions. | _____ |
| 20 points | Describe two examples of discrimination faced by this person and then tell how the problems were overcome. | _____ |
| 20 points | Outline form, informative, includes page numbers for each item listed. | _____ |
| 10 points | Page numbers on outline correctly correspond to the pages in the book. | _____ |
| 10 points | Presentation: well-planned and organized. Three minutes minimum presentation time requirement met. | _____ |
| 10 points | Evaluate the book by describing its strengths and weaknesses. Do you recommend the book? Why or why not? | _____ |
| 100 points | TOTAL POINTS | _____ |

Teacher comments:

**OPPORTUNITIES FOR REFLECTION:**

1. What types of preparatory work must a teacher complete before assigning a project to students?

2. What information should be included on a project requirement sheet?

3. What are the important parts of a grading rubric?

# TESTS (AND QUIZZES)

A proper definition of the word "test" is "a set of questions, problems, or exercises for determining a person's knowledge, abilities, aptitude, or qualifications; an examination; a trial" (*Webster's New World Dictionary of the American Language*).    Teachers think in terms of the first two definitions, and students closely relate to the last of the three definitions. Most people could easily and accurately define the word "test", but many disagreements exist between educators when discussing the rationale for tests, the qualities of a well-written test, and the validity of test results.  At any rate, the expectations are that teachers will give tests to students.

Tests and quizzes are generally accepted as a method of documenting student learning or mastery of content or skills (or lack of those accomplishments).  National tests are given to measure general levels of advancement or development and provide individual comparisons to the norm.    Those tests are well-researched and carefully written, yet still questioned.    A very different type of test is written by the classroom teacher whose test is designed to determine if the students in a particular class have "learned" certain information which was presented in the course.  The questions which are asked, the design of those questions, and the manner in which the answers are graded can have a great impact on the students' test scores.

Classroom tests or quizzes are given for a variety of reasons.  First, testing is done in an attempt to evaluate the students' success in understanding a new topic, or more simply stated, to document learning.  By giving a test or quiz the teacher may be able to determine which students have successfully learned new information and which students have not.  The teacher may also learn which students need extra help.  If many students performed poorly on the test the teacher may decide to repeat parts or the entire unit, or re-examine the test.  The second reason for testing is to encourage (force) students to learn defined curriculum content.    The students realize it is "do or die" time.    Often the pressure of an approaching test is sufficient so students accept the necessity of self-education, personally gaining an understanding of course content. A third reason for testing is to comply with stated school district and/or department policy. Generally, school policy related to student testing within an academic discipline is quite flexible. Seldom are teachers told how often to test students but they are informed that tests are expected. Some tests, such as mid-year or final exams are required at established times, while other tests are left to the discretion of the teacher. Testing is simply a part of the educational life of students (and teachers) within the school setting.

Test or quiz construction is difficult for many teachers. It was for me. Writing a test which is a valid indicator of a student's success in learning subject content takes teacher effort. When a teacher combines a content test with an opportunity for the students to apply their learning, the job of test construction becomes a true challenge.

The ability to write valid tests is a learned skill; however, the teacher does not have to write every question to be included in a test. I wrote most of my own tests, but whenever possible I would incorporate commercially prepared questions. Since test construction was difficult for me, I regularly ordered prepared unit tests which accompanied the textbooks used in my courses or copies of tests prepared for similar textbooks. Those prepared tests had many usable questions, yet by writing my own test I included only the questions I purposely chose. Well organized class presentation notes provide another source of information which can assist the teacher with test construction. Additional test questions can be gained from tests written by teachers of other sections of the same course. One of my colleagues and I regularly exchanged our unit tests.

In large high schools it may be possible for all the teachers of a particular course to work together to write one final exam for all sections of the same course; however, I do not think such a method would be successful for unit test construction. Some obvious problems with group test construction include different items stressed by different teachers, teachers finishing study units at different times, a lack of cooperation between teachers, lack of time to work together, or difficulties keeping the test secure.

There are many concerns and problems for teachers when constructing tests. Some teachers are very careful to include both objective and subjective questions. Some teachers are overly concerned about point distributions and totals. Other teachers are concerned about grading time; they want their tests designed so grading is easily and quickly accomplished. Some teachers delay writing tests for as long as possible then, just before the test is to be given, they write a few questions. At that point there is little concern about the validity of the test it is just something that must "appear" as scheduled. Some teachers are quite disorganized and so are their tests!  Still, other teachers are concerned with the length of the test rather than the quality of the test.

Remember:  test construction is a demanding activity for teachers and it takes time to write a test which will provide a challenge to students and still reflect an evaluation of their learning.

Many teachers construct tests based on recall and those tests are just a re-write of homework or class work assignments.  Tests based on recall alone are not sufficient to measure learning.  For example, when I was in college, one of my final exams was almost entirely based on workbook sheets.  I memorized two hundred fifteen multiple choice questions and answers in order to gain a certain score on the test.  Fifty of the questions I memorized were on the test.  I missed only one question.  Was that a valid test?  Did I learn the information or just the questions and answers?  Rote learning has a place in the education of an individual, but there is so much more to knowledge than just rote learning.

During the first few years of my teaching career, I was not always pleased with the tests I wrote.  Then I realized that tests should present three basic challenges.  First, tests must provide opportunities for students to demonstrate their newly acquired knowledge (recall).  Second, tests should provide students an opportunity to draw valid conclusions from their recently mastered information (think and apply).  Third, when possible, tests should provide students with an opportunity to state and/or defend their own opinions related to the learned material (personal interaction with learned material).  For example, an American History class studying the United States Government may be asked to define the word "petition" (recall).  Then, for a think and apply response, students could be asked: "Why is this an important right of citizens?"  Finally, the teacher writes a short petition and students are asked if they would sign the petition, followed by "why or why not?" This question requires personal interaction with previously learned material.  English literature teachers could name a particular character in a book and ask students to identify and describe the person.  Then, list a situation from the book (or invent a new situation), and ask students to describe how the character would be expected to respond, and why.  Finally, ask students to describe how they would feel about the character being a family member or a friend.

It is not always possible to include the personal interaction portion on tests, but both recall, and think and apply opportunities, can and should be a part of every major test. Math teachers could give word problems which include extra numerical information.  The students are then to sort through the information, keep what is needed, discard the unnecessary information, and correctly solve the problem.  Science teachers could describe "what if" situations and have students explain results.  Language teachers could tell a story in the foreign language and have the students supply the ending. Students would not be able to complete this assignment correctly if they were not familiar with the vocabulary and rules of grammar. In all of the above-mentioned examples, students would use recall along with think and apply skills. Tests should be a fair challenge; they should require more than just recall skills and they should be possible to pass.

Teachers can judge the results of a test without much difficulty. If all students perform poorly on the exam, take a look at the exam. Discuss the exam with the students, and ask them if they know why they did so poorly. It is helpful for teachers to discover the reason for the poor grades. Was the test too difficult? Were the students inadequately prepared for the test? Do the students have the necessary ability to do well? Did the students neglect to study for the test? If all of the students scored well on the test, again look at the test. Maybe the test was not the challenge it should have been.

Generally, there is a correlation between students' performance on a test and their success in other activities within the classroom. The able student usually does well on tests, and the not-so-able student has a difficult time with tests. There may be times when an able student will have a bad day and score a low grade on a test, while the less-able student will have an occasional good score; but ordinarily there are few surprises when it comes to test scores.

What are the students' responsibilities when it comes to testing? Although teachers assist students in the learning process, there is a time when students must put forth individual effort in the learning process. Students simply must adequately prepare themselves in order to do well on a test.

Teachers should always review graded tests with their students. Usually, students are interested in their earned grade and what was well-done on the test. They are also interested in knowing the correct answers to test questions which they answered incorrectly. You may find it helpful to re-read the description on the third page of this chapter (under the heading of "Homework") for a quick question review procedure.

Once you have succeeded in writing the perfect unit test, be sure to save it. Place the test (and key) along with class notes and other support papers for the unit of study just completed into a folder and then file the unit for future reference.

## OPPORTUNITIES FOR REFLECTION:

1. **What course related student testing policies exist within the district in which you are employed?**

2. What are your main concerns when writing a test?

3. What testing practices will you use, for example, will you curve test grades, give re-tests when a student fails the test, require students to correct tests with a failing grade, require parental signatures on tests with a failing grade?

# Chapter 13

# IS THERE JOY IN GRADING PAPERS?

Is there joy in grading papers?  Yes, it is partly that small, but wonderful feeling gained every time another stack of papers is finally graded, most especially when those papers had been ignored, but not forgotten!  There is also a sense of accomplishment when students score well on a test or produce an impressive "piece of work" whether it is the results of research, perseverance, or personal creativity.

Grading papers is probably the most time consuming work performed by teachers, it literally takes hundreds of hours per year.  Reducing the amount of time required for grading papers is a goal of many teachers.  Suggestions for efficient scoring processes are presented in the following segments.

## GRADING CONSIDERATIONS

Many teachers grade all of their students' papers without any assistance.  It takes time and effort, but to some teachers it is simply accepted as a necessary part of the job.  Some teachers save themselves the work of scoring objective papers by having students exchange papers and mark them during class time while other teachers use the Scantron grader because it is available, accurate, and quickly grades objective student assignments.

There are two basic approaches used by teachers when scoring objective student responses:  counting correct responses or counting incorrect responses.  Teachers should choose one of the approaches and use it consistently.  Over the years, I found it usually was faster to count the number of incorrect answers on a student's paper for two reasons.  First, although it does not always hold true, there usually are fewer incorrect responses than correct responses to count! Second, I often used a Scan-A-Score sheet (described later in this chapter) to figure the student's percentage score.  The Scan-A-Score sheet lists percentage scores and is based on the number of wrong responses compared to the total number of available points.

When a teacher scores students' papers, it is very important to use a brightly colored pen or marker. The bright color makes it easier for the teacher to count responses, or points, and for students to notice teacher marks and comments. Most teachers use red pens or markers, but any bright color which is easy to read will suffice. At times, it is less threatening to students (and a nice variety) if the teacher uses green, orange, or purple pens or markers when grading students' papers. Pastels or shockingly bright colors should be avoided, they are simply too difficult to look at for any length of time.

There are several different styles used in scoring objective papers. Illustrated below are examples of the scoring methods used by five different teachers (represented by the letters A - E) to grade the same student answer sheet, followed by a comparative evaluation of the strengths and weaknesses of each method.

| A | B | C | D | E |
|---|---|---|---|---|
| 12C / 5X | 12C | 5X | | 71 |
| 1. D ✓ | 1. D ✓ | 1. D | 1. D | 1. D |
| 2. A ✓ | 2. A ✓ | 2. A | 2. A | 2. A |
| 3. C ✗ | 3. C | 3. C ✗ | 3. C ✓ | 3. C |
| 4. A ✓ | 4. A ✓ | 4. A | 4. A | 4. A |
| 5. B ✓ | 5. B ✓ | 5. B | 5. B | 5. B |
| 6. D ✓ | 6. D ✓ | 6. D | 6. D | 6. D |
| 7. D ✓ | 7. D ✓ | 7. D | 7. D | 7. D |
| 8. C ✗ | 8. C | 8. C ✗ | 8. C ✓ | 8. C |
| 9. A ✓ | 9. A ✓ | 9. A | 9. A | 9. A |
| 10. B ✓ | 10. B ✓ | 10. B | 10. B | 10. B |
| 11. C ✗ | 11. C | 11. C ✗ | 11. C ✓ | 11. C |
| 12. A ✗ | 12. A | 12. A ✗ | 12. A ✓ 5 | 12. A |
| 13. B ✓ | 13. B ✓ | 13. B | 13. B | 13. B |
| 14. B ✓ | 14. B ✓ | 14. B | 14. B | 14. B |
| 15. A ✓ | 15. A ✓ | 15. A | 15. A | 15. A |
| 16. D ✗ | 16. D | 16. D ✗ | 16. D ✓ | 16. D |
| 17. C ✓ | 17. C ✓ | 17. C | 17. C | 17. C |

TEACHER A: Outrageous over-kill! Valuable time is wasted in scoring both correct and incorrect answers and obtaining an accurate count of correct or incorrect answers is more open to error. Some students would not even bother to read through the teacher's marks. A very poor method which encourages grading errors.

TEACHER B:  Only correct answers are marked.  This teacher wrote 12 correct ( C ) marks.  The more marks one writes, the more time it takes.  The total of correct responses is written at the top of the paper.  One cannot use a Scan-A-Score sheet to figure percentage grades unless additional math is done to compute the total number of wrong responses.

TEACHER C:  The letter "X" is written next to incorrect responses.  It is best to write the "X" next to (rather than on) the incorrect response thus making it easier for students to compare their answer to the correct answer.  Even though the teacher counts the number of wrong responses, scoring speed is reduced because writing an "X" requires two pen strokes in opposite directions.  The total of wrong responses is listed at the top of the page.

TEACHER D:  Using a check mark ( √ ) for noting incorrect responses increases speed, an advantage over the "X".  The total number of wrong responses is written at the bottom of the page.

TEACHER E:  Two styles are shown here:  a one-stroke slash mark is made across or next to the student answer thus indicating an incorrect response.  The total number of wrong responses can be written anywhere on the paper where it is easily noticed.  The percentage score is written on the top of the paper for quick recognition when recording the grade in a grade register or on a computer grading program.  Of the five methods illustrated, this is the most efficient method for scoring papers.  Writing a slash mark is faster and requires less effort than writing other marks shown above.  After marking the papers and counting the number of incorrect responses, one can quickly use the Scan-A-Score sheet to convert the total number of incorrect responses into a percentage grade.

You may be wondering why so much attention has been given to such a seemingly trivial point regarding different marking indicators used on a student's paper.  You probably will be greatly surprised by the many hours needed for grading papers.  It often seems as though teachers spend more time grading papers than preparing for class presentations, a very discouraging realization.  Consider the following information and you; too, will be interested in time-saving methods which make the scoring process more time efficient.

|  |  |
|---|---|
| 125 | average number of students per year (for each teacher) |
| x 15 | average number of papers to grade per student, per term |
| 1875 | total number of papers to grade per term |
| x 4 | number of marking terms per year |
| 7500 | average number of papers to grade per school year |

The 7500 papers to grade is only an estimate, there may be many more. If, on average, it takes five minutes to grade each paper, those papers would consume at least 625 hours each year. Objective papers can be graded quickly, but subjective assignments are very time consuming. Essays, reports, labs, research papers, and projects require intensive teacher attention and involve many hours of concentrated work. Is it easier to understand the need for efficient, accurate grading methods?

# CALCULATING GRADES

Every teacher should have a dependable calculator. An inexpensive calculator which performs the four basic math functions is sufficient for most teachers.

With or without a calculator, teachers should know how to convert the number of correct or incorrect student answers into a percentage grade; that formula is:

$$\frac{\text{number right}}{\text{total available points}} = \text{percent correct}$$

For the sake of example, let's assume that a student has completed a homework assignment which had 17 equally weighted questions. The student correctly answered 12 questions. What percent of his answers were correct?

$$\frac{12}{17} = 70.5 \ (71)$$

Some teachers count incorrect responses when grading papers. This, too, can be quickly changed into a percentage score. You may subtract the number of wrong answers (5) from the total number of points available (17), finding the difference (12), then proceed using the formula given above. A second method for calculating a student's grade also based on the total number of incorrect responses (5) divided by the total number of points available (17); the quotient is 29. To find the student's final score, subtract 29 from 100; the answer is 71. A third and the easiest method for finding a student's score based on the number of incorrect answers is to use a Scan-A-Score sheet (partially reproduced in the next section). On the Scan-A-Score sheet, find the column numbered "17" and look opposite number 5 - you will find the score is 71.

The process described above can also be used for grading tests or projects having more than one hundred responses or points. An example of this would be a final exam with one hundred thirty-three objective questions and a twenty point essay question.

$$
\begin{array}{rl}
133 & \text{equally weighted objective questions} \\
+\ 20 & \text{point essay question} \\
\hline
153 & \text{total test points available}
\end{array}
$$

A student missed forty objective questions and lost two points on his essay answer. What was the earned percentage grade for the test?

$$
\begin{array}{rl}
153 & \text{total points on test} \\
-\ 42 & \text{total points lost on test} \\
\hline
111 & \text{total correct points}
\end{array}
$$

$$
153 \overline{)\ 111.0000}\ ^{.7254} = 73\% \quad \Rightarrow \quad \text{Exam Grade: 73\%}
$$

Once a teacher knows how to figure a percentage grade all assignments and tests are easier to construct because the teacher is not bound to working within a point spread based on one hundred points.

# THE "SCAN-A-SCORE GRADER"

Often, to make percentage scoring easier, teachers will construct a test so that it is based on one hundred points. For example:

$$
\begin{array}{lll}
20 \text{ fill-in} & = & 20 \text{ points} \\
20 \text{ multiple choice} & = & 20 \text{ points} \\
20 \text{ identifications} & = & 20 \text{ points} \\
20 \text{ true/false} & = & 20 \text{ points} \\
1 \text{ essay} & = & \underline{20\ \text{points}} \\
& & 100 \text{ total test points available}
\end{array}
$$

The obvious temptation here is to include less-meaningful or unnecessary questions simply to have a "sufficient" number of questions to meet the point requirements. By using the Scan-A-Score Grader (or a calculator), the teacher can avoid this pitfall and construct a test which includes all desired questions without the addition or deletion of questions simply to have the necessary number of points. On the next page, there is an example of a test design based on including only desired questions.

Desired test questions include:

| | | |
|---|---|---|
| 16 fill-ins | = | 16 points |
| 24 multiple choice | = | 24 points |
| 8 identifications | = | 8 points |
| 11 true/false | = | 11 points |
| 1 essay | = | 15 points (relative value) |
| | | 74 total test points available |

The base for this test is 74 and a percentage score can quickly be obtained by referring to the Scan-A-Score sheet.

So, what is a "Scan-A-Score Grader? It is one of the most valuable teacher tools I have ever used. This printed sheet helps one to quickly find a percentage grade for a student's paper based on the total number of points available and the number of incorrect student responses. The "Scan-A-Score" sheet includes a percentage score for all numbers from three through one hundred.

A small portion of the "Scan-A-Score sheet is reproduced below:

| Wrong | 25 | 24 | 23 | 22 | 21 | 20 | 19 | 18 | 17 | 16 | 15 | 14 | 13 | 12 | 11 | 10 |
|---|---|---|---|---|---|---|---|---|---|---|---|---|---|---|---|---|
| 1 | 96 | 96 | 96 | 95 | 95 | 95 | 95 | 94 | 94 | 94 | 93 | 93 | 92 | 92 | 91 | 90 |
| 2 | 92 | 92 | 91 | 91 | 90 | 90 | 89 | 89 | 88 | 88 | 87 | 86 | 85 | 83 | 82 | 80 |
| 3 | 88 | 88 | 87 | 86 | 86 | 85 | 84 | 83 | 82 | 81 | 80 | 79 | 77 | 75 | 73 | 70 |
| 4 | 84 | 83 | 83 | 82 | 81 | 80 | 79 | 78 | 76 | 75 | 73 | 71 | 69 | 67 | 64 | 60 |
| 5 | 80 | 79 | 78 | 77 | 76 | 75 | 74 | 72 | 71 | 69 | 67 | 64 | 62 | 58 | 55 | 50 |
| 6 | 76 | 75 | 74 | 73 | 71 | 70 | 68 | 67 | 65 | 63 | 60 | 57 | 54 | 50 | 45 | 40 |
| 7 | 72 | 71 | 70 | 68 | 67 | 65 | 63 | 61 | 59 | 56 | 53 | 50 | 46 | 42 | 36 | 30 |
| 8 | 68 | 67 | 65 | 64 | 62 | 60 | 58 | 56 | 53 | 50 | 47 | 43 | 38 | 33 | 27 | 20 |
| 9 | 64 | 63 | 61 | 59 | 57 | 55 | 53 | 50 | 47 | 44 | 40 | 36 | 31 | 25 | 18 | 10 |
| 10 | 60 | 58 | 57 | 55 | 52 | 50 | 47 | 44 | 41 | 38 | 33 | 29 | 23 | 17 | 9 | |
| 11 | 56 | 54 | 52 | 50 | 48 | 45 | 42 | 39 | 35 | 31 | 27 | 21 | 15 | 8 | | |
| 12 | 52 | 50 | 48 | 45 | 43 | 40 | 37 | 33 | 29 | 25 | 20 | 14 | 8 | | | |
| 13 | 48 | 46 | 43 | 41 | 38 | 35 | 32 | 28 | 24 | 19 | 13 | 7 | | | | |
| 14 | 44 | 42 | 39 | 36 | 33 | 30 | 26 | 22 | 18 | 13 | 7 | | | | | |
| 15 | 40 | 38 | 35 | 32 | 29 | 25 | 21 | 17 | 12 | 6 | | | | | | |
| 16 | 36 | 33 | 30 | 27 | 24 | 20 | 16 | 11 | 6 | | | | | | | |
| 17 | 32 | 29 | 26 | 23 | 19 | 15 | 11 | 6 | | | | | | | | |
| 18 | 28 | 25 | 22 | 18 | 14 | 10 | 5 | | | | | | | | | |
| 19 | 24 | 21 | 17 | 14 | 10 | 5 | | | | | | | | | | |
| 20 | 20 | 17 | 13 | 9 | 5 | | | | | | | | | | | |
| 21 | 16 | 13 | 9 | 5 | | | | | | | | | | | | |
| 22 | 12 | 8 | 4 | | | | | | | | | | | | | |
| 23 | 8 | 4 | | | | | | | | | | | | | | |
| 24 | 4 | | | | | | | | | | | | | | | |

© Perfection Learning Corporation   Used by permission

To determine a student's grade on an assignment with 17 possible points, find the column headed with the number "17". If a student had three incorrect answers, look down the column until you see the number "3" and in the column to the right, you will find the earned grade of "82".

Although the Scan-A-Score Grader is no longer available for purchase, a copy of it is provided to you through the generosity and special permission of the Perfection Learning Corporation. This company has been in operation since 1926 and is a supplier of educational textbooks. If you wish to obtain a copy of their educational catalog, you may contact them at:

Perfection Learning Corporation
1000 North Second Avenue
Logan, IA 51546

Telephone Number: 515-278-0133

A copy of the Scan-A-Score Grader has been provided to you along with this book. It is suggested that you place the Scan-A-Score sheet in a clear plastic protector sheet or laminate it in order to increase its durability, then, keep it in your grade register for easy access.

# EVALUATING STUDENT ASSIGNMENTS

The two basic grading methods most commonly used by teachers for evaluating student assignments are objective grading (limited possible responses, right versus wrong) and subjective grading (based on the teacher's interpretation of the student's work and how well the stated goals were met).

Objective grading can usually be done quickly by the teacher, by students within the classroom, by teacher aides, or by a grading machine. It is definitely easier to grade objective papers, but one must ask what type of learning they truly represent.

Grading subjective student assignments is difficult and time-consuming because the teacher evaluates how effectively the student integrated resources and completed a variety of tasks. Subjective grading is the interpretive review of student work as found in essays, posters, research papers, poetry, and fine arts expressions. Evaluating content, grammar, appearance, originality, and success in meeting stated requirements are important parts of the grading process. Most teachers write additional comments on each student's submission to correct or compliment the presented work, explain the teacher's evaluation, and encourage continued student effort. The teacher's comments are important, necessary, and usually appreciated by students.

Subjective assignments are much easier to grade when students have been given well-developed guidelines from which to work. A teacher should not say "Write an evaluation of the book after you have read it," and then judge the book report against a list of ten later developed items of which the students were unaware. Instead, the teacher should clearly inform all students of the requirements, allow students the opportunity to meet those goals, then, evaluate the students' work in relation to the stated directions and goals. Teachers should clearly define all directions and requirements, write them on a sheet of paper, distribute those directions to each student, and review them so each student clearly understands the assignment. The directions then form the basis of the grading rubric.

Teachers from all academic disciplines should assign subjective work to their students. It is important for students to obtain knowledge and learn thinking skills in many different disciplines and then to be able to combine their knowledge and skills into a well developed presentation.

There are a few practices which teachers can adopt, to make the process of grading subjective assignments somewhat easier:

1. Maintain a work station in a quiet (free from interruption) area.
2. Sit in a comfortable (but not too comfortable) chair.
3. Collect necessary supplies - marking pens, a copy of the directions given to students, and the grading rubric or grading chart.
4. Write an evaluation form which you will complete as you review the student's assignment, and photocopy a sufficient number of the forms so students will receive your written evaluation of their work.
5. Refer to your rubric so that teacher consistency and fairness in grading practices is maintained.
6. Alternate objective and subjective assignments to allow for sufficient time to grade subjective assignments.
7. Collect major assignments close to the beginning of a marking term rather than near the end of a marking term.

It is difficult to evaluate students' subjective assignments and it is difficult knowing the stream of incoming student papers never ends until the school year is over. One of my colleagues aptly stated: "I dislike the mound of paperwork under which I am constantly buried." Those feelings can tempt a teacher to move toward more objective assignments and fewer subjective assignments; that is a mistake. Subjective assignments require students to do more than just memorize facts or find key words within the textbook; they require students to expand their knowledge into a deeper understanding and then to interpret and apply the learned information. This process requires students to think - a primary goal of education.

Both objective and subjective assignments are necessary in order to aid the learning process, manage the classroom experience, and justify posted grades.

Two additional types of subjective student evaluation which are utilized by some teachers are student self-evaluation and an option for teachers in which they may add extra points to a student's final term averages based on student participation in class. Before using either method, teachers must establish guidelines and explain the process to students.

Evaluating students' work is difficult, challenging, and time-consuming; it will probably always be that way. The truly rewarding part of grading papers and evaluating students' assignments is when teachers recognize expanded student knowledge and improved student skills. Noticing student improvement, having an opportunity to encourage students, and sharing with them the satisfaction of intellectual growth - well, I might even call that "joy in grading papers!"

# PART V

# TECHNO-TEACHER

**(THREE NECESSARY WORDS:  ON, OFF, HELP!)**

# Chapter 14

# ENHANCED TEACHER SKILLS

Careful, creative use of technology greatly increases teacher impact and efficiency. By using available technology teachers are able to prepare improved lessons, include a wider variety of resources, vary their presentation methods, and use time efficiently - all of which will result in increased student knowledge, interest and class participation.

Several different machines and equipment are available within most schools which can assist the teacher with lesson preparation, classroom presentations, scoring objective student papers, recording and computing student grades. Teachers ought to be aware of the variety of machines available for their use within their school and they should learn the correct method of operation including expanded use or application for each machine.

# PHOTOCOPIER

There are numerous ways in which teachers can effectively use a photocopy machine. Entire articles can be copied and used as teacher resource materials. Current information can be given to students as resource reading assignments. Teachers use photocopy machines to mass produce review sheets, tests, quizzes, assignment descriptions, sample problems, resource readings - the list goes on. Teachers with limited keyboard experience can photocopy material and then blend information from several sources to create a new document. By so doing, a teacher can eliminate many hours of typing and, if care is taken when combining and taping items to a clean sheet of paper, the finished product is neat in appearance. In addition to text manipulation, teachers can incorporate pictures, graphs, charts, or maps for document based assignments with little extra work involved for the teacher.

When distributing assignments or tests to students, it is preferable that the written work be typed rather than hand written. The paperwork appears more professional along with being much easier for students to read. When photocopying papers for distribution to students, be sure to keep several extra copies for your records - one as a clean master and another as a correcting key.

The photocopy machine is without question a great asset to teachers. It makes possible the development and quick production of a wide variety of classroom activities; however, there are some limitations. Many laws exist to protect copyrighted materials. Although teachers routinely ignore many of those laws when copying material for classroom use, it does not excuse their actions or relieve them of legal liability.

# THE "SCANTRON" GRADER

There is a machine available in many schools which assist teachers by grading objective student papers; its name is "Scantron." This machine is designed to electronically score and correct pre-printed objective answer sheets. There are several different answer forms available which can be used for objective assignments, quizzes, or tests. While grading each student's answer sheet, the Scantron grader will mark incorrect answers with a red line then print the correct answers at the end of the answer line. It will also total the number of correct student responses and print the total at the bottom of the answer sheet. After grading all of the answer sheets, the Scantron grader will also complete an item analysis listing the number of incorrect student responses for each question.

The Scantron grader has several advantages. It grades papers quickly and accurately, thus reducing the amount of time teachers spend grading objective papers. The item analysis can assist teachers as they review the effectiveness of their questions.

There are a few concerns associated with the Scantron grader. Some teachers complain that the Scantron machine is quite noisy when grading papers and is irritating to teachers who work in nearby areas. There is an increased cost to the school district for the required answer sheets. There is also some concern about teachers relying too heavily on objective assignments because the Scantron grading process is so easy to use.

Many school administrators are willing to obtain a Scantron grading machine and purchase the necessary answer sheets as a means of providing a benefit for their teachers. If a Scantron grader is available for your use, learn how to use it and enjoy the extra time it gives you.

# COMPUTERS

Computers, printers, and scanners can be of great assistance to teachers and there is a wide variety of affordable packages from which to choose. Educational computer programs are countless and vary in quality, usefulness, cost, and user friendliness. Different programs can be used to increase content knowledge, provide individual student assistance (practice), and assist teachers in record keeping responsibilities. The power point program offers versatility limited only by a teacher's creative ability and preparation time.

If you need to improve your computer skills, consider enrolling in a computer course offered through a nearby college, local adult education program, or an in-service course provided by any number of educational service providers.

It is important to become familiar with the computer programs used within your school building and district. Within a particular school, there are a number of specific academic programs (available or required) for classroom use. There are communication systems available for use between administrators, faculty, staff, and parents. Additional programs may be available for student grade and attendance reporting methods. Training for district specific programs is usually offered to new teachers, so if needed, one should accept the training opportunities.

# VISUAL PRESENTATIONS

Most teachers have overhead projectors available to them for classroom use along with the most popular viewing aid, the video tape player. Many schools also provide computers in the classroom which teachers may use during their instructional presentations. Power Point presentations can be specifically designed by the teacher, and when used in conjunction with a "Smart Board" each lesson can be adapted to answer specific student questions.

Before actually viewing media, all students should be specifically prepared with regard to media content. They should also be instructed as to what is expected of them such as: watch and listen, take notes, answer questions on a review sheet, write a content summary after viewing.

It is necessary for the teacher to know the length of time required for viewing audio-visual media. This knowledge allows the teacher to plan activities related to the media such as stating an introduction, reviewing terms and ideas, or answering students' questions. Usually, the running time is listed in the multimedia catalog and on the media storage case.

# VIDEO TAPE PLAYER

The video tape player generally has a much greater impact and appeal in the classroom than other audio-visual media. Often, the information presented by a video tape is current (something which can be lacking in many other media forms). Since health issues, scientific findings, political, social, and economic situations can change so quickly, taped programs are not only interesting to watch, but they present vital information which must be included in our students' educational experience.

Teachers quickly learn how to operate the video tape player available for their use. Some schools have mobile units while other schools have permanently mounted video tape players in each classroom. Often, a video tape player must be set on a particular channel to allow for viewing. It is important for the teacher to know the required channel number, for occasionally, a student will change the channel indicator on a tape player as a "source of frustration" to an unsuspecting teacher.

When a video tape is to be shown to more than one class (and cannot be completed within a single class), the teacher should use the counter to identify the ending-beginning point for each class. The teacher should note the counter reading in the plan book or on teacher class notes. The next day, the teacher can quickly remind students of content viewed the previous day and advance the tape to the correct place for continued viewing.

It is important to be aware of course related programs to be presented on television. If there is a person or educational service available to record programs for you, inform them of your recording requests as soon as possible; otherwise, record programs yourself on an as needed or desired basis.

Classroom activities are enhanced by using the video tape player; however, video tapes should not be used so often that they replace other teacher presentations. Also, some students watch course related programs shown on television, so teachers should choose video programs and the frequency of use, with care.

Teachers should read carefully the descriptions given in audio-visual catalogs and preview all videotapes. Most teachers agree that previewing audio-visuals is crucial; a few will also admit they seldom, if ever, consistently preview -- it just takes too much time. If a teacher is going to present a videotape in class it must be previewed for content. Teachers should evaluate the information presented on the videotape and ascertain that it is within curriculum guidelines, in accordance with school district guidelines, and of a non-offensive nature.

When viewing audio-visuals for the first time, teachers should write notes to obtain an overview of the general ideas, major concepts, and terms presented. From those notes the teacher can develop an outline to use in class or a worksheet for students. A copy of any notes, outline, or student worksheet developed from viewing the videotape should be attached to the audio-visual reservation slip and saved for future reference. Those collected papers are valuable to teachers for they describe the audio-visual used, assist with developing different classroom presentation methods, and make future re-ordering easier. If the quality of the audio-visual is poor, the information outdated or otherwise of little use, record that information somewhere on the reservation slip or in your class notes so it is not re-ordered in following years.

# OVERHEAD PROJECTOR

For the teacher who is giving detailed notes, presenting a diagram, reviewing a map or an outline, explaining a difficult problem and its answer, or illustrating an idea or process, it is physically much easier to use an overhead projector with a transparency than writing on a chalkboard or marker board. Writing on a board can be laborious for the teacher because one must reach high or bend low, write large neat letters, spell words correctly while explaining content and maintaining a logical flow of information. Then, the chalkboard needs to be erased producing chalk dust in the air and chalk-dried hands. The process must be repeated in each class of the same preparation. When teachers are writing on a chalkboard or marker board they are not facing their students and they lose eye contact, thus the teacher's ability to easily converse with students is limited and classroom control can become more difficult to maintain. In many schools chalkboards have been replaced by marker boards, yet most of the disadvantages remain. An important alternative to writing on a chalk or marker board is the use an overhead projector. After using an overhead projector once or twice, most teachers quickly accept it as a tremendous teacher aid.

Teachers can easily prepare transparencies. One simply composes class notes or other informational material using a black ink pen or a pencil on plain white paper, photocopies the notes, then makes the transparency from the photocopy. When the notes are presented in class, dim some of the classroom lights, turn on the overhead projector, show the transparency, and begin the presentation.

When an entire page of notes is shown all at once, students will copy all the material and not hear the teacher's explanation. To increase the students' attention to the teacher's instruction, simply limit the amount of the transparency which is projected. There are two ways to limit the amount of the transparency viewed by students. The teacher can either change the position of the transparency on the projector so only a limited amount of the transparency is viewed (using a roll transparency is effective) or cover part of the transparency with a piece of paper - be sure to use only lightweight paper. The lightweight paper found between boxed transparencies serves as an effective cover sheet. Medium and heavy weight paper (including some photocopy paper) will absorb the heat produced by the overhead projector and may cause the transparency to crinkle rather quickly. Another advantage to using the cover sheet is that while the students cannot see what is on the transparency until the cover sheet is moved, the teacher can continue to read what is on the transparency. By reading what is under the cover sheet the teacher can make a smooth transition in note presentations and explanations. The overhead projector allows the teacher the opportunity to face the students, keep eye contact, improve interaction, and quickly answer students' questions - all of which assist the teacher in maintaining student interest and classroom control.

Each year in September, I always secured an overhead projector for the entire school year from the audio-visual department. I learned how to replace a burned-out bulb and kept an extra bulb in my desk. It seemed the bulbs always burned out when the projector was first switched on at the beginning of a lesson presentation; an event which greatly excited the students and effectively interrupted my plans if I was without an extra bulb.

Teachers have several different methods available to them when using the overhead projector. Transparencies can be prepared before class time and simply reviewed in class, or they can be written during the class presentation. Writing on a transparency during class time allows students an opportunity to observe an explanation of a problem, see the development of a logical answer, be instructed in the drawing and labeling process, or copy major ideas from a teacher's presentation. Writing on a transparency during class time can also provide an opportunity for student involvement in class activities. Using a transparency need not always be a teacher-to-student activity; it can be successfully used as a means of collecting and sharing student comments and observations. In addition to the teacher's individually designed transparencies, there are many excellent commercially-prepared transparencies available for class use.

The overhead projector is a valuable teaching tool which assists the teacher in classroom presentations and is an effective substitute for the chalk or marker board. Why not use it during your classroom presentations?

# CASSETTE TAPE PLAYER

Teachers of some courses, such as music or foreign languages, may be able to successfully use a cassette tape player without additional support materials. Some teachers may be able to use audio machines when accompanied by a script for students to follow, such as while reading a play. However, most teachers know that using audio-only media with students can be difficult. After my first year of teaching an economics course, I ordered a series of eight tapes discussing major economic concepts. I used one tape in the classroom, one time. The tape was fair-to-good in its presentation, but the student reception (more accurately, rejection) was what convinced me that using those tapes was an unworkable idea. I am sure those tapes are still stored somewhere on a closet shelf, never noticed or used, and now outdated. If you choose to use audio-only media, choose it very carefully and you probably should not spend your own money to purchase it!

# SUMMARY

Audio-visual media and machines contribute in countless ways to classroom activities; however, it is necessary to learn how to properly use the machines before a classroom presentation. Teachers who follow that rule will save time, audio-visual equipment, media items, and embarrassment! Always rewind video tapes before returning them to the loaning agency; that is expected practice. A short note, describing audio-visual media which did not work correctly or that was damaged while in the teacher's possession, should be attached to media being returned to any lending institution. Return borrowed multimedia items on time, or earlier if you have finished using them, for another teacher is often awaiting their arrival. Finally, do not be afraid to learn how to use new machines as they are introduced into your school system. School district administrators will purchase expensive equipment when they believe it is desired by teachers and will be used by them to enrich the educational experience for their students. When machines and equipment are available and will enhance classroom presentations, increase student interest and knowledge, and decrease the teacher workload, there is no excuse for not learning how to effectively use them.

# Chapter 15

# AUDIO-VISUAL MEDIA

Using audio-visual media is vital for the enrichment of course content and to stimulate student interest. There is an unbelievably large quantity of audio-visual media available for the teacher to order, examine, and use effectively. The most commonly used media aids are videotapes, transparencies, and computers. Also, a teacher may occasionally incorporate the use of a cassette tape to listen to music, a speech, or a play.

# CHOOSING MEDIA

At the beginning of the school year, teachers must take time to learn what multimedia materials are available for their use. Some public school systems maintain their own media libraries but due to inadequate budgets, those libraries are often limited in scope and depth of items available. A common practice of school districts is to join a regional multimedia sharing system which supplies a catalog to each teacher at the beginning of the school year and media throughout the year upon request. Media catalogs are usually arranged by grade levels: elementary, junior high (middle school), and high school. The classification of media into those categories is done to assist teachers in choosing media which is age and grade appropriate so teachers should pay close attention to the defined categories.

Teachers are skillful in discovering additional media resources, so seek suggestions from colleagues as well as visiting local libraries or college and university libraries (generally open to teachers who are enrolled as students or to those who are alumni).

Professional organizations, such as the American Bar Association or medical research societies, provide multimedia materials for use in educational environments. The educational or public relations offices of many large corporations, banks, insurance institutes, and governmental agencies also produce materials which they provide to schools upon request.

It takes time to read through media catalogs, make telephone calls, or write letters in an attempt to locate quality teaching resources which are low-cost or free. It is a job which should be done only once a year!

The most efficient method for reading catalogs is to turn to the table of contents, mark all areas which contain media related to your courses, then, read through those sections. While reading the short descriptions of media items, write the name of the course in which the media is to be used next to the media title. Sometimes teachers are told not to mark their catalogs since the catalogs will be collected at the end of the school year and used again in future years. If "no marks in the catalog" is requested, seek permission to mark your catalog by promising to use the same catalog next year -- a tremendous advantage for you. Then clearly write your name on the catalog. The next year when the catalog is returned to you, it will be very helpful since the desired media titles will already be marked. You will need to review only the supplemental pages. After marking items to be used, there are several different ways to organize your list of chosen audio-visual items.

One method for organizing your list of desired media is to remember the items that you want to order, and simply check the catalog on occasion. The advantage to this method is that there is no additional work involved in listing the items. The disadvantage of this method is teachers become so busy they seldom order media of any type. An even greater disadvantage to this method is that many good materials are forgotten or ordered so late they cannot be used in the unit at the most appropriate time. Also, a teacher may waste additional time searching through catalogs in order to find the few items that were "remembered."

A second method for organizing media selections is to write a list of the desired items. The more organized the list, the more useful it will be, so begin by writing the course name at the top of a sheet of paper - use a separate sheet of paper for each course. Specific, identifying information is important, so draw several columns on the paper and write the following column headings: title, catalog number, catalog page number, and study unit (in which media is to be used). Next, review the sections of the catalog related to your courses, and write the necessary information for each desired media item. If you are choosing items from different catalogs, identify the different catalogs as well. The advantage to this system is having audio-visual items organized by each course and related topic. This system also allows a teacher to quickly locate a particular item in the catalog in order to check its desirability for a specific unit. The primary disadvantage of this system is that the classification process takes time, and to be effective it needs to be done early in the school year - a time when all teachers are extremely busy. Another disadvantage to this system is that the teacher will have to write the media information a second time when ordering it for classroom use.

Most school districts in New York state belong to a regional educational support service called the Board of Cooperative Educational Services (BOCES). One of the services provided by BOCES is to make available to teachers a wide variety of media resources. Teachers are given a large catalog listing many different titles and types of media available on a loan basis. Media reservation forms are also provided. On the reservation forms, teachers write identifying information such as: date of request, media number and title, different request dates for media use, name of school, course, and teacher. Using those forms could be the basis for a third method of organizing a list of desired media. While reading through the catalog, indicate chosen items with the course name in which the media will be used. Then, simply write the title and media catalog number on the reservation slip for each item to be ordered. The reservation slips could then be arranged according to units and the audio-visuals could be ordered before the unit is started. To save time, and for future reference, it is helpful to write the catalog page number and viewing time somewhere on the teacher copy of the reservation form. The remaining information requested on the media reservation form would be written just prior to requesting the media. The advantages to this system are writing the name of multimedia items only one time, and being able to place reservation forms in order of planned use. Thus, the teacher is more apt to request media before it is actually needed and receive it when most beneficial to classroom presentations.

# ORDERING MEDIA

Once you have chosen certain audio-visual items and decided when you want to use incorporate them into your lessons, complete and submit the reservation forms. Allow sufficient time for the delivery of the media. It may be necessary to state several different dates for which you prefer to receive the item. Choose different times in your lesson plans when the audio-visual items would contribute to your class presentations and make your requests accordingly. Remember, too, audio-visual media requests are usually scheduled according to the age-old standard "first-come, first-served," so send in your request forms as early as possible.

After viewing the multimedia in class the teacher should write a short evaluation of it on the reservation form. Comments related to usefulness, grade/level appropriateness, student interest, and student reaction will be of assistance in the future. The reservation form can be attached to any notes, worksheet developed for use with the media, or lesson plan and filed with the related unit. Then, if you repeat the unit in the future, you will know if you wish to use (or avoid) a particular media item and you will know how you used it. Also, by saving the ordering information it will reduce your work time if you wish to re-order.

After receiving notification of the delivery date for requested media, clip the notice in your plan book according to the week in which the media is to be received or write the media name in the plan book when scheduled to be used.

# USING MEDIA

Preparation, preview, and presentation are the keys to successfully using multimedia materials in the classroom.

The first key, preparation, includes choosing the media, ordering it, and securing the necessary audio-visual equipment; but that is only a part of the preparation "key." The students must also be prepared. They must have sufficient background to make the media presentation valuable, which explains why previewing is so vital.

Previewing media is the second key for successful media usage. We all know previewing audio-visuals is very time consuming especially for first year teachers, since all of the audio-visual items are new to them; however, it is necessary. While previewing is the preferable method of teacher preparation, many teachers still rely heavily on the catalog descriptions of audio-visual items. Previewing media makes it possible for the teacher to evaluate its appropriateness, write notes for classroom review, or develop a worksheet for student use. Teachers who choose not to preview audio-visuals should write notes during the first viewing of media in the classroom. Since students learn more from audio-visuals when major ideas, new concepts, and unfamiliar vocabulary words are reviewed by the teacher, those previously developed teacher notes will be useful when emphasizing or explaining information contained in the media.

The third key for successful media usage, presentation, involves the students, teacher, and the media. The attitude of the teacher toward the media, the specific reason(s) for using the media, the teacher's classroom introduction of the media, the learning aids utilized, and the quality of the media itself are all very important ingredients in presentation. Valid educational reasons for including multimedia usage in the classroom must exist.

Audio-visuals are to assist, not replace, the teacher.

One time, I showed a video tape (which I had previewed) to my students. The tape contained some important ideas, but lacked excitement. After watching the tape, some of my students told me it was "boring" (the one word teachers find impossible to tolerate). Before showing the video tape to my second class, in an attempt to be honest with my students, I informed them that some students in the previous class decided the tape was not exciting. I then listed the ideas I wanted the students to notice and made some encouraging statements about the tape. My introduction was not yet completed when I noticed a few students settling down in their chairs for a short nap. They had already decided the video tape was not worth watching. I learned an important lesson that day: present and use media in a practical, positive, educationally beneficial way or do not use it at all; and never inform students that an activity judged by their peers to be "boring" is about to be sent their way!

A copy of notes, worksheets, and other materials developed to accompany multimedia items should be saved for future use. Teacher exchange of valuable audio-visuals is important (including teaching methods used), so inform colleagues who teach similar courses whenever you have received quality media items, and share both media and methods when possible. Teachers might also try working together for the purpose of ordering media. At times, depending on available space, it may be helpful to join two or more classes for viewing a video tape.

# EVALUATING MEDIA

There are several important considerations for teachers when evaluating which audio-visual media to use and when to use them. Teachers know that audio-visual media can add value to a lesson plan and increase the students' interest in classroom activities, complement course goals, and aid the student in the learning process. It is absolutely essential to select and use audio-visual items for their value to the overall plan of a particular lesson; and students should be made to feel responsible for knowing the major ideas, concepts, and vocabulary presented in any audio-visual item shown as part of the lesson. A sense of responsibility can be encouraged in the students by requiring them to take notes while viewing media. Their notes should include major ideas presented and new vocabulary words used. If note-taking is too difficult an assignment, the teacher should prepare a worksheet to be completed during or after the media is viewed. In some cases, a written quiz could be given to students after the media has been presented; however, I think it is necessary to forewarn students that a quiz will be given after viewing the media. To maintain a sense of fairness, it is important to review media ideas, vocabulary, and answer any student questions before distributing a quiz to the students.

Student reaction to the multimedia being presented is very important. If the media is acceptable to students they will learn from it. Occasionally, a teacher will choose what appears to be a useful video tape only to discover while using it in class that it is worthless (a problem which previewing would prevent). One day, I ordered a well described tape from a catalog. I did not preview the twenty-three minute long tape (mistake number one). I planned to review the main ideas after viewing the tape in class and I had an assignment for the remainder of the class time. Shortly after starting the tape, I realized that it was far removed from what I expected it to be. The outdated, simplistic ideas being presented were completely ineffective in terms of teaching my class anything. In a short time all the students (along with their teacher) were laughing hysterically. The tape was so bad that I stopped the video tape player and said it was useless to continue. There were loud protests throughout the room, for by now the students were really enjoying themselves. After a quick discussion, we decided to take a vote on whether or not to continue the tape (mistake number two). Of course, the vote was in favor of continuing. Again, I turned on the tape player (mistake number three), and we finished viewing the tape! We did not discuss the tape or refer to it in class notes; we quickly went on to other things. Of course, as my students left the room that day, some complimented me on my choice of "extreme tapes," while others shook their heads and wondered aloud where I had ever found that one! Needless to say, I saved the media request form for that tape and wrote on it in very large letters, "Never Order Again!" Sometimes written catalog descriptions and good intentions are just not enough!

Evaluating audio-visual media is not difficult. Teachers consider and evaluate both the information presented and the presentation method. The contents of the media should be appropriate to the age and grade/level of the students and should be presented at an appropriate time within the unit of study. Main ideas should be reviewed, explanations offered as necessary, and student questions answered. Teachers should have a sense that using the media was purposeful and provided their students another opportunity to learn new information or gain a new understanding.

Student reaction to all audio-visual media used in the classroom is also very important. Audio-visual media should complement course goals and aid the student in the learning process. If the media being used are acceptable to the students, then the students will learn from them. Therefore, teachers should note their students' reaction to both the information given and to the presentation method. If the method of presentation is poor, few students will be able to focus on the information being presented. There are some audio-visual media which will be helpful in all sections of a course and some that will not work as easily. It is, therefore, necessary for teachers to factor the class personality to the proposed media and prepare each class for a positive experience with the media presented.

Advanced planning and thorough preparation, teacher media preview, and positive, thoughtful presentations are the keys to incorporating audio-visual media into your classes for the fullest educational impact. When those keys are followed, evaluating the usefulness of media to student instruction and enrichment is not difficult. From the examples cited, it is clear that all three keys are needed when using audio-visual media. Are all three key indicators practiced when you use audio-visuals in your classroom?

# ONE FINAL NOTE:

At the end of the school year when you are busy cleaning your room, finalizing grades, sorting and filing papers, ordering some supplies for the next year, or fulfilling department requirements, take a few minutes to order several media items you wish to use in the fall. You should order two or three audio-visual items for each class for the month of September; this will help tremendously when the next school year begins. Your classes will be improved by the addition of quality media. Since you will not have to do the catalog search during the first week or two of school, your new school year duties will be somewhat lighter. The most important advantage to early ordering is that you will probably receive those ordered items on the dates requested since your request forms were submitted in June - long before request forms are sent by most teachers. As I left school each June to begin the summer vacation, one of the last items accomplished was to submit my media booking reservation forms. Often several of my colleagues gently teased me for doing this, but completing that early ordering always paid off in September.

# PART VI

# PROFESSIONALISM

**(AN INDIVIDUAL'S CHOICE)**

**Chapter 16**

# THE TEACHER'S IMAGE

Henry Adams wrote in his book *The Education of Henry Adams*: "A teacher affects eternity; he can never tell where his influence stops." What determines the effect of teachers on their students? I believe it is, in addition to academics, a combination of our attitudes, actions, and appearance.

# TEACHER ATTITUDES AND ACTIONS

As teachers, our attitudes and actions are very important. Our attitudes are often seen in our actions, and our attitudes determine the manner in which we meet our responsibilities as teachers, how we relate to those around us, and our effectiveness as teachers.

It is vital to our survival and effectiveness as teachers that we enjoy young people and our teaching position. It is of utmost importance for teachers to have a genuine, positive feeling toward students and to establish a purposeful relationship with them before attempting to teach course content. Occasionally, there will be days when things do not go as planned or days when we do not feel well. There may even be a particular class we do not enjoy and the unpleasantness presented by this class may last for an entire year, but we still must maintain a high standard of performance, presentation, and interaction.

## What determines how we view our teaching career?

Some of the satisfaction derived from our teaching position comes from our belief in the importance of the course content we teach, and some satisfaction comes from recognizing our abilities to successfully instruct students. We must have a genuine appreciation for our course content, a desire to constantly increase and share our knowledge, and a willingness to improve our instructional practice.

Satisfaction derived from our job is vital to our performance. One of the courses assigned to me in my first year of teaching was listed as "consumer economics." It was a course for less able students and I eventually learned it was a low priority course in the school system. When I arrived at the school during the summer to obtain textbooks and other course related materials, I was informed that, for this course, there were no textbooks, no curriculum guide, and no required standards. I was given a list of topics which could be taught in the course, some addresses to which I could write for free material, and a "good luck with the course" statement. At first, it was a challenge to find topics and materials for the course; however, the course soon became stale to me. Then I realized my boredom with the course was probably creating a similar situation for my students as well. At that point, I began to seriously build the course curriculum and requisitioned many resource materials. The defined purpose of the course was to provide students with a foundation for successful personal financial management. As I searched for new ideas to increase my students' abilities for successfully dealing with their financial future, I found many different topics to include in the curriculum. As I put forth more effort into developing the course, it became more exciting to me. However, the most beneficial change in the course occurred for my students since many new and improved topics were presented to them and a wider variety of teaching methods were used.

Maintaining a personal sense of integrity is vital for a positive teacher attitude. It is essential for teachers to meet commitments, act responsibly, set a good example, deal fairly with students, and control their tempers. Teachers must be respectful in order to be respected; they must set standards for themselves and then see that those standards are met. The importance of maintaining one's integrity while assisting students, meeting with their parents, and working with colleagues cannot be understated.

One year, I had a total of eighty-four students in three sections of a Regent's American history course. I assigned a project and gave a due date. Since I had so many students and a limited time in which to grade the projects, I determined the due date would not be changed. Students were encouraged to complete the project early and give it to me as soon as it was completed. For those who procrastinated (most of the students), I often repeated the due date, followed by the comment, "Even if you are sick and out of school, the project is still due on the announced date. Late projects will not be accepted." I strongly believe that students should be given some absolute deadlines so they learn to meet requirements. Only one girl failed to deliver her project to me by the stated date. Two days later, she tried to give me the project and I refused to accept it. The next day, the girl and her mother came to see me at the end of the school day. The mother was livid because I had refused to accept her daughter's project. We discussed the project requirements and due date. I asked the daughter if she had understood the project requirements including the due date. She said, "Yes." When we finished that discussion, the mother said to me, "So are you going to accept my daughter's project?" I answered, "No." With my one word answer, I put the mother's mouth into overdrive! As she verbally attacked me, I simply answered any question she yelled. She threatened to go to the principal to discuss my unreasonable decision. I told her she could do so if she desired. Since her threat did not move me to accept the late project, she said she would go to the superintendent and have me fired. I acknowledged her right to visit with the superintendent. She asked again if I was going to accept the project, and I again replied, "No." She turned to her daughter and said, "This is useless, let's leave." Without even saying "good-bye," they both left the room. After the dust settled in my classroom, I reflected on our meeting. I was relieved it was over, but even more, I was pleased that I did not respond to the woman according to her style, and I was glad I had not lost my integrity. I never did accept the girl's project and I had no regrets. Presumably, the woman did not go to the principal (I never heard from him) or to the superintendent (I was not fired!).

Successful teachers also realize it is necessary to control their ego. It is very easy to become involved in many school activities and to develop a sense of importance, based upon one's position of authority in the classroom and with extracurricular activities. Enjoy the feelings of accomplishment you gain from your professional efforts and contributions, but try not to become excessively impressed. It is so refreshing to work with accomplished teachers who maintain a casual, realistic view of themselves.

During my first five years of teaching I had no children, so I was often involved in extracurricular activities. I taught eleventh and twelfth grade classes and enjoyed my involvement in school activities. My job was very important to me and I believed I was an important part of the school system. My life and my teaching position were merging. Then, during one school year I began a maternity leave. I was home for a little over one year. After returning to school I recognized two major changes in my own perception. First, incredible as it was, the school had somehow survived without me! Second, I realized that my priorities had changed. I still enjoyed teaching and took my position seriously, yet I also realized my job no longer defined my life in the manner it once did. Those realizations assisted me greatly in maintaining a balanced view about my teaching position and the importance of my contributions within the school community.

Another attitude vital for a successful teaching career is a desire to work with one's colleagues and act responsibly toward them. We teachers are not an entity unto ourselves; we are a part of the entire school community. We should not be competing against each other; rather, we should be assisting, supporting, and encouraging each other.

Teacher actions are as important as teacher attitudes when defining successful practices. One action which is very important within the school setting is to extend a compliment. When you notice something another

183

teacher has said or done which has merit, compliment that teacher. If you hear a positive, insightful comment from a student about another teacher, share it with the teacher. It is not necessary for you to scurry around each day handing out compliments to every teacher, but when something is well done, commend your colleague. Teachers work hard and they seldom receive encouragement from fellow teachers or administrators. As a group of educators working within a school system, we need each other and we benefit from encouraging one another. Toward the end of my teaching career, my department chairperson started a practice I very much appreciated. At the end of each school year he wrote a letter to each department member summarizing the successes of the year, thanking each one for contributions made, and congratulating us for a job well done. I think he was the only department chairperson to write such a letter. I appreciated his recognition of what we in the social studies department had accomplished, and was grateful to him for taking the time to say "thank you."

Other important actions of teachers are punctuality and promptness. Teachers are expected to arrive on time at school each day, fulfill required supervisory duties, begin and end classes promptly, and attend required meetings. These requirements are very important to protect the school from lawsuits involving unsupervised students and to maintain a smoothly operating school building and district. Building administrators are rightly upset by a teacher's failure to meet established requirements. Promptness in the "paper chase" is also important. In addition to grading papers, there are many other obligations to which a teacher must respond including: writing student recommendations, requisitioning school supplies, completing reports, designing and evaluating curriculum, and contacting parents.

To summarize: teachers can and should enjoy their career! As individuals, we must develop and maintain attitudes which promote our best efforts towards our students. We can and should act responsibly towards our colleagues by helping a troubled colleague and encouraging others. Teachers ought to seize opportunities to learn new skills and grow professionally. We should expand our knowledge of curriculum content and include new topics were possible. We can constantly refine and expand our classroom presentation methods in order to increase the value of our instruction. We should reach for something new instead of settling for the status quo. We must be fully participating members of the team that makes a school into a place of true learning. Too idealistic? I do not think so. I respect teachers for who they are, what they attempt, and most of all, for what they accomplish.

# TEACHER APPEARANCE

Often there is no stated dress codes for teachers; however, that does not mean the teacher's choice of clothing is of little importance or influence. It is important to be comfortable and safe in your choice of clothing, but there are other factors to consider such as: your own personal tastes, what you own, what you wish to purchase (and can afford!), and your specific course assignments such as art, technology, home and careers, or physical education. Remember, too, that school furniture and facilities are very rough on clothes. If you make it through the day without a snag in your clothes, consider yourself lucky! Even more, chalk dust, pens, pencils, dust, or smudges from photocopied material all leave their "mark" on clothing.

## What will the teachers in the 2000's say by their appearance?

Whatever your choice in clothing happens to be, it is important to appear neat, confident, and professional. Teachers should not be sloppy to appear stylish, rather use your appearance as another means of gaining respect; let your choice of clothing show that you care about yourself and what you are doing.

OPPORTUNITIES FOR REFLECTION:

1. What constitutes professional attitude? Appearance?

2. Does overall teacher attitude affect students' attitudes? If yes, then how?

3. What actions will you incorporate into your practice of teaching which will be of benefit to your students? To your colleagues? To yourself?

**Chapter 17**

# TEACHER PROTECTIONS

Teachers, like most individuals, want their interests known, their desires met, and their jobs protected. In order to gain and protect employment rights, teachers formed associations and found in them a successful method for continuing representation. Additional teacher protections are provided through tenure and seniority laws. Tenure provides job security based on a three year probationary period during which teachers are observed and evaluated several times each year. Seniority rights enhance and complement the benefits provided by tenure.

The rights to form and join associations, receive tenure, and gain seniority benefits are all very important legal protections for teachers, and teachers should be knowledgeable regarding those safeguards.

# THE TEACHERS' ASSOCIATION

Each teacher is given freedom of choice in deciding whether or not to join an association (designated word meaning unions), although at times one might feel somewhat pressured to join. Some teachers prefer not to join their local and state associations because they do not have faith in unions or they believe associations accomplish very little. Others fear joining because of the possibility of a strike and the personal problems and financial loss which can result. Still others prefer not to pay the membership fees since they will receive all the benefits of a negotiated contract whether or not they join the association.

Teachers usually decide whether or not to join an association at the beginning of each school year. Methods of paying association dues often are by payroll deductions or lump sum payment, the choice being given to each individual member. Due to differences in association activities, fees vary from one district to another. Specific membership fee information is available from an association representative in each building or district.

In many school districts the contractual agreement calls for an agency shop. This contract clause requires all teachers to pay union membership fees whether or not they chose to join the association. Shares of the membership fee which are used for political matters are returned to those who chose not to join, but all other portions of the membership fee are to be paid by all teachers. Usually the political refund represents a very small portion of the total membership fee.

Whether or not teachers join an association, they should receive a copy of the contract between the school district and the teachers' association. Teachers should read through the contract to learn of their negotiated rights and responsibilities as employees within the school district.

Often, people new to the teaching profession do not understand much related to teacher contracts. When offered a teaching position within a school district, the beginning teacher is given an "employment agreement" to sign. This statement, often only one page long, is a basic job offer and acceptance. After accepting the position, the new teacher should be given a copy of the contract negotiated between the district and the teachers' association. The contract, often fifty or more pages in length, addresses many issues such as: academic freedom, teacher duties, grievance procedure, teacher's hours, observation and evaluation of unit members, personnel file, teacher assignments, transfers, leave policies, class size, academic load, and employee benefits.

There are some advantages to joining a teachers' association. As a member your viewpoints and opinions concerning the contract are considered, and that is especially important when new contracts are being negotiated. Legal assistance is available to member teachers if they become involved in a contract grievance, although this assistance may also be given to a non-member teacher involved in a precedent setting case. Association members may also become involved in a variety of different association activities including union leadership, fund raising, problem solving, and social events.

Upon joining a local association, a teacher usually becomes an enrolled member of a statewide teacher organization. Many times, through the statewide organization, a member can purchase life or disability income insurance at reasonable rates. Some organizations make available to their members special purchasing plans which can reduce the cost of buying items such as furniture, cars, appliances, and jewelry.

Whether or not you choose to join an association, the decision, based on personal preference, is yours to make.

# TEACHERS AND TENURE

Tenure is a controversial topic; it provides job security to teachers and occasionally can be a source of problems to school administrators and boards of education. There is a need for teachers (and the general public) to be informed about the nature of tenure, how tenure recommendations are determined, and how school districts are protected against having to keep poor teachers.

Tenure is a desirable benefit to teachers in that it grants job security. Teachers are protected from arbitrarily being dismissed from their jobs due to personality conflicts with a building administrator or other school official, or for union activities. It is a valuable protection. Tenure is also important to the individual teacher, for it is a statement of acceptance into the teaching profession and into a specific district.

Teachers desire and enjoy the protection that tenure grants; however, it does not grant an unlimited job protection. Tenure provides job security so the free expression of ideas which differ from the administration may exist. Tenure also allows teachers the freedom to engage in union activities without fear of losing their jobs. Yet, all of those expressions and activities must be within the limits of the law. Tenure is not designed to protect a teacher who does not meet basic standards in teaching skills or those who fail to meet the responsibilities and duties of their position.

Tenure is not a total, irrevocable protection granted to all teachers upon receiving a teaching position; it is an earned recognition of one's professionalism. The tenure law and the policies of a school district related to tenure should be fully explained to all new teachers. In New York State, tenure is usually granted for the first time to a probationary teacher after three years of successful teaching service in one school. During the probationary period, the teacher is usually observed by several people including the department chairman, building principal, and possibly the district superintendent. Those official visits provide an opportunity for the teacher to be evaluated "on-the-job." The classroom evaluator will write a report stating observed practices and skills. Based on the collected evaluations of the teacher's abilities, knowledge, contributions, and professionalism, tenure is granted or denied. In New York, school districts can grant tenure to a teacher in less than three years if the teacher had previously been tenured in another New York school district. However, if tenure is not granted to a teacher by the end of three years of employment, the teacher's employment in that school district will end. Occasionally a fourth year of probationary status is granted, but it is usually due to extenuating circumstances.

It is the responsibility of administrators and the department chairperson to evaluate new teachers and to accurately document observations. Positive teacher practices and areas in need of improvement (along with suggestions for improved performance) should be noted. In the case of inadequate teacher performance, active intervention related to identified deficiencies or difficulties should begin immediately.

It is much easier to deny contract renewal to a probationary teacher than to terminate a poorly functioning tenured teacher. However, any teacher who is not performing well after having received tenure can be investigated and evaluated by school officials. If a teacher is found to be incompetent, insubordinate, immoral, physically or mentally incapable, or has failed to maintain certification, the teacher's employment in the school district can be terminated. Sometimes the termination is resolved by a settlement reached between the school district and the teacher, while other cases are presented at a hearing for resolution.

There are times when, due to a general lack of teaching skills or major personal problems, a teacher is unable to continue in the profession. There are cases in which teachers were very good, but gradually over the years lost much of their ability, zeal, and impact. If the ability of a teacher to instruct students is so impaired or diminished as to render the teacher ineffective, it is the responsibility of the school administrators to document that situation and take necessary steps to deal with the defined problem. Those teachers must be identified, re-vitalized (if possible), re-evaluated, and then retained or replaced based upon performance. It is a difficult, time-consuming, and costly process to end the employment of a tenured teacher, but it is a possibility. Dismissal of poor teachers can and should be done to protect the educational rights of students and preserve the reputation of the teachers and the school district. Some incompetent teachers have been allowed to continue in teaching positions because administrators refuse to involve themselves in the fight to dismiss those teachers. School administrators should be held accountable for the quality of the teachers within their school buildings, just as teachers should be held accountable for properly instructing their students and fulfilling all requirements of their position.

Teachers have also learned that along with tenure, seniority rights are an important teacher protection for they enhance and complement the benefits provided by tenure. Seniority rights are based on the number of years "on the job" at a particular school, and are related to job assignments, transfers, and layoffs.

The legal protections which teachers enjoy provide a quiet security - it is nice to know those protections exist. However, after all the discussions about teacher associations, tenure, and seniority are voiced, teachers still know that the most important aspect of job security they can possess is a dedication to high ideals and a determination to perform at the highest educational level possible.

# PROFESSIONAL GROWTH

Wonderful opportunities exist within the teaching profession for the continuing development of one's personal expertise. Through a variety of means, teachers can increase their knowledge, refine their classroom techniques, hone their leadership abilities, expand their ability to positively interact with people, investigate different career options within the field of education, and begin to network with many other professionals. So much to be gained!

There are many ways to pursue professional growth. Teachers can read publications focused on general teaching practices, curriculum specific magazines, or educational journals. They may enroll in interest specific courses at a nearby college or university - or on the Internet. If there is a teacher center within one's geographic location, teachers can visit the site and learn of available curriculum resources and training sessions. School district budgets include funding to provide for conference or workshop attendance by teachers. The funding is often limited by departments or grade levels, but teachers are encouraged to attend presentations which are school, grade, or curriculum related. Teachers may choose to join discipline specific organizations such as the National Council for Social Studies - often these groups have regional, state, and national levels. Department chairpersons often have information on many professional organizations and opportunities related to out-of-district workshops, seminars, and conferences, so teachers should express their interests to their chairperson and gain the requested information.

Often, due to career and family demands, teachers often find it difficult to include professional growth activities on their calendar - until they truly find an area of great interest. Soon, they become involved in a new learning experience. As their expertise expands and their network grows, their professional growth experience is self-sustaining and effective changes appear in their practice of educational delivery. Opportunities for professional growth abound - to enrich your life and improve your educational practice, include them on your calendar!

# DISTRICT ORGANIZATIONAL DESIGN

In each local school district, the board of education is the highest ranking authority. The board of education is comprised of a group of elected individuals who formulate district policy, set educational direction, and determine financial matters. School personnel are organized according to the positions held; the superintendent is the primary leader of the district and is responsible for the day-to-day operation of the district. Next in line are other district wide (central office) administrators, followed by building administrators, teachers and teacher assistants (faculty), and then support staff such as secretaries, aides, custodians, bus drivers, cafeteria workers, and maintenance personnel.

All of these people contribute their time and skills to meet the educational needs of students or to provide other support services. In a well functioning district these groups work together, for they each have defined, necessary functions. Take time to talk with staff members and show a genuine interest in them; respect them for the work they do and be on a first-name basis with them. Staff members work hard and contribute much to the school community. They also appreciate being recognized as members of the educational team, and often they will go out of their way to be helpful to the teachers who have been kind to them. The staff members can provide valued assistance to teachers during the school year, so treat them with kindness and gain their friendship before you need their services.

## OPPORTUNITIES FOR REFLECTION:

1. Is teacher association membership important to you? Why or why not?

2. Why is the contract negotiated between a school district and a teachers' association of importance?

3. If you are presently employed by a school district, have you received a copy of the contract negotiated between the school district and the teachers association? Have you read it, and do you have any questions related to it?

4. Are you aware of the observational process (pre-conference, observation, post-conference) and the actual evaluation form used within your school district? Are you aware of your right to respond to any comment written on the evaluation form related to your classroom observation?

5. What categories of professional growth are of greatest interest to you? What actions will you pursue to ensure your own professional growth?

# PART VII

# ROUGH TERRAIN AHEAD

## (BE PREPARED!)

**Chapter 18**

# CONQUERING THE MOUNTAIN PEAKS

Teachers face many different situations during a school year. Some situations provide delightful, encouraging, inspiring, or satisfying times. There are also occasions which are not so pleasant, for teachers encounter disappointing, frustrating, distressing, and anxious moments as well. Some of the difficult times are the result of disagreements with students, their parents, or school administrators. Other difficulties result from conflicting educational philosophies, social standards, or self-perceptions. Sometimes a difficult circumstance grows with time into a more serious situation, some difficult circumstances develop quickly, and sometimes what first appeared as a difficult situation fades away almost as quickly as it appeared. Learning to deal with those challenges in an effective way comes through formal education, discussions with colleagues, understanding school policies, maintaining personal standards and goals, and actual experience. Although teachers may not face all of the situations described in the following readings, it is likely that they will face some of them.

# PROMOTING STUDENT HONESTY

Honesty in academic pursuits is an attractive and desired quality. It is also learned behavior. Teachers should encourage the development of this quality in their students by discussing the desirability of it and the importance of establishing a positive work ethic and reputation. Student honesty can be promoted by occasionally rewarding students for it. Teachers can also help their students to be honest by reducing cheating opportunities whenever possible and by disciplining students who are caught cheating on school work. Those teacher actions clearly inform students cheating will not be tolerated and that, too, is an important lesson for students to learn. However, for any efforts promoting student honesty to be truly effective, students must want to be honest.

During one of the first days of the school year, I discussed in each class what I expected from my students. One topic of discussion was the practice of individual honesty when completing course assignments and taking tests. I asked students not to place pressure on their friends by seeking to copy their work. Students were also asked not to give away their efforts and hard work by allowing another student to copy their work.

Students must be told that they are expected to complete all of their assignments on their own without copying the work of another. Students were also informed that on any assignment in which they were caught cheating, a grade of zero would be given for the assignment, a letter "C" would be written inside the zero entered in my grade register to indicate cheating, and in some cases a telephone call would be made to the student's parents.

Honesty in the preparation of course assignments and the completion of tests can and should be actively encouraged and rewarded. Teachers can write a note of encouragement or recognition to a student on an assignment or test which was completed carefully and correctly. One time after writing a high grade on a student's test paper, I wrote the word "Thanks! As the student was about to leave the room at the end of class, he approached my desk and asked why I had written the word "Thanks" on his test paper. I told him I appreciated his great effort on the test and again congratulated him for the high grade he had earned. He was somewhat surprised by my comments and obviously pleased to have his efforts recognized. He left the room feeling complimented and rightly proud. It is a sad fact that we teachers sometimes overlook our students' efforts and hard work because we expect good work and often believe a good grade is reward enough. It is not. We need to encourage our students to do their best, then notice and compliment their efforts.

Another method for encouraging student honesty in school work is to occasionally have the students write a note to the teacher on the bottom of a homework paper. Once or twice during a marking term my students were asked to write "I did/did not receive answers from another person, and I did/did not give answers to another person while completing this assignment" and then mark each statement to indicate how the assignment was completed. Students were asked to respond honestly and were told there would not be a penalty for admitted cheating. I read each statement and sometimes was surprised by my students' responses and admissions. Occasionally, I learned that students discussed the questions for increased understanding; sometimes they made bets on which response was the correct answer, and sometimes they traded answers. Although at times I was disappointed by the students' methods, they were never punished for their statements nor were any points deducted from their papers. I wanted the students to realize I valued honesty, wanted honesty from them, and was honest with them. Many times it seemed as though the students appreciated the chance to honestly reply and admit their cheating. The next day in class I would comment generally on the student statements and encourage them to continue to write honestly to me, but more importantly, I would encourage them to do their work honestly. I have no proof that this system changed any students' methods of completing homework assignments, I only hope it did.

There were times when I made a mistake while grading a student's paper. After examining the paper, if additional points should be added, they were and the student received an apology from me. If I had written more points on the paper than the student earned, and the student informed me of my mistake, I would not reduce the grade but did promise to be more careful the next time! This, too, encourages student honesty and gives the student the opportunity to gently tease a teacher about making a mistake - students love those opportunities!

It is also important for a teacher to reduce the opportunities which tempt a student to cheat. When preparing tests for several classes of the same course, teachers often change the essay questions. It is not really necessary to write entirely different tests for there is a limit as to how many questions can be accurately remembered and passed on to other students. When students are taking a test, the teacher should observe students and occasionally walk around in the room. Students who are trying to cheat will be very much aware of the teacher's location, for they do not want to be caught cheating. Teachers who sincerely do not want their students to cheat will never sit at their desks and grade papers or read a book while their students are taking a test. Some students simply cannot resist the temptation to cheat when an opportunity is readily available.

When students are to make up a test or a major assignment, require them to do the work with you in a study hall or in an after school session. Many times when students are making up an assignment or test, they are not sufficiently supervised by another teacher in a study hall or in the library to guarantee that cheating will not occur. It is also unfair to expect another teacher to proctor your students involved in completing an assignment or taking a test. Some cheating on homework papers can be reduced by discarding the papers after reviewing them in class. Other papers, such as lab reports, term papers, major tests, or special projects should be reviewed in class and then kept by the teacher and discarded at the end of the school year. Those teacher actions may prevent some student work from being passed on to succeeding students.

Finally, it is important to the promotion of student honesty that teachers take some well-defined action when cheating is discovered. Cheating cannot be condoned and it cannot be ignored. If students are successful in cheating experiences, the attempts will spread and include more students. The teacher should establish guidelines based on stated school policies. If no policies exist, then teachers should develop their own guidelines. After explaining to students what will be done about student cheating, teachers should consistently follow the outlined course of action when cheating is discovered. Often a grade of zero plus a private discussion is sufficient action.

Instituting a zero tolerance plan with regard to student cheating can at times produce difficult consequences for the teacher. An interesting article in July, 2002, *Reader's Digest* (page 39) details the actions of a teacher after a board of education ordered her to give partial credit to students who had cheated on a major project. The article goes on to describe how plagiarism is an increasing problem in academia and that fewer teachers have enforceable standards against it.

Honesty can be a difficult quality to learn. It involves an individual choice about integrity which can be vigorously attacked through peer pressure. It is a personal interpretation of "how to act and why." Not only is honesty difficult to learn, it can be difficult to practice, and even more difficult to teach. We as teachers tackle difficult course curriculum, and step-by-step we bring our students through the course; that is the same way we ought to approach the topic of student honesty. Step-by-step we must establish fair rules, inform our students of those rules, and then apply those rules.

# STUDENT CHEATING: SUSPECTED / OCCURRING

Some students do not cheat in completing their school work, some cheat occasionally, and if you read and believe statistical reports, many cheat regularly. After spending a considerable amount of time encouraging students to prepare their work honestly, it is disappointing when cheating is suspected or discovered.

Teachers' views related to student cheating vary greatly. A few teachers are totally oblivious to student cheating in their classrooms, thus nothing is done about the problem. Some teachers are obsessed with the possibility that a few students may be cheating in their classes. In their attempt to reduce student cheating possibilities those teachers often succeed only in creating large amounts of extra work for themselves. Some teachers reprimand an entire class for the cheating done by one student. There may even be a few teachers who are so frustrated by student cheating or who are so determined to avoid confrontation that they simply ignore the problem and the cheating continues unchallenged. Some teachers take preventative measures which effectively limit student cheating. The teacher's attitude toward, and awareness of, student cheating are of utmost importance in dealing with the problem.

## What is a teacher to do when student cheating is suspected or discovered?

It is very important for teachers to talk to their students about cheating before it becomes a problem. This discussion should take place during one of the first days of the course when all students are present. Teachers should take a "no-nonsense" approach toward the topic of student cheating. They should clearly state their opposition to this method of completing course assignments and inform their students of the penalties for cheating. The discussion gives the student some insight concerning the teacher's point of view regarding cheating, as well as an opportunity to think about cheating and its consequences.

When a teacher begins to suspect that cheating is occurring, it is disappointing but not overwhelming. Teachers should take some class time to remind students of the discussion held at the beginning of the course related to student cheating. Remind students why it is so important for them to individually complete their work and review with them all previously stated consequences for cheating.

At some point in time, if suspected student cheating continues, teachers must take increased corrective actions. Teachers can observe student behavior, check papers for similarities (but realize many papers may be the same by nature of the assignment), question students, rotate the order of test questions, and change seating assignments. Teachers must also realize it is difficult to stop students who are cheating on assignments completed outside of school; teachers simply cannot constantly supervise students' work methods.

Most importantly, with regard to student cheating, teachers must maintain a sense of balance. Some teachers become very angry and verbally assault all the students in the classroom when one student is caught cheating. Many students understandably resent the lecture since they were not involved. The class lecture, after one student has been caught cheating, is not an effective way to deal with a cheating problem. The most effective method for dealing with a cheating problem is to discuss it with the student(s) involved in a calm, quiet way after class or at the end of the school day. In most cases, I have found it very difficult to accuse a student of cheating except for when a student is actually caught in the act of cheating. It is easier to show students similar papers after noticing an established pattern and ask for an explanation, followed by a teacher silence. Many times the teacher's silence and patient waiting for an explanation is much more effective than many accusations, it certainly is much less emotionally charged and much less draining. When the student is placed in the position of having to explain a questionable paper or defend the completion method used, the teacher does not need to accuse the student for often the student will simply admit to cheating.

One year there were two girls in my class who were best friends. One girl was an above-average student; the other was not as able. After distributing a test in their class, I began to notice the poorer student glancing at her friend's paper quite often, so I reminded the entire class membership to pay attention only to their own test. After grading the tests, I noticed that the thirty objective answers on the two friends' papers were exactly the same. The only difference between their papers was their essay answer. When I returned the test papers to the students, I asked those two girls to stay after class for a few minutes. I showed them the similarities on their answer sheets and asked if they knew how that happened. Then I waited. One girl spoke immediately and claimed she did not cheat on the test. I knew she had not copied any answers from the other girl, but I thought she had allowed her friend to view her paper. The second girl then spoke. She admitted she copied answers from section one of her friend's test, but insisted she had answered section two completely on her own. She "could not imagine" how her section two answers were the same as her friend's test. I told her I did not believe she had copied section one and not section two, especially since both sections on the answer sheets were exactly the same. We finished discussing the tests, and I told the girls that this would not happen again. They agreed, and never again sat together in my class while taking a test.

Assigning a grade to those tests was difficult. I allowed the first girl's test to be without penalty for at the time I still was not sure if this girl purposely allowed her friend to copy her test answer sheet. The second girl received a grade of zero on the test. Several weeks after submitting term grades for report cards, the academically stronger girl came to my classroom to talk with me. She admitted she had allowed her friend to view her answer sheet. After firmly telling her I did not appreciate what she had done during the test, I thanked her for telling me the truth; I also informed her that no further action would be taken regarding her grade.

If a teacher suspects some students are cheating on tests, there are several different actions which can be taken. Teachers can change the seating plan just for the day of the test. As students enter the classroom, have them fill in the rows of desks in a random order. It should be standard practice during testing that student desks are cleared of all books and papers other than those distributed by the teacher. Books and papers belonging to the students can be put on the floor, in the student's desk, or at the back of the room. Teacher attention to the students during the testing period will reduce cheating, and teachers should remind students to pay attention to their individual papers alone.

If a teacher believes students from one class are passing test questions and answers to students in another class, there are some effective actions which can be taken. The most obvious action is to change the test questions, especially essay questions. It takes valuable time to completely change tests, and I do not think that is totally necessary. Sometimes, it seems if students can correctly remember a question and its answer, they have truly learned something!

Another effective teacher action to reduce student cheating is to check the tops of students' desks for "valuable" information. I always had a can of desk cleaner and a cleaning rag stored in my closet. Several times a year, before a major test, I would inspect the tops of the desks in my classroom. If any test related information was discovered, a little "magic spray" took care of it. Many times as I walked around the room with the desk cleaner in hand, students would ask me to spray their desk for they were tired of looking at certain obscenities which another student had written on the desk. I obliged. I did not scrub all the desks; I just took care of a few little, necessary cleaning jobs.

Cheat sheets present an interesting class event. Some students will go to great extremes to write a usable cheat sheet while others will write special notes on their arms, their shoes, or their clothes. One day while giving a test, I saw a student with a piece of paper about one inch square. He saw me watching him and quickly tried to hide the paper in his hand. I asked him what the paper was, and he denied having any paper. I asked him to open his hand, and when he did we "found" this small sheet of paper there. I examined the piece of paper to make sure it was what I suspected. It was. I then very quietly told the student to place his test paper in the wastebasket near my desk. Most students noticed this quiet conversation. That was the one and only time I found a student with a cheat sheet in that class. I believe the "quiet approach" is the preferable course of action because the problem is dealt with immediately and the class membership learns of consequences without a heated interruption during a test. The student was assigned an automatic zero on the test. When I recorded the zero in my register I wrote the letter "C" inside the zero to indicate student cheating.

Students can be very inventive when it comes to cheating methodology. Teachers have reported some interesting, yet foiled, attempts. One student wrote answers on a small piece of paper, and then taped the piece of paper to a tissue. He looked at the tissue for an answer then pretended to wipe his nose. Some students write answers on their arms and then wear long sleeve shirts to cover the writing. One dexterous student placed her textbook on the floor, took off her shoe, and proceeded to use her foot to turn to the page containing the needed information. Some students write answers on a small piece of paper and tape it to the back of their watches. The very brave students may enter the classroom a day before the test is given, and if it is available, take a copy of the test for previewing. Still others will try writing a few answers on the chalkboard before the test period. Once in a while a student will "neglect" to turn in the test at the end of the test period. When the test is missing the student suggests that the teacher must have lost it. Of course, the student wants an opportunity to take the test again. That situation is a tough one to call. If a teacher suspects such a situation has occurred, a new test should be written and it should present a real challenge to the student!

Sometime during your teaching experience you will have students who attempt to cheat - and they may be successful. Students cheat for a number of reasons which are often based on a sense of necessity or laziness, for adventure or challenge, or to be part of a group activity. Do not take student cheating as a personal insult from your students. There are few teachers who have not had to deal with this problem. When you suspect student cheating, take notice of it and become more aware of student activities. When you discover student cheating, take positive actions to stop it. Do your best to limit the opportunities for students to cheat. Often, a call to parents is most helpful in dealing with students who are known to be cheating in your course. Although the situation in which you find yourself may for a time be unpleasant, you simply cannot allow that type of student activity to continue.

Teachers must learn to deal with a cheating problem in a rational, kind, yet firm, manner. This type of teacher action includes every step from introductory remarks about cheating, to suspicion, discovery, discussion with the involved student(s), punishment, forgiveness, and even a healthy forgetfulness. Remember, teachers: you must establish reasonable standards and present reachable goals. Those guidelines allow for students to succeed in a course without feeling that it is necessary to cheat in order to complete an assignment or earn a good grade.

# SUSPECTED SUBSTANCE ABUSE

Substance abuse is generally defined as an excessive and uncontrollable use of alcohol and/or drugs (prescription and illegal). The problem of substance abuse and the problems created by that abuse are enormous in American public schools. I have seen far too many young people ruin their lives through substance abuse. Schools have failed in many attempts to educate young people about the dangers of substance abuse and I believe that teachers are woefully unprepared to recognize and deal with the problem of student substance abuse. For a description of physical and emotional symptoms which may indicate substance abuse in young people I have quoted a noted psychologist from his book entitled: *Dr. Dobson Answers Your Questions*. Tyndale House Publishers kindly granted me permission to incorporate the following material into this chapter.

Enumerated items listed below in bold print are commonly observed by teachers.

## What should parents and teachers look for as symptoms of substance abuse?

1. **Inflammation of the eyelids and nose is common.** The pupils of the eyes are either very wide or very small, depending on the kind of substances internalized. Eyes are often red, and eye movements are imprecise. Face is often pale.
2. **Extremes of energy may be represented.** Either the individual is sluggish, gloomy, and withdrawn, or he may be loud, hysterical, and jumpy. Often there is a noticeable change from active competitive interests to a more passive, withdrawn personality.
3. The appetite is extreme - either very great or very poor. Weight loss may occur.
4. **The personality suddenly changes**; the individual may become irritable, inattentive, and confused, or aggressive, suspicious, and explosive. Many times, there is an inappropriate overreaction to mild criticism.
5. **Neglect of personal appearance.** Body and breath odor is often bad. Cleanliness is generally ignored.
6. The digestive system may be upset - diarrhea, nausea, and vomiting may occur. Headaches and double vision are also common. Other signs of physical deterioration may include change in skin tone and body stance.
7. Needle marks on the body, usually appearing on the arms, are an important symptom. Those punctures sometimes get infected and appear as sores and boils.
8. **Moral values often crumble and are replaced by new, way-out ideas and values.** Distinct lessening in social warmth; less care for the feelings of others.
9. **Significant drop in the quality of school work** which is a result of reduced drive and ambition, diminished attention span, and impaired communication skills.
10. **Friendships change dramatically.** Associations with people who fit the above-mentioned descriptions, and who refuse to identify themselves on the telephone.
11. There is an increased secretiveness about money or the disappearance of money or valuables from the house.

Some of these symptoms will not be readily observable to teachers, but many are. I do not propose that it is the duty of teachers to investigate their students and continually be "reporting" cases of suspected substance abuse. However, when it is obvious that a student is in trouble, teachers should notify school administration personnel. Since few teachers have the expertise needed for substance abuse counseling or accessibility to available assistance programs for young people, they should report their observations to the school psychologist, qualified guidance personnel, or building principal. Teachers must be aware of legal requirements and obey reporting laws, yet they must also be discreet about their reporting and maintain confidentiality.

It is important to remember that most teachers are not equipped with the expertise to deal with a student who is abusing drugs or alcohol. One year I caught a student using his "favorite, self-made pipe." Since there were only ten days left to the school year and he was a senior about to graduate, I tried to obtain help for this student without going through the proper school channels. I was afraid the young man would be expelled from school and not be allowed to graduate if I reported him. Although my intentions were good, I was not successful in helping my student because he did not want my help. I eventually went to the principal and asked for his help. He met with the student, offered assistance, and was able to enroll the student in a counseling program; however, the student discontinued his counseling after the first session. Looking back on that situation I believe the student would have been better served had I gone directly to the principal at the very beginning of the problem. The student was allowed to graduate with his class and I was happy about that fact, but his substance abuse problem was not improved. From this experience I realized how unprepared I was to deal with a student's substance abuse problem. I simply did not have the authority, resources, or expertise to deal with the situation.

It is important to remember that the goal in identifying students involved in substance abuse should not be to punish them but to assist them in dealing with their problems and overcoming their addiction. It is also vital in this situation that the teacher has administrative support, for without that support, little progress will be made with any student.

## SUSPECTED DRUG DEALING

This unit will be short. Drug dealing within the school system must not be tolerated; however, in many schools, it is. I believe the most dangerous students found within the school are the ones who are selling drugs. Those students are a very real threat to all other students. Many young people who would normally avoid drug involvement are pressured into drug usage at their schools - a place which should be a safe, learning environment for students. Drug dealers (who are part of the student body or walk-ins off the street) must not be allowed to carry on their trade within school buildings or on school property. Teachers should report all suspected drug dealing activities to the proper school authorities; those school authorities should fully investigate any reports received from teachers and call in the police as required.

After writing the previous paragraph, I realized how easy it is to state my opinion while not facing any threats of reprisal. I do remember the personal fear which became a part of my life whenever I reported a suspicion or observed action. I am aware that teachers are attacked, their vehicles vandalized, and their families threatened because the teacher reported suspected drug dealing. Teachers face threats from students and often, insufficient support from administrators who are unwilling to take action against drug dealing within their schools. In light of those situations, it is understandable that not all teachers are quick to inform school administrators about suspected drug activity. The issue quickly becomes very personal and each teacher must answer a variety of questions: "What are my responsibilities?" "What are my priorities?" "What are the consequences of my action or of my failure to respond?" Whichever direction you choose to take, there are consequences. Your decision must be based upon your evaluation of what is in the best interest of the students in your school combined with consideration for yourself - two ideas which may create upsetting conflict in your mind.

If and when teachers report suspected drug dealings, they should clearly state all reasons for their suspicion and deliver the report to the designated building administrator as quickly as possible. Should teachers discuss the details of the report among themselves? Some teachers believe the reports should be kept confidential. Those teachers see no reason for discussing the matter with anyone not directly involved, and they understand that confidentiality can be a means of self-protection. Other teachers believe that sharing observations, suspicions, and knowledge of administrative support increases their involvement and effectiveness in reducing drug dealing within the school. Both viewpoints are valid, and teachers sometimes change viewpoints depending on the specifics of each case. Whether or not the report is kept confidential by the reporting teacher, the next important step is taken by the administration. If administrators take quick, well-defined action, teachers recognize the support and their involvement will be maintained. If administrators take little or no action, teachers will interpret the lack of action as a lack of support and their involvement in reporting suspected drug dealings will probably decrease or even end. After reporting suspected drug dealings, teachers should always check with the administrators to learn what action was taken. Teachers and administrators must work together, support each other, and encourage each other in order to reduce drug dealing within schools.

205

The problems created by drug dealing (and drug usage) within schools are very serious. Policies with well-defined procedures must be established and followed. It will take a determined effort from the school administration, teachers, students, and parents to successfully terminate drug-related activities within our schools. The solutions will not occur quickly and they will not occur without the cooperation of many people. Teacher involvement is absolutely necessary due to their close proximity to the problem. Carefully consider your responsibilities in this matter and know this: ignoring the problem of drug dealing within the school setting will not cause the problem to disappear but adult intervention may help to reduce it.

# TEEN SUICIDES ARE PREVENTABLE

More and more schools are facing the problem of teenage suicides, but many schools do nothing about this problem until after a student suicide has occurred. In many cases, faculty members and administrators are unprepared to deal with this problem before it happens. Although school systems are developing and improving grief management teams, many educators, as well as parents, believe "it could never happen here." Few faculty meetings are devoted to the discussion of teen suicide - always there are more "immediate issues" which must be solved. Then, when a teen suicide occurs, many are at a loss as to what should be done. School administrators, teachers, and other professionals are called upon to deal with the problem in a constructive way, and precious few people know where to begin. In this situation it is very difficult to establish a well-planned program.

Few teachers are trained to recognize the warning signs of teen suicide, yet many teachers are at the forefront of the problem. As schools continue to take on more responsibility for meeting the social needs of their students, educators must be made aware of the scope of the problem, suicide indicators, and preventative actions available to them. A booklet entitled: *Teen Suicide Prevention* written by Mr. Ray Allen, Chairman of the Teen Suicide Prevention Task Force (Washington, D. C.) contains fourteen articles related to teen suicide including topics defining the problem, listing warning signs, and describing prevention strategies. For additional information related to teen suicide prevention you may call the Teen Suicide Prevention Task Force at (301) 627-1595.

In the booklet listed above, Mr. Allen lists the following "Warning Signs of Impending Suicide." Items listed below in bold print are often noticeable to teachers. If you recognize several of these items in a student and it is a change from the normal behavior of the student, talk with your department chairperson, a guidance counselor, social worker, or principal. A determination should be made as to whether or not a parent should be contacted, and if so, by whom.

1.   **Depressed mood.**
2.   Changes in sleep and/or appetite patterns.
3.   **Decline in school performance.**
4.   **Increased social withdrawal.**
5.   **Loss of interest and pleasure in previously enjoyable activities.**
6.   **Preoccupation with themes of death.**
7.   **Increased irritability and behavior problems.**
8.   **Verbal expressions about self-death.**
9.   Giving away important possessions.
10.  Use of alcohol or drugs.
11.  History of previous suicide attempt.
12.  History of physical, mental, emotional, or sexual abuse.
13.  **History of learning disabilities combined with sense of failure.**
14.  Frequent sleeping disorders or complaints.
15.  **Sudden interest in dangerous activities or uncharacteristic risk-taking.**
16.  **Inattention to personal hygiene.**
17.  **Rebelliousness, belligerence.**
18.  **Depression or grief following loss of emotionally supportive "significant other" relationships.**
19.  **Sudden lifting of severe depression.**
20.  Recent withdrawal from therapy or psychological counseling.

Reprinted with permission from Teen Suicide Prevention Task Force.

Although teachers cannot be expected to act as trained experts in the area of psychology, they should be knowledgeable about the early warning signs of teen suicide. If teachers are successfully trained to recognize the danger signs displayed by their students, and if teachers are to have any impact on solving those students' needs, it follows that there must be someone with whom the teachers can discuss their concerns. Even more important, there must be someone to whom students can go for help. This support system will not "just happen." School administrators and their faculty members should be informed about the seriousness of the suicide issue and they must be taught the warning signs. Students must also be informed of assistance programs in existence, the type of support offered, and how to contact the program providers.

Along with suicide prevention programs, the leadership of a school system is wise to develop a plan for responding to student and faculty trauma, grief, or threatened or actual violent acts within a school or with individuals closely connected with the school community. Counselors should be trained and ready to deal with a variety of unexpected situations which cause widespread disruption and/or sadness within the school community. Schools should not only prepare to deal with a wide variety of difficult situations, but the district needs to inform students, staff, and parents of the availability of assistance or support groups. It takes time, recognition of need, and a desire to provide services before a crisis team is developed, but school districts which have prepared for those challenges are able to respond in a positive, supportive manner that assists its students and staff.

# WHEN A STUDENT SWEARS AT YOU

How carefully did you read the title to this reading? Did you notice the title begins with the word "When" not the word "If"? When a student swears at a teacher it is unsettling, and when it occurs to you (and it will), you will be upset.

A situation in which a student swears at a teacher usually erupts quickly, leaving little time for a teacher to plan a course of action. Teachers do not want to say: "What did you call me?" or "Would you repeat that please?" Take a few minutes right now to think about how you would like to react; it may help you in the future.

Unfortunately, in a reaction to this type of situation, a few teachers may have a totally incorrect, spontaneous thought about slapping the student's face. This action by a teacher is completely unacceptable and should be absolutely avoided for several reasons. As the adult authority in the classroom and in order to maintain credibility, the teacher must control that reaction. Also, the teacher runs the risk of injuring the student and of incurring a civil lawsuit and/or criminal charges by the student or his parents. The principal or the board of education may take action against the teacher. Then, too, the teacher may become physically injured, for a student who will swear at a teacher may also hit a teacher.

Another spontaneous reaction which might occur is for the teacher to use similar language directed toward the student or threaten the student with bodily harm. This, too, is fully unacceptable for it continues the teacher-student conflict, arouses class sympathy for the unruly student, may result in legal action against the teacher, and sets a poor example. If the teacher swears at a student a serious leadership problem is created for the teacher. How, in a sense of fairness, can a teacher punish a student when the teacher has acted in the same manner?

When a student swears at a teacher, it cannot and should not be tolerated or ignored. Teachers destroy their own credibility and authority if this problem is allowed to occur and continue. So, what action should a teacher take? It is most important for the teacher to remain as calm as possible. If back-up support is needed the teacher can call the building administrator and request immediate assistance or seek assistance from another teacher who is nearby. At this point in time, the student may need to be directed (and possibly assisted) to leave the classroom. At some point in addressing this problem and finding a solution, the teacher must explain to the student why the comments are totally unacceptable. Lastly, the teacher must determine a punishment which is in accordance with school guidelines/policies and report the incident to the main office for possible administrative action. Often, the teacher can have the student removed from class until a parental conference is held, or until the student offers a genuine apology to the teacher. Some teachers believe that when an offense of this nature is committed in the classroom in front of all the class members, an apology should be given to the teacher in the same manner. A requirement such as this is very difficult for most students to fulfill, and in most cases will not yield satisfactory results.

In dealing with this type of situation there are several things to keep in mind. First, in many homes parents and their children fight and in the general course of the fight, swearing often occurs. So, at the beginning of the school year, students should be informed of your standards and expectations related to this topic. Teachers should clearly state that their classrooms may be different from their students' homes and that swearing (and other offensive language) will not be tolerated. This can be a difficult lesson in the area of self-control, but it is a lesson which students need to learn. Second, teachers must remember they are to be examples of self-controlled individuals and they are to provide a positive classroom environment in which respect for all is fostered. Teachers are role models, whether or not they want to be. Third, teachers should remember that if they put themselves on the student's level in dealing with this problem (e.g., swearing back at the student), they lose the opportunity to set a punishment based on fairness. Additionally, teachers may lose the respect and cooperation of other class members. So, this difficult problem must be handled in a respectable manner. It is acceptable to be angry, and few teacher would not get "hot under the collar" just remember to control the anger. You should not lose your ability to treat a student, even a troublesome one, as a person. In this way you will keep the respect of your other students, and in time possibly even gain the respect - or at the least the cooperation - of the one student who is not well-behaved.

# A STUDENT FAILS YOUR COURSE

The time comes in every teacher's professional life when a student has not earned a passing average in one's course and therefore, fails to pass the course and in some cases, fails to graduate. This can be a difficult time of mixed emotions for a teacher. It is a time to proceed with careful consideration.

During each year of my teaching career, I taught senior social studies courses and there were only a few years when I had no seniors who failed to graduate. In most cases, it is disappointing when a student fails to graduate because s/he did not earn a passing grade. To be frank, it is somewhat less stressful if the student has failed a number of courses, but there are times when the senior has failed only one course, and you are the teacher who makes the final decision related to the student and graduation.

Teachers can maintain a strict "you get what you earn" attitude about grades or they can exercise discretion. In most school systems, there are no absolute patterns of action for a teacher facing this problem, but there are many thoughts which come to the teacher's mind before final failure grades are delivered in the main office. Teachers consider the ability level of the student, the effort extended by the student, and the basic learning accomplished by the student. Teachers think about fairness to all of their students, not just to the one who has failed the course.

Teachers quickly acknowledge their many responsibilities toward a student who is failing a course. Most importantly, the teacher knows the importance of working with the student whenever possible during the school year to increase the opportunity for success while reducing the chance of failure. Teachers also must be careful to warn the student often, encourage the student to improve, contact parents or guardians, and inform guidance personnel and/or the principal. When teachers have met their responsibilities to their students, then they come to realize that most of the responsibility for passing or failing a course truly belongs to the student. Sadly, many students fail to realize that in order to earn a passing grade one must display consistent effort in attendance, assignment completion, and most importantly, they must demonstrate increased knowledge and/or skills.

Students offer many explanations as to why they failed a course, ideas such as: they did not like the course, too much work assigned, saw no reasons for having to take the course, lacked time for attending class and assignment completion, the course was beyond their ability level, personality conflict with the teacher, or any number of additional extenuating circumstances. Whatever the explanation is for the failing grade, the teacher may be asked to review the situation and decide if the grade will be changed so the student can receive credit for the course, and if a senior, graduate.

### Should a teacher pass a student regardless of the earned grade?

In both of the school systems in which I was employed, an average of sixty-five was the lowest possible passing grade. Depending on the circumstances, my quietly held policy was "a final grade average of sixty-three or sixty-four was negotiable." I did require the student to complete certain assignments so the grade was earned, not just given. Students were required to come into my classroom and complete assignments which included correct completion of previous incomplete work, correction of one's final exam, and additional reading and writing assignments.

If a teacher decides to pass a student who has failed a course, I believe it is most important to require the student to satisfactorily complete some assignments. It is important for the student to learn that certain requirements must be met. It is necessary for some of the work to be done to improve the earned average. I believe it is also important for the student to earn the passing average, rather than just receive it as a gift. A high school diploma is a mark of achievement and people look on it as an accomplishment. No one wants to know for the remainder of her/his life that the diploma was given, not earned. It is also important for the teacher's own credibility to require students to make up work. When a passing grade is simply given to a student who had earned a failing grade, other students in a school soon know how to obtain a passing grade from a particular teacher. In fairness to all of the other students in a class, the teacher should not add two-to-four points to a student's failing grade without adding those same points to all students' averages (top students would love to receive additional "gifted" points!).

There are times when a student will fail a course, and the teacher is not inclined to make any grade changes. After an entire semester or year has passed and a student has an average in the thirties, forties, or fifties, there is no sane reason for trying to pass the student. The student has not and cannot complete course requirements and, therefore, should not receive a passing grade for the course.

At times, the teacher may have to explain to parents or administrators how the failing grade was determined. Teachers should clearly explain the course requirements and grade averaging method. Next, teachers should review actions they have taken to assist the student and describe the student's response. Finally, teachers should describe the parental contacts (warning notices and telephone calls) initiated by the teacher. After a clear presentation to the parents and/or administrators, people usually understand the teacher's decision - although they may never appreciate it.

When a student fails to earn a passing average in a course, does a teacher have any options related to the earned average? Generally, yes, the teacher can review the merits of each case and then decide whether or not to work further with the student. There are few general rules other than be fair, consider the overall situation, be consistent, do not be afraid to allow a student to fail, and do not blame yourself for a student's failure if you have consistently met your responsibilities to the student.

### What would you do in each of the following situations?

A student was assigned to your senior elective courses in order to allow the student to meet all graduation requirements. This student was not interested in the curriculum content and she was very angry about being "forced" into the course by guidance personnel. You have been informed of this student's above average ability although you see little evidence of it during class. She does, however, have an above average ability to sustain anger! Every day this student enters your classroom with a disgusted look on her face, sits down at a front desk so her classmates will notice, and promptly puts her head down on the desk in an attempt to fall asleep. Each day you interrupt her nap plans. She completes as little work as possible. Warning notices were sent to her parents and she was informed she would not pass this course if she failed to earn a grade of sixty-five. This goes on for twenty weeks! At the end of the semester, she needs a high-eighties grade on her final exam in order to pass the course. If she had less than a sixty-five average and had been accepted by a college for fall entrance, would you allow her to receive credit for your course and proceed with her college plans? What would you do in this situation? Answer the question before you continue your reading.

On her final exam, this girl received two points more than what was needed in order for her to pass the course. I was quite pleased when I was informed that she had photocopied another student's notebook and studied intensively for her final exam. In this case, I fully intended to postpone her graduation if she had not earned the necessary points for a passing average. Years later I learned of the career choice of this student - she is now a teacher - how I would love to sign up for one of her classes for a week or so!

Another senior student seldom attends your class and completed only an occasional assignment. She is a pleasant girl and has sufficient ability to pass your course; she just does not have the time to come to school and learn. Although it should not have been a surprise, she found it hard to believe she was not going to graduate. She meets with you and tries to convince you to just give her a passing grade. Would you grant her request?

Before grades were final, this girl met with me several times. Our conversations were pleasant; she questioned my position and presented her point of view. She even tried flattery, informing me that I was a very good teacher (an opinion based on only a few days of observation!). Graduation day came for the senior class, but not for this girl. Several years later I was greatly surprised to see her name on my class list for the next semester. She came to class for several days and informed me she now realized what she needed to do to pass the course. She assured me this time she was going to meet course requirements because she wanted to graduate. Her new attitude lasted approximately two weeks when, once again, she failed to attend class or complete assignments. Shortly thereafter she dropped out of my class. Occasionally I see her in our community, and almost thirty years after she failed to graduate, she still reminds me of her anger towards me for not allowing her to graduate.

Sometimes the most valuable lesson students can learn in school is that they must meet their responsibilities and when they fail to do so, they face consequences. At times, it is a painful lesson to learn; but it is still a valuable lesson.

For very low functioning students, the teacher must modify assignments. Teachers can seek the involvement of special education teachers for advice and in-class assistance if the student is identified as a student with special needs. Along with task modification, the teacher can offer additional time to tutor the student during study halls or in an after school session. On occasion, I have read final exams to students whose reading ability level was so low they probably would not have passed the test even though they knew the content. Teachers, in the past, have had considerable amounts of flexibility when working with low ability students, but with increasing requirements related to meeting state standards as documented by state testing, this flexibility is disappearing.

I have had many students with a wide variety of problems, including physical abuse, parental divorce, a death in the family, poverty, mental/emotional problems, substance abuse, and illness. A teacher must be willing to consider extenuating circumstances and difficulties, and then work with students so that the individual is cared for and educational goals are met. It is important to keep the difficulties from becoming a reason or excuse for failure; rather they must be viewed as a personal challenge which can be overcome. Students need help when facing major obstacles, yet at the same time they need to succeed through their own efforts.

Working with a student on a one-to-one basis is an especially effective method for helping a student through a difficult time; often the extra attention stimulates sufficient motivation which then encourages the student to produce good work.

In reviewing extenuating circumstances, I always thought about the impact on the student of failing the course verses the benefit of passing the course. Some students learn a valuable lesson from failing a course; they overcome the problem and go on. Some students are overcome by the failure; they never finish high school and continue to have many problems. How would you handle the following situation? You have had this student in class for two different semester courses. He has basic ability, a definite lack of interest in his own education, and he put forth minimal effort in meeting his academic responsibilities. You notice that he is a follower-type, who has been quite bothersome in class. In the second semester course he had a low but passing average prior to taking the final exam. After the final exam he had a failing average for the course. After being notified of his failure to meet graduation requirements, he comes to school and talks with you; he informs you of his military service plans and apologizes for his disruptions in class. He pleads with you to allow him to graduate. He had passed all of his other courses. Is graduation going to happen for this student? Answer the question before continued reading.

In this case, I believed there was no purpose in keeping him from graduating. This student was given a number of assignments to complete in my classroom. For three days he arrived at my classroom by 8 A.M., and he worked throughout the day. He correctly completed all of the assignments which I gave him. I believed he increased his knowledge of course content, learned the value of completing requirements, and earned his right to graduated with his classmates. He also joined the military as scheduled.

# EXPELLING A STUDENT FROM CLASS

"Get out of my classroom - as far as I'm concerned, you are out of my course!" This is a statement of utter frustration and total futility. It is a statement of last resort, usually voiced in anger, and should rarely, if ever, be said. Seldom do teachers win when they use this statement, for in a short time the student is back in the classroom and must be accommodated.

There probably are no teachers alive who cannot recall a student who deserved to be suspended from their class or expelled from school. Yet in today's public school system, to deny a student's right to an education means a long, involved, and sometimes costly process.

In most cases, the removal of a student from one's class is not a planned action. Usually there is a disagreement between the teacher and a student which leads to an argument, followed by the teacher ejecting the student. The problem between the teacher and the student is not solved by dismissing the student and almost immediately new problems begin. Where does the student go? What other problems does the student create? How will the problem between the teacher and the student be resolved? If a teacher dismisses a student from class, how is the student allowed to return without the teacher losing credibility and the respect of other students?

When a teacher is having a major problem with a student, the teacher should inform the principal or department chairman of the problem and ask for advice or assistance. One of those individuals should review the options available to the teacher for dealing with the student and solving the disagreement. Teachers must learn how to work with students and how to resolve problems with them, but occasionally some assistance is required.

If a teacher becomes embroiled in an unexpected dispute with a student and the teacher decides to remove the student from class, the teacher should verbally limit the removal. For example, the teacher should not say "get out of my classroom and do not ever come back - as far as I am concerned you are permanently out!" Teachers seldom have the power to permanently expel a student from a class. Preferably, the teacher should say something like this: "get out of my classroom, go to the main office (or detention room), and we will solve this problem later." When a student is expelled from class, the teacher should clearly state that the student is removed from class until a solution is reached. The solution may include a meeting with the parent, the principal, or both. All of those actions allow the teacher to re-admit the student without losing the battle. The ousted student learns he is not going to have some time off and then return to class as a hero. Meanwhile, the other students in the class learn that certain behaviors will not be tolerated.

It is very difficult in such a case not to lose one's temper, but teacher self-control is of utmost importance. The teacher has to maintain credibility as an adult who is in control. The teacher should attempt to maintain fairness and sensitivity, yet at the same time the teacher should not be forced to capitulate to student insolence or threats. Also, the teacher must have a working situation in which life in the classroom is not only tolerable, but in most cases, enjoyable. One will not be able to teach students any course content or be a positive role model if there is constant turmoil in the classroom. So, the troublesome student must be dealt with for the student's own good, for the good of all other students in the classroom as well as for the good of the teacher. The teacher should try to solve in-class problems without involving the administration. However, there are those times when the disciplining of a student must include the involvement of administrator(s) and teachers want to know (and have a right to expect) that the administration will support them.

When the disciplined student returns to the classroom, the teacher should not constantly remind the student of past problems. The student should be given the opportunity to demonstrate a changed attitude or improved behavior without being subjected to teacher criticisms. If it becomes apparent that there are no improvements in the student's attitude or behavior, then the teacher may continue to discipline the student and again seek administrative assistance.

# WHEN IN TROUBLE, ASK FOR HELP

At various times throughout one's teaching career help is needed and some of the best people from whom to seek assistance are your colleagues! They understand the difficulties and frustrations of teaching. They can listen to you, analyze the problem clearly, and offer solid advice based on experience. They can also give you much-needed encouragement. There are, however, times when more is required than just general suggestions or encouragement. When a teacher has a major problem, it is advisable to talk with the department chairman or the building principal. The assistance and support of the building administrators are vital to the successful resolution of major problems faced by school teachers.

Any teacher in a given year can experience difficulties within the school setting. However, first-year teachers or those who are new to a school district are especially vulnerable for they have few means of knowing how well they are doing and often do not have a support system. Since their experience may be limited, it is difficult for them to accurately judge their successes or failures. There is the occasional classroom observation, but over all, new teachers are "on their own".

At times it is also difficult for new teachers to judge the seriousness of a problem. Some teachers will make a mountain out of a mole hill; others will face mountainous problems and may not even realize the seriousness of the situation until the problem is well developed. One must learn to recognize the difference between an annoyance and a serious problem.

During my first year of teaching, one of my senior classes was very difficult to control. The class contained far too many talkative people. They were a nice collection of personalities, but they had so little self-control. It seemed most of the students felt free to say whatever they wanted, whenever they felt like it, I was continuously telling my students to stop talking and pay attention to class activities, and that bothered me. Finally, I decided I had given sufficient warnings and something more had to be done. I went to the principal and discussed the problem. He suggested I remove the most troublesome student from class until the student agreed to control his comments. We agreed that the next time my students did not do as instructed, I would choose the most disruptive student and send him to the office. It didn't take long to choose my candidate! The next day in class, a large outdoorsman-type fellow tested my patience. I told him to go to the main office, find the principal, and tell the principal he could not behave in my class. However, that big, brave young man refused to go. Now what was I to do? I could not take his arm and walk him to the door and he continued to refuse to leave. So, I sat down on my chair behind my desk and said, "I will not teach anything more in this class until you students learn to do as you are told." Then I just sat quietly and looked at all of my students. They all began to show their embarrassment at their poor behavior and eventually began to call for "Peter" to leave. He finally left, and I immediately began teaching again, this time with improved student behavior. What happened to Peter? The principal informed him he was out of my course unless he could convince me to allow him to return. As soon as class was over, Peter was at the door, very apologetic and asking to be reinstated. We had a rather long discussion, followed by my accepting him back into the class. His behavior never was a problem again, and the general behavior of all of the class members improved noticeably as well. My students finally realized they must improve their behavior in order to stay in my course. A word of caution: Beware! It's not always that easy to solve a class behavior problem.

Looking back on the classroom situation just described, I believe that I made a mountain out of a mole hill. When the problem first began to be irritating, I should have used the school detention system or contacted a few parents on the telephone. Clearly, that type of problem should be resolved by the classroom teacher. On the other hand, if a teacher has a student who is uncontrollable in the classroom or a threat to the health and well-being of the other students in the classroom or to the teacher, the principal should be informed and expected to take immediate, definite action. To allow serious situations to continue is to not even see the mountain.

What are some of the indicators which show you may need the help or support of colleagues or administrators? When you dread going to one (or all) of your classes, something is wrong. When one or more students in a classroom are uncontrollable and able to totally disrupt a class, you need help. When many students are failing your course, changes must be made.

When it becomes obvious that a problem exists and you do not have a solution, choose a friendly teacher who appears to be well-respected professionally and with whom you feel comfortable. The teacher to whom you go may or may not be from your department. Ask that person if she/he would be willing to meet with you and give you some advice. Few teachers would refuse to talk with a troubled teacher. Be honest in your description of the problem(s) and then listen to the advice given. When more than one solution is offered, choose the suggestion which you think would best solve your particular problem. If you believe the problem is beyond your ability to solve or you desire the support of your department chairman or principal, then meet with one or both of them.

Some teachers are too afraid or too embarrassed to ask for help from another teacher, their department chairman, or principal. Troubled teachers often believe that if they seek help from others they are showing themselves to be weak or unable to meet performance expectations. They may also fear the possibility of losing their job if their classroom problems are discussed. Therefore, troubled teachers often continue to struggle in silence, and their problems not only persist but often grow to be more troublesome. What teachers with major problems fail to realize is that serious classroom problems are quickly noticed by competent administrators and unresolved problems will often affect the administrator's decision concerning contract renewal offers.

There are times when new teachers have serious difficulties and they receive little or no assistance or mentoring. Maybe those teachers were afraid to ask for help or too embarrassed to admit they needed help. Maybe the teacher experiencing difficulties failed to receive some very much needed support from colleagues since many teachers think they should not offer unrequested advice and others believe that "all teachers must learn to make it in the classroom on their own." For whatever reason, it is disappointing when a new teacher is not adequately assisted and mentored and then permanently leaves the teaching profession.

All experienced teachers should recognize a professional responsibility to new teachers and remember to offer needed assistance to any new teacher or veteran who is experiencing a difficult time. Ask how things are going in the new teacher's classroom. When possible, give the teacher an honest compliment. Allow that person the freedom to discuss any teaching problem, and be sure to let new teachers know that even the best teachers have some difficult situations each year.

During my first year of teaching, I was greatly encouraged by a teacher in a department other than my own. We had many of the same students and the same free period. We discussed numerous ideas. She often gave me insights into the art of teaching and how to form positive working relationships with the students. She passed on complimentary statements made by our mutual students. She assured me that I was performing well and her encouragement was of utmost importance to me. That kind of assistance is what most new teachers need. New teachers do not want someone to do the work for them, but they often do need just a little assistance, a little encouragement, someone to talk with and from whom they can learn. I never forgot that teacher's kindness to me nor her willingness to advise me, and later on I assisted other teachers in the same manner.

Some school districts have an established mentor program to assist new teachers in each building. The new teacher is assigned to an experienced teacher who has volunteered to work in the program. Usually the mentor teacher is from the same department as the mentee and may also teach on the same grade level. During my first year of teaching I was included in such a program. My mentor teacher and I shared a classroom, and taught some of the same courses so we shared ideas about tests, projects, grading, and classroom control methods. She also guided me as I became familiar with the policies, practices, and programs available in the high school. Her support was vital to me and so was her friendship.

The greatest advantage of a support system is that it gives new teachers security. There is someone available from whom to seek advice without creating a threatening situation for yourself. Many new teachers are hesitant about too quickly approaching a department chairman or building principal with problems; however, the mentor is readily available and not part of the administration.

Another difficulty faced by all teachers at one time or another is a feeling of isolation from their colleagues. There is very little unclaimed time in which to share ideas, develop new programs, solve problems, or even to vent.

Some teachers are so busy with their own classes, students, and other activities, that they seldom notice their colleagues. It may sound trite, but interaction between teachers is important, so necessary and beneficial - take the time, even if it is only a few minutes, to visit with or come to know another teacher in your building.

There are many different problems found within a school community, but there are an equal number of solutions! There are many different personalities, educational philosophies, and personal beliefs represented among a school faculty - a fact which can bring extraordinary strength and resiliency. It is vital for those people work together to improve their teaching skills and their impact within the school community. Encourage the free flow of ideas, build a spirit of cooperation, and enjoy the give and take which comes from people who care about one another.

**Chapter 19**

# OVER THE FOOTHILLS

Most of the problems faced by teachers within a school year are easily categorized as irritations, some being more serious than others. Those problems can raise teachers' blood pressure and add to the stress familiar to many, yet those problems should not be overwhelming. Learning to cope with the "less than desirable" situations seems to be a necessary part of a teacher's career.

# THE DREADED OBSERVATION

From the very first day you enter the school building as a teacher, you are noticed. Your department chairman and your principal(s) will observe your attitude, appearance, language, and your relationships with students, faculty, and staff. Each day you are actively building your reputation, so create a positive reputation by consistently acting in a professional, courteous, and confident manner!

Shortly after school opens, you will begin to hear about observational visits for the purpose of evaluating your performance as a classroom teacher. Usually the observations are completed by the department chairperson or other building administrator. The number of observations required for non-tenured and tenured teachers varies within different states and is usually defined in the teacher's contract. An observation usually lasts for one class period, and it can be pre-arranged or unannounced. The administrator will complete a written report describing the academic environment and teacher effectiveness. Within a few days the observer is required to review the written evaluation with the teacher to compliment the positive observations and, if necessary, review suggestions for improvement. Teachers are usually given the right to reply to any comment included within the report.

One time when I was observed, the principal made note of the fact that I arrived late for my class (not the type of comment a non-tenured teacher wants to have on an observational report). After explaining to the principal, that I was at another assigned duty which did not end until the same time my class was scheduled to begin, I was given the opportunity to include my response on the observational report and the criticism was neutralized. The scheduled class and duty time conflict was not resolved; I continued to go to the duty and arrive late for my class.

The observational report (or evaluation) becomes a part of a teacher's employment file within the school district. The reports are reviewed by the administration, usually the superintendent and building principal, when deciding whether or not to renew a probationary teacher's contract for another year or to recommend tenure. Those observational reports are, therefore, very important to one's teaching career. After each evaluation process is completed, the teacher should be given a copy of the evaluation report and it should be kept at home in an employment related folder.

Most teachers categorize an observational session somewhere between unsettling and artificial to downright nerve-wracking. From my first through my last classroom observation many years later, I was always stressed and felt as though the class period would never end.

There are some ways to reduce the nervousness associated with an observation. Read a copy of the observational form so that you are cognizant of the teaching skills and practices to be evaluated. Always be well prepared for class presentations; then if you are unexpectedly observed, you have a workable plan. If you are having a pre-arranged observation, include a student assignment which you can supervise. Although it is important to include all students in class activities, remember that your students may be somewhat hesitant to "perform" with an observer in the room, so do not put students "on the spot." Sometimes students think they are the ones being observed so they are especially quiet and well behaved! If you wish to have involved student responses, give the students a few minutes to organize their thoughts and then build from that point.

Observers evaluate the total classroom environment including lesson content, instructional methods, student involvement in planned activities, teacher rapport with students, and teacher classroom management skills. Teachers should try to change classroom activities several times during each class period in order to maintain student interest and involvement (this holds true whether or not the teacher is being observed). The change of activities should be smooth and related to the overall lesson plan. When students are working individually, teachers should walk around the room and question students about their work (this, too, should be done even when not being observed); this is relaxing for the teacher and helps the students to feel comfortable as well.

There are some ideas teachers should keep in mind while being observed. Teachers should not constantly look at the observer; without being rude, try to ignore the observer for you are teaching a class not starring in a performance. Do not develop an on-the-spot quiz to use up class time; it will be obvious that the quiz was not a part of the planned lesson. Do not be intimidated by a particular student's poor behavior; correct the student and insist on appropriate behavior, then go on with the lesson.

Finally, teachers should be pleasant, enthusiastic, and conscious of students' needs and their behavior. Remember, even though the observation period seems to last forever, it does end.

# TEMPORARY LEAVE POLICIES

There are a number of different types of paid leave available to teachers. Temporary and long-term leave policies, as well as the number of days available in each leave category, are defined in the contract between the teacher's association and the school district. It is advisable to become familiar with the different types of leave provided and how to apply or qualify for the available days. Most teachers have some or all of the following types of temporary leave granted to them: sick, business, bereavement, professional (conferences), jury duty, and association business days for elected association members.

At the beginning of every school year, teachers are usually notified of the total number of sick days credited to them. When given the new total, teachers should check the total with their own records. If any discrepancies exist, review the records with personnel in the administrative office. If there is a mistake, it should be rectified as soon as possible.

My school district gave fourteen days per year, and I used approximately seven to nine sick days each year. Some teachers used few sick days; others took all fourteen days each year. The New York State Board of Regents wants teacher absences to be no more than a total of seven days per year for any reason. (Somewhat idealistic?)

There is absolutely nothing wrong with taking sick leave from school when ill, but teachers should not abuse this privilege. Since teacher attendance is vital to learning opportunities for students, teachers should be in school when able. It is also important to save some sick days, if possible; they may be needed in the future.

Temporary sick leave, referred to as sick days, is available to teachers for short-term use; they do not provide long-term protection at the beginning of a teacher's career. Sick leave is usually cumulative, meaning unused days are saved by the teacher and are added to the next year's allotment. Often there is a limit placed on the number of accumulated sick days which can be credited to a teacher (200-250 days). Those days, once accumulated, can be especially important in the case of long-term teacher disability resulting from illness, accident, or for maternity disability leave.

Some contracts between school districts and teachers' associations allow teachers to use a limited number of their temporary sick leave days for family illness as well.

If, by contract, you are given the opportunity to join a sick bank, it is advisable to do so. When teachers join a sick bank they are usually required to donate several of their temporary sick days to the pool and in exchange they are entitled to a stated number of sick days for a serious disability. The sick bank days are not available to an individual teacher until after all of the individual's accumulated sick days have been used. The sick bank ordinarily provides paid sick days only for long-term illnesses or disability. In my school district, a teacher joining the sick bank contributes two sick days and receives two hundred days of protection for an extended illness or disability. The long-term protections of joining a sick bank are obvious, but there is another important advantage. If a teacher decides to purchase disability income insurance, the policy could be written with a two-hundred-day waiting period, thus greatly reducing the cost of premiums without decreasing protection.

Business leave or personal days are also made available to teachers and those days are usually non-cumulative. Some contracts between school districts and teachers' associations restrict the use of personal days by stating specific conditions for their use, such as for conducting business which can only be done during school hours, attending a funeral or a graduation, or for religious holidays. Some school districts make no limits on the use of personal days, thus some teachers use them for shopping, golfing, or a long weekend. Here again, teachers should be prudent in their use of personal days, but if an absence is necessary and fits the category then use a personal day.

Many school districts also grant teachers paid bereavement leave to be used when a death occurs in the teacher's immediate family or to a corresponding member of the spouse's family. Again, the specifics of the bereavement leave policy are defined in the contract.

In addition to sick and personal leave, teachers have many opportunities to attend special-interest conferences and are often encouraged to do so. It is important for teachers to take those opportunities as they are presented. Attending a conference provides teachers with an opportunity to learn new ideas and trends, meet other teachers and educational leaders, and exchange viewpoints with other professionals. Informed, intellectually stimulated teachers bring new ideas back to their school district and make valuable contributions to their school community.

Teachers should keep records of all days off due to sickness, personal leave, and conferences. I wrote the dates of absences on a "Notes" page in the back of my plan book. Often, plan books must be returned to the school district office or to the building principal at the end of the school year. So, if you record your days absent from school on a page in the plan book, remember to remove the page before leaving your plan book in the main office; then, save the page with your personal records.

In all cases, each teacher must decide whether or not an absence from school is necessary. If you are ill, have personal business which can only be completed during school hours, or are attending a conference, take the day off and do not feel guilty about it.

The difficulty with being absent from school is the expectation that the teacher will supply lesson plans for the substitute teacher. Some teachers use emergency lesson plans - written for use anytime within a school year. Emergency lesson plans generally are curriculum general and simply provide students with an opportunity to practice or review course content. A more difficult and time consuming lesson plan to write is a current content lesson modified for a substitute teacher.

In addition to temporary leave policies, many contracts between school districts and teachers associations contain extended leave policies. Extended leave policies are for long term absences due to child rearing, military service, or other personal reasons. Often, but not always, extended leave is granted with restrictions and without pay. When granted an extended leave, the teacher must honor any listed restrictions in order to maintain the leave and protect a teaching position to which she/he can return.

# THE "BEE" IN THE CLASSROOM

Whenever your classroom windows are open, there is a potential crisis - the entrance of a yellow jacket or a hornet! This event can totally disrupt even the best-behaved class receiving the most well-planned lesson. Often hornets will stay near the ceiling or the lights, but yellow jackets like to dive at both students and teachers sending them in all directions! Flies are annoying; bees and hornets are dangerous. Many students and teachers are allergic to bee stings, so the panic which occurs in the classroom is not just frivolous activity.

What should teachers do when the classroom is interrupted by a yellow jacket or hornet? Since hornets like to stay near the lights or ceiling, they may be successfully ignored, but yellow jackets are more troublesome. Observe the yellow jacket's "flight plan" for a few minutes, and try to determine if you will have an opportunity to knock it out of commission or convince it to go back out the window. You might as well accept the interruption and make the best of it (with a little luck, this will not be the class in which your principal is completing a classroom observation!). It is suggested that you keep a fly swatter in your room; it's a most effective weapon against all insect intruders. A magazine or newspaper is a good second choice, but please, not the book you are presently reading! Once the insect is destroyed your students will settle down quickly and everyone can get back to work. Crisis over!

# STUDENT HEALTH ISSUES

Some students come to school even when they do not feel well. Sometimes an illness will strike students as they sit in the classroom. Often you can tell by looking at certain students that they are not well. If a student who is obviously sick requests a pass to the health office, give him one! Quickly! It may be advisable to send a dependable student along with the sick student to insure the student's safe arrival at the health office. Much to my relief, I have never had a student pass out, vomit, or have a seizure in any of my classes.

Every teacher should know how to handle certain situations of student accident or illness just in case they occur in the classroom. What should the teacher do for the student? Should you send for the nurse? Should you empty the classroom? Generally, schools give teachers a list of students with health problems. If you learn that one of your students has a serious health problem (such as seizures, allergic reaction, diabetes), ask the school nurse for advice on how to handle problems the student might experience before they occur in the classroom. You could also talk privately with the student or with the parents to learn what should be done if the student becomes ill.

A teacher must use good judgment concerning students and health problems. Teachers must realize they have limited ability to deal with sick or injured students, but teachers do have the responsibility of deciding from whom to seek help. The health office is in existence to evaluate a student's health situation, determine if a parent should be informed, or call for immediate health assistance.

There have been times when I have allowed a student to go to the health office, and later learned about an instant recovery the student enjoyed several minutes after arriving in the health office. The student's quick recovery even allowed him to complete a homework assignment for his next class. Needless to say, some students would have a difficult time obtaining another pass to the health office from me! Most students, however, will not abuse the privilege of requesting a pass to the health office.

When students asked for a pass to the rest rooms, I almost always granted their request, especially for girls. When certain students formed a rest room habit, I discussed the situation with them; if a valid reason was stated a pass would continue to be given, otherwise passes would be denied.

Occasionally, the school nurse will give prescribed medications, but only after receiving a physician's written orders. Teachers should never voluntarily give any medications to students. Remember this: Do not give any medications to students and do not allow students to "help themselves" from your personal supply of non-prescription medicines. Teachers can create serious situations for themselves if they dispense medicine.

There are some actions a teacher can and should take when a student becomes ill or is injured in class. Teachers should keep a box of tissues in their rooms for student use especially during the winter months. Often the health office will supply boxes of tissues if requested to do so. If a student develops a nosebleed, give him some tissues and ask him what he would like to have done for him. If a student is seriously coughing, ask the student if he would like to go to the water fountain for a drink. If a student vomits in class, send the student to the health office accompanied by another student. Take the remaining students to a study hall and stay with your students (do not just add your students to the study hall teacher's responsibilities), then, send for the custodian!

All teachers could benefit from taking a first aid course; however, science, industrial arts, and physical education teachers, as well as coaches, are often required to take such a course. Red Cross First Aid courses are often available on a local basis, and teachers may be able to receive in-service credit for completing the course. Although an accident is more likely to happen in one of the above mentioned classes or situations, students can get hurt in any class. If an accident does happen, assess the situation quickly, take necessary action to help the student or other injured person(s), send for help if needed, then panic! Remember, too, there are usually other people in the building who can assist you: teachers in other rooms, students in your classroom or in the hallways, or you may be able to call the main office through the intercom system. It is much better to be prepared for this type of situation and not ever need to use your knowledge, than to need the knowledge and not possess it.

# OOPS, I MADE A MISTAKE!

Occasionally, a teacher makes a mistake in class. The teacher may state incorrect information, make an error in grading, or wrongly answer a student's question.  Once, on an American history test for my students, I misspelled the word "illiterate."  That was especially embarrassing for me because I was absent from school the day the test was given and the substitute teacher found and corrected the error in class!

All teachers at one time or another will make an embarrassing error and there is no "best way" to deal with such a situation.  It can cause a range of emotions:  embarrassment, silliness, irritation, or even anger.  When you make a mistake in class, do not deny it or feel you must explain it.  Admit the mistake if need be and go on.  Sometimes everyone can enjoy a good laugh about it, even the teacher.

Occasionally when I made a mistake in class, I would explain to my class that I always allowed myself the privilege of making one mistake each year in order to keep me humble.  If the mistake occurred early in the year, I told my students I would have to be very careful for the remainder of the year.  If the mistake took place late in the year, I told my students I wanted to get my mistake in before the year was over.  Some students laughed, some did not know how to react, and I think a few students really believed my speech!  Once in a while a student would speak up and tell me I said the same thing the last time I made a mistake.  Interestingly, sometimes students accurately remember what we tell them!

There have been times in my classroom when I have made a mistake and it became a humorous situation.  It is great when a sense of humor can help you get through a mistake.  Using your sense of humor can also increase your ability to keep students interested and involved in classroom activities.  Most students enjoy a teacher who not only has a sense of humor, but who is willing to use it.

The most unforgettable mistake I made in class occurred in one of my senior elective courses.  It was by far my most embarrassing moment in the classroom.  I was presenting information related to advertising and had taken a variety of advertisements out of magazines.  I planned to discuss the different approaches and motivations used by advertisers to increase sales.  I also wanted to show students how advertisers tie their product to other totally unrelated ideas.  One of the advertisements I had chosen was for hope chests.  I discussed how the company attached the idea of love to their product.  I should have said, "How can a wooden box be related to love?"  Instead, I said, "What can be romantic about a chest?"  I instantly knew I was in trouble for that question and would pay dearly.  One man-about-town young fellow spoke up and said, "Would you like me to answer that question, Mrs. Johnson?"  At that moment, I was wishing most of my students were engrossed in private conversations, doing homework for another class, or even sleeping.  Instead, every student in the class was paying close attention to my statements, and then, laughing hysterically while thoroughly enjoying the vibrant rainbow of reds appearing on their teacher's face. Once I was again able to speak, I simply said, "Is anyone interested in what I have to say about the next advertisement?" They all answered with an enthusiastic "Yes!"

There are some mistakes teachers make in the classroom which are not humorous and should be avoided. There is no valid reason for a teacher to swear, use obscene or crude words within the school setting. There is no need for ethnic jokes, demeaning names, or extreme criticism. How we talk to students in our classrooms and throughout the school does make an impression. Language should be used to set an example of responsible adult behavior, to foster respect, and to encourage those around us.

Teachers must exercise care not only in the choice of words they use, but also in the choice of topics for discussion with their students. Teachers should not discuss with their students major personal problems such as marital problems, legal difficulties, on-the-job disputes, nor should they discuss their salary. Students should not be the people to whom teachers air their problems, vent their frustrations, or go to for sympathy. This does not mean teachers cannot mention their family, an enjoyable vacation, a sick child, or the desire for a new car; it simply means teachers must be prudent in their conversations with students.

The classroom should not be a place where students are allowed to discuss their opinions of other teachers or their disagreements with them. One cannot control students' opinions about their teachers, but the classroom is not the place for those discussions. Along the same line, teachers should not discuss with their students their dislike or lack of respect for a particular school administrator, nor should teachers allow an in-class dissection of another student's personality, grades, or past record. The classroom simply is not the proper forum for those discussions.

There are times when a student may be having a serious problem with another teacher and the student comes to you for advice. During your discussion it is possible that criticisms may be made against the other teacher. The statement of criticisms should not be fostered, rather the student should be directed toward possible actions which could be taken to solve the problem and improve the situation. Encourage the student to talk about the problem with the teacher involved. If that fails, suggest an intermediary to meet with both the teacher and the student. It is important to assist students who are having problems with interpersonal relationships; yet at the same time it is a mistake to become the one to whom most students go whenever they want to complain about another teacher.

Mistakes are bound to happen during each year of a teacher's career. Even though a teacher may be frustrated or embarrassed, it is not the end of the world. Each of us should learn from our mistakes, make needed corrections, and then move on to the next challenge.

When speaking to your students, remember what you say and how you say it makes a difference. Your speech has an impact and it can influence your students' opinions and actions. Remember, too, that along with the freedom to choose the topics of conversation in the classroom comes the responsibility to have proper discussions. Teachers have been given the authority and the responsibility to create a positive classroom atmosphere; make sure the atmosphere is protective of individual rights and encourages respect, tolerance, and decency. Classroom discussions can and should be constructive, supportive, and ethical.

# WHERE SHALL I LIVE?

Shortly after signing an employment agreement with a school district, most teachers begin to think about housing. Based on the current levels of teachers' salaries, few teachers will seriously consider an immediate purchase of a home or the renting of a penthouse apartment. If by accepting a job one must make a geographical move, there is a very important question to contemplate: "Shall I live inside or outside of the school district in which I am employed?"

The type of apartment or home in which a teacher chooses to live is largely determined by personal preference. It seems most teachers can find very acceptable housing inside or outside of the district in which they are employed, so the decision of "where to live" becomes important for other reasons.

Living in the district in which one is employed has some important advantages. There is little time wasted in traveling to and from school, an important consideration especially in a geographic area known for difficult winter driving conditions. Also car expenses for gas, tires, insurance, and car replacement are reduced.

For teachers who have children, it can be very important to live and work in the same district. As teachers, they will become acquainted with faculty members who will instruct their children and as parents they will have the same school calendar as their children including the same weather related days off - it works well.

Many teachers who live and work in the same school district appreciate the sense of belonging in the community. Teachers feel they have the opportunity to know their students better because it is easier to attend more after school activities such as clubs, socials, and sports events. It is also easier to meet more of their students' parents and to get in touch with them if necessary. Teachers who live and work in the same school district often know some of the business, religious, and social leaders in the community and they tend to learn more about the community and its issues. With that background teachers can better assist their students in dealing with both individual and community concerns. For teachers who are both pragmatists and homeowners in the district in which they work, there is the opportunity to see their taxes at work!

There are some very important disadvantages to be reviewed by the person considering living and working in the same school district. A major problem, especially in a small district is the loss of privacy. In a rural district news of where a teacher lives, and what a teacher does, travels fast. During my first year of teaching, I began to date the man I later married. His home was located at the northern part of the school district and my apartment was located at the southern part of the district. To get to my apartment from his home, I had to travel through a small town with a village square. Early in May, the older students from the high school would gather there and "hang out" until midnight or so. One night, when I came driving through the community, my students were all standing around waving at me! The next day one of those students asked me if I had completed grading the last test I had given. I said "No." He jokingly told me that if I would get home at a reasonable hour I would have time to grade those tests! He was right but I was not going to agree with him. I simply replied, "There's more to life than grading papers!" Eventually I finished grading the tests. I also continued to see the students late at night at the village square!

Another disadvantage about living and working in the same school district is the impossibility of going to any store, library, church, or social function without seeing someone from school, be it a student, parent, school administrator, staff or faculty member. Sometimes it is nice to be unknown.

Not all of the times when one sees students outside of the school setting are pleasant. There have been times while driving in the community that I received deliberate, unprovoked obscene gestures from students. There have also been times when I felt somewhat threatened by a student's comments related to knowing where I lived. Those times are understandably upsetting, but they do not happen often.

Short travel time between school and home was discussed as an advantage, but it can also be a disadvantage. Sometimes teachers need some down time between when they leave school and when they collect their children and continue active parental responsibilities. Maybe a half-hour ride each day would have been therapeutic.

Approximately half of my colleagues lived outside of the school district for reasons of preference and privacy. Some of the teachers lived in the urban area of Albany; others lived in the communities surrounding our district. As with living in the district, there are also advantages and disadvantages to living outside of the school district in which one is employed. Those who live in an urban area such as Albany enjoy the many conveniences, services, and wide choice of entertainment available. The extra travel time is not considered to be a major problem because of the easy access provided by major highways. Often, teachers car pool, thus reducing individual car expenses. Car pooling also provides an opportunity for teachers to share ideas and problems with colleagues as well as time to vent. The travel time to and from school provides time to make the transition from home, to job, and back to home. Even though mornings may be somewhat rushed, most of the teachers who live outside of the district feel it is worthwhile to do so.

A few of the disadvantages to living outside of the district in which one is employed are related to distance. There is a loss of useful time due to increased travel. Car expenses are increased and winter travel can be hazardous and stressful. Additionally, some teachers who are also parents may have a different school calendar from that of their children.

So, where shall I live? The choices available to each teacher offer many opportunities, advantages, and disadvantages. Before making a choice, maybe it would be a good idea to talk with several teachers who live within the school district to learn something about that district. Decide what factors are important to you, and then make your choice accordingly.

# THOSE EXTRA-DUTY BLUES

In many schools teachers are assigned certain duties or responsibilities which are in addition to teaching one's classes. Throughout my teaching career, my colleagues and I have been assigned all of the following types of duties: monitoring study halls, patrolling the hallways during class time, searching lockers, monitoring smoking areas (no longer an assigned duty although a continuing problem for schools), checking the student parking lot, policing the cafeteria during lunch periods, directing homeroom activities, monitoring exams, checking student rest rooms, attending assemblies with students, conducting emergency bus exiting drills, chaperoning extracurricular activities, advising clubs, and coaching sports teams. Most of the extra duties are not particularly enjoyable; they simply must be done in order to effectively guide student behavior.

Extra duties must be conducted by a responsible adult, but it is not legally required or totally necessary for teachers to be assigned to all of those duties. Many school districts employ adults who are not teachers to fill teacher aide positions. Those aides then conduct most, if not all, of the extra duties so teachers can devote more time to their students and course work. If a school district does not employ teacher aides, teachers might try to negotiate the hiring of aides during contract talks.

There are some problems with the hiring of teacher aides. It is often difficult to find qualified people who can adequately handle the job and want to be so employed. Since the job is usually a low-paying one, it can also be difficult to keep good teacher aides on a long term basis. Students often perceive a difference between a teacher and an aide, and at times will offer more resistance to an aide. The hiring of aides also increases the expenditures of a school district.

As long as teachers are obligated by the contract to monitor extra duties, it is important that they perform the duties as assigned. Some of the extra duties are tolerable and others seem intolerable; yet the teacher is expected to attend all the assigned duties, not just complete the ones of personal choice.

School administrators alone cannot be responsible for a smooth-running school; they need the help, support, and cooperation of teachers. Although many of the extra duties assigned to teachers are undesirable and often have us questioning the professionalism of our teaching positions, they must be performed when agreed to by individual or association contracts. School administrators generally do not assign teachers monitoring duties to make the teacher's life more difficult; the monitoring duties are assigned so students are properly supervised at a reasonable, affordable cost to the district.

# STUDENT TARDINESS

It is important for teachers to begin classes promptly. To do this it is necessary for students to arrive on time with all their required classroom supplies such as pen or pencil, textbook, notebook, and completed assignments.

Motivating students to arrive promptly for class is usually not a major problem. At the beginning of the school year teachers should discuss the tardiness issue with their students and clearly state their rules concerning tardiness. Teachers should know the school's policies regarding student attendance, tardiness, and passes. Those policies should then be incorporated into the teachers' expectations.

In an attempt to keep students (and teachers) on schedule, most high schools have a bell system which rings when classes are to begin and end. Many schools have policies which require students to have a pass before entering a classroom after the bell indicating classes are to begin has sounded. Some school districts hire hall monitors to keep students moving toward their next classroom. Sometimes teachers are required to position themselves in the hallways to encourage students to go to their next class. All of those systems can be effective in getting students to class on time; however, those methods do not require students to assume responsibility for arriving at the proper classroom, on time, and with all necessary supplies in hand. It is far less irritating to both students and teachers when students assume the responsibility for promptly arriving in the classroom - students are not hassled, teachers are not upset, and the class is not interrupted. When taught that promptness is required and penalties for tardiness are enforced, most students will arrive on time as required, and ready for class activities.

When students are allowed to linger in the hallways, they often have (and sometimes take) the opportunity to create disturbances away from classrooms. Teachers who allow students to enter the classroom late without penalty contribute to the problem of unsupervised students. Those teachers also create problems for themselves since their classes will be interrupted many times. Colleagues may also be offended since some of them may be required to deal with the student disturbances in the hallways

Students will on occasion have an excellent excuse for arriving late for class without a required pass. It is nice to be able to believe the explanations offered by students and exhibit your trust in them, but it is not always possible. It is also a "must" for teachers to treat everyone with the same consideration. If you allow a reliable student to enter your classroom late and without a pass, you should also be willing to allow a less reliable student to enter your classroom late and without a pass. Sometimes you overlook a student's late arrival if it is an unusual event for the student. - it can be a tough call. When a teacher does not allow students to enter the classroom without a pass after the late bell has sounded, other problems may be created. Where can students go to obtain a required pass and how long will that take? What other interruptions will occur to other classes and again to your own if you require students to obtain a pass from another teacher or the main office? Is there room for "reasonableness and consistency"? Teachers need to have an effective method for working with late arriving students which will cause the students to arrive on time of their own volition. It is possible to guide students so they do as you want –

simply make the alternative unattractive to students without greatly increasing your own work load.

One year I had a class of seniors who very much enjoyed the social aspects of high school. About ten or twelve of those nice people simply could not get to class on time. They were always visiting a "special friend," discussing the latest sports game, busy looking in their locker for their notebook, etc., etc., etc.

The tardiness problem started very gradually and just continued to grow. I was always waiting for those people to arrive and class presentations were beginning as much as five minutes late. I decided it was time to take definite action to encourage prompt arrival by those students, so for three days I told my students: "Starting on Monday, late arrivals are not going to be without penalty, so make sure you get yourself to class on time."

Over the weekend I prepared a "Late Sign-In Sheet." The sheet had four columns with the following titles: Name, Date, Time, and Number of Minutes Late. On Monday, just before my class was to begin, I placed the sign-in sheet on a student desk in the front of the room. When the bell rang indicating it was time to start the class, I closed the door and immediately started teaching the lesson. One by one as the "late arrivals" came into the room, I told them to sign-in on the sheet and what time to write in the "Time" column. The students were told that we would discuss the sheet at the end of class. A few minutes before the class was to end, I picked up the sign-in sheet and began to explain what was happening. I reminded the students that they had been told to arrive on time as of this day. Then I stated that our class was going to start on time and student tardiness to class was going to end. Students were told the late sign-in sheet would be used in their class for the remainder of the marking term. Each day when students arrived late for class without a valid pass, they were to sign-in on the sheet. When a student accumulated a total of ten late minutes, an afternoon detention with me would be assigned and a telephone call would be placed to the student's parent. If the student missed my detention s/he would be reported to the assistant principal who would assign two detentions. If students were caught writing the incorrect time on the sign-in sheet they received an additional five late minutes to their total.

What were the results of this plan? It worked well! Students arrived on time without being hassled and I was able to start class on time without many interruptions. The students accepted the new system as fair to all. A few students came to class a minute or two late once in a while, but the major problem ended. Only one student collected over ten minutes. She was assigned a detention, skipped it, and received two detentions from the main office which she did attend. The record keeping for this system was simple. Every so often I reviewed the sheet and totaled the late minutes for each student. The sign-in sheet was only three-quarters full by the end of the school year. One student, who had received three late-minutes during the course, waited outside of my classroom on the last day of class for six minutes (so he would have a total of nine late-minutes). He claimed my system had "inconvenienced him" and this was his way of protesting. He also said he did not want to receive a detention on the last day of class so he kept his total to nine late-minutes instead of going for ten. At that instant I realized my system was quite effective and even more successful than I had expected.

# TODAY'S NEWS...

Teachers should begin each day listening to the news report on the TV or radio. Knowing about changing world events and incorporating the information into class discussions broadens the students' understanding of their world and improves the quality of classroom discussions.

Also, while listening to the TV or radio, teachers may hear an announcement related to their school district. Occasionally, schools are unexpectedly closed due to inclement weather, water problems, boiler failure, or power outage. Since it is much more enjoyable to learn of the school closing before driving to school, you have one more reason to develop the habit of listening to a news broadcast in the morning while you are preparing for the day.

# PART VIII

# ENRICHING OUR LIVES

**(SPECIAL MOMENTS IN TIME)**

Your students —
each one is unique, each one is important!

# Chapter 20

# STUDENTS ARE "AMAZING PEOPLE"

In order to be successful in teaching, individual teachers must first be truly interested in each one of their students. We must care about our students while assisting them to grow academically and personally. Without caring for our students we will not have much success in teaching them. Most students, whether or not they are experiencing difficulties, want to know they are important to their teachers and are very appreciative when a teacher responds to them. It is of utmost importance to reach out to students who are experiencing especially difficult times and show them by our actions that we care. Students need the educational opportunity and structure we provide throughout our courses, but they need more. They need our kindness, our attention, and our guidance. Reaching out to students can take many forms.

At the beginning of one school year, one of my eleventh grade students suffered the loss of a brother due to a tragic motorcycle accident. I had not known the older brother, but it was obvious that my student was very sad. Many of the teachers in the school were also quite upset by their former student's death and sent sympathy cards to "Mr. and Mrs. and Family." I carefully chose a sympathy card, and after writing a personal note, I mailed it to my student. Within a week the student returned to class and I assisted him in making up back work. He was very quiet, yet he seemed much more responsive to me after returning to school. Shortly thereafter, I left school on a maternity leave. When I returned to school a year later, this student was in one of my second semester classes. He took his school work much more seriously and he worked harder for me than he had during the previous year. At the end of the year he wrote a note to me as he signed my school yearbook. He stated that he worked hard in my class "because I respect and care for you, and I wanted to become one of your better students." I believe his increased desire in my class was due to receiving the sympathy card I had sent and for the extra attention he received from me during his difficult times.

There are many elections in a school year and of the many who "throw their hat into the ring," only one person can win each position. The winner is congratulated many times during the day or week after the election and gains increased status, but what of the losers? One year, a student of mine was running for student council vice president. He was not a popular student, although he thought he was. Many students made fun of him and considered his election bid nothing but a joke. During the middle of the day, the election results were announced, and he learned he was not elected. While he was waiting to board his bus for home at the end of the election day, I watched him. He was obviously very disappointed. I was in the faculty room near a window so I opened the window and called to him. He came over and we visited for a few minutes. I tried to encourage him. As he left to board his bus he thanked me for taking the time to talk with him. A few years later while swimming, he drowned. How glad I was for having taken a few minutes to ease his disappointment after he lost the election. It did not take much effort on my part, only caring put into action - something we all can do.

During one school year I volunteered to coach a girls' softball team. I had to learn the many rules of the game. We practiced three days a week after school. When we had games, I seldom got home before 6 p.m. The softball season was about ten weeks long. Although this was an unpaid position, it was lots of fun and the beginning of three years of girls' softball for me. I got plenty of exercise, and I worked with many students that I would have in class during the next year or two. We became friends as we practiced the game, rode the bus, and played games against other schools. It is amazing how quickly mutual respect can grow in this type of situation. Whenever possible, try to be involved with some type of extracurricular activity and you will form some good friendships, too.

Seniors are always celebrating: a birthday, a sporting event, a friend's purchase of a car, or a new romance. One day there was a very special anniversary celebration for one of my students - he was celebrating a doctor's declaration that he was "cured" of cancer. He had now been cancer free for five years. As we were both walking toward my classroom, I commented to him that I had just heard about his five-year anniversary. I congratulated him and told him how happy I was for him. He seemed pleased that I knew of his victory and cared enough to mention it to him. Every so often I see him at the bank where he works. He is still healthy and doing well.

Each year a number of students become pregnant -- it's simply a fact of life in high schools. One year a girl in my course became pregnant. She was very quiet, yet determined. She decided to keep her baby and make a good home for her child, even without a husband. Her baby was due a few months before my first child was due. We often talked about our hopes for our unborn children and shared news about our progress. She graduated from school about a month before her baby was born. A year or two later she was married. She eventually went to work as a secretary in an office, and I saw and talked with her on occasion. We both had a second child. After my third child was born we often joked that I was ahead in the "baby-making race." One day we met in a store and she informed me that she was going to even the score - her third child was due in a few months. Then about a year later when I was in the office again, she informed me that this was her last day of work. I asked her why she was resigning. She smiled and very calmly told me, "Because I am taking the lead in our competition; I am going to have another baby!" She was planning to stay at home and care for her children as long as possible and her family was soon to move into a larger house. She's very happy and her family is doing well. I miss seeing her at the office but our paths still cross every so often; it's always good to see her again.

Many times a teacher will have the opportunity to offer guidance to a student searching for educational direction. One year a boy of superior abilities was in my Regents American Studies course. He had only a few friends and never seemed very happy, but he was a good student and did very well in my course. I asked him about his future educational plans. He told me of his interest in law, but doubted his financial ability to attend college for seven years in order to become an attorney. We continued to discuss his future during his senior year. He matured much during his last year of high school and became more friendly, confident, and outgoing. This was about the time when paralegals were becoming an important part of the legal profession. I suggested he investigate local colleges to learn of the availability of paralegal programs and he did so. After graduating from high school, he attended college for two years and became a paralegal. He secured a job as a paralegal and was very happy about his career choice.

A major problem for high school students occurs when their parents divorce. For many students it presents a very difficult situation for a long time. During the year that I served as senior class advisor, one boy was working through this situation. He would come into my classroom after school, sit on a student desk, and talk. We discussed many things - he simply needed a pair of ears to listen to him and a person to show him understanding and give him some guidance and much support. For a while, our sessions after school were quite regular, then, as the year progressed, he seemed to have regained emotional strength and self-confidence. He was coming to my classroom less often as the school year was coming to an end. At the end of the school year he so wonderfully informed me of his appreciation for time spent with him when he signed my yearbook. He wrote: "You smiled into my heart this year and have caused me to incur an unpayable debt. Many thanks is all I can pay and hopefully lots of memories. You're one person that always cared and was there when I needed someone to talk to. Thanks again and please keep smiling and touching people." Those are the times when, as a teacher, you realize the true impact of reaching out to people. The stated thankfulness of a student to his teacher for efforts and caring is one of the highlights of the school year. Although I eventually lost contact with this student, I recently learned that he is married and is a successful businessman.

One of my closest friends is a former student. Although she was in one of my courses for only five months, we began a friendship that has lasted for over thirty years. Throughout those years we have shared happy and disappointing times; we have encouraged and helped each other; and we have discussed many hopes and dreams. She was the first student in school that I told of my first pregnancy. When I had my fortieth birthday, she sent me two cards because there were so many great cards for the person reaching that milestone! She is now a high school English teacher, and has been a great help to me in the writing of this book. Ours is a friendship that I feel privileged to have; a treasured benefit of my teaching career.

It is often difficult in a highly time-structured day to make human contact but it is so important to do! We, as teachers, can greatly affect the lives of our students when we actively care for them. It is rewarding when our efforts toward our students produce positive results and often, in this process, we recognize that our own lives have been enriched! Perspective is important at this point - so we must remind ourselves that not all of our attempts to assist students will be successful. There are times when we genuinely try to assist our students, yet for some reason, we simply cannot reach them. We need to accept this possibility, yet foremost in our minds, we should still be encouraged to help our students when we recognize a need.

## OPPORTUNITIES FOR REFLECTION:

1. How will you build a positive relationship with your students?

2. What types of support or assistance will you give to students?

3. What types of support or assistance do you believe are beyond the scope of the teacher / student relationship?